Going for the Jugular

A Documentary History
of the SBC Holy War

Also from Mercer

The Struggle for the Soul of the SBC.
Moderate Responses to the Fundamentalist Movement
edited and with an introduction and conclusion
by Walter B. Shurden
(1993)

The jacket illustration is from an engraving by (Paul-)Gustave Doré (1832–1883) in *The Holy Bible with Illustrations by Gustave Doré* (London and New York: Cassell, Petter, and Galpin, ca. 1866) and as reproduced in *The Doré Bible Illustrations: 241 Illustrations by Gustave Doré*, Dover Pictorial Archives Series (New York: Dover Publications, Inc., 1974) plate 89.

Going for the Jugular

A Documentary History of the SBC Holy War

compiled and edited by
Walter B. Shurden
and Randy Shepley

Mercer   1996

ISBN 0-86554-456-5   MUP/H377

Going for the Jugular.
A Documentary History of the SBC Holy War.
Copyright ©1996
Mercer University Press, Macon, Georgia 31210-3960 USA
All rights reserved
Produced in the United States of America
First edition, June 1996

We gratefully acknowledge permission to reproduce the documents,
both copyrighted and uncopyrighted,
by the copyright holders (articles, etc.) or by the authors (sermons, addresses).
Sources are indicated at the head of each document.

The paper used in this publication meets the minimum requirements
of American National Standard for Information Sciences—
Permanence of Paper for Printed Library Materials, ANSI Z39.48-1984.

Library of Congress Cataloging-in-Publication Data

Going for the jugular.
A documentary history of the SBC holy war.
edited by Walter B. Shurden and Randy Shepley

CIP, unavailable at press time,
will appear in subsequent editions
and is available from the Library of Congress.   **CIP**

Contents

Part I. 1979–1983

1979

1980

1981

Part II. 1984–1987

Preface

During the Fundamentalist-Moderate Controversy in the Southern Baptist Convention (SBC), which may be dated from 1979 to 1990, the historical half of my mind was very much aware of the need for collecting and preserving the documents of the controversy. Like others, however, I was too consumed in the struggle itself to take time out to be a historian. I made some modest effort to remedy this situation by calling together some leading moderates on 8 October 1992 at Mercer University and getting them to record something of their roles in the controversy. Some results of that conference are in *The Struggle for the Soul of the SBC: Moderate Responses to Fundamentalism* published by Mercer University Press in 1993. In that book I included a beginning chronology of the controversy. That chronology has been extended and elaborated upon in this volume, although it yet remains limited in scope.

While *The Struggle for the Soul of the SBC* represented narrative accounts of the controversy from the perspective of moderate leaders, I realized that the public documents needed to be collected. At my encouragement and under my supervision, Randy Shepley, a senior honors student at Mercer in 1993, began collecting some of the major documents. After we decided to compile this book, Shepley began foraging more extensively for documents. He made two trips to Nashville to the Southern Baptist Historical Commission and worked assiduously in the library at Mercer and other places in collecting these documents. In addition, he did much of the laborious proofreading of the final manuscript.

I have written the interpretive introductions and conclusion, made the final selections, and edited the documents where necessary. Much of the introductory and concluding material is taken from chapter 7 of the revised edition of my *Not a Silent People* published by Smyth & Helwys in 1995, and I am grateful for permission to use that material here.

The plan of the book is obvious and straightforward. The controversy is divided into three chronological periods, 1979–1983, 1984–1987, 1988–1991. Within each of those three periods, the chapters are organized according to each of the years of the controversy. I did this for a couple of reasons. One, this helps to tell the story of the controversy sequentially. Two, for those acquainted with the general developments of the controversy, it will facilitate finding the desired documents.

This project is only a meager beginning. What we have tried to do is to bring together some of the basic public documents of the controversy. There are two significant limiting words in that last sentence, "some" and "public." Because of space restrictions, we have published here only "some" of the public documents. The most difficult part of putting this book together was deciding which documents to include. Others might compile the same kind of book and include some very different documents. But at least this book provides in one place a ready reference for such major public documents as the Peace Committee Report, the sermons of Rogers and Robison at the 1979 Pastors' Conference, the Holy War Convocation Address of Honeycutt, "The Higher Ground" sermon by Russell Dilday, the "Address to the Public" issued by the Cooperative Baptist Fellowship, some of the major resolutions, such as those regarding doctrinal integrity (1980), the role of women (1984), and the priesthood of believers (1988), and controversial motions, such as the Slatton motion, at the Southern Baptist Convention. In addition, we have included some of the important news releases, such as that on Paul Pressler's "jugular" line, on the initial meeting of "the Gatlinburg Gang," James Dunn's interview regarding the Baptist Joint Committee, and Daniel Vestal's announcement to seek the SBC presidency. These help tell the story of the controversy.

The other qualifying word about these documents is "public." Personal letters, correspondence, notes, and other crucial documents of an individual nature are not found here. We may hope that in time such will appear in print, because they would help clarify the behind-the-scenes machinations that eventuated in many of the public documents. Historians and the general public relish reading others' mail. To read the private and very personal correspondence of Paige Patterson, Paul Pressler, Adrian Rogers, Cecil Sherman, Kenneth Chafin, Russell Dilday, and others is going to be necessary in order to "get a read" on this controversy. Even then, the historian must weigh those letters critically and carefully. The only way ultimately to get at this controversy would be to listen in on telephone conversations and personal chats. A friend once told me that eventually technology would discover a way of retrieving and recording every word we have ever spoken. My guess is that all who played even the smallest part in this controversy would then run for cover.

Some of the sermons, especially those of Rogers and Robison at the 1979 Pastors' Conference, are taken from tape recordings. They have all the marks of spoken rather than written material, and the oral idiosyncrasies have been maintained. These sermons have very few if any deletions; the few deletions are only because the tape could not be deciphered.

We express special gratitude to the SBC Historical Commission and to some of those associated with it, especially Lynn May, Bill Sumners, Slayden Yarbrough, and Carolyn Patton. Also, to Susan Broome, Special Collections Librarian, and Beth Hammond, Collection Development Librarian, at the Mercer University Library in Macon, Georgia, we extend special thanks. They make life easier, happier, and more productive for researchers and writers of all kinds. Andy Rawls of Southern Seminary went to great trouble to transpose valuable 1979 sermons from reel-to-reel to cassette tapes so they would be usable to us. Nancy Stubbs, administrative secretary for the department of Christianity at Mercer University, created a valuable historical treasury over two "slow" summers when she "input" the documents (much more than one sees in this book) onto computer disks for us.

Macon, Georgia   —*Walter B. Shurden*

An Overview
of the SBC Controversy

"We will have a great time here, if for no other reason than to elect Adrian Rogers our president." Those apparently casual, throwaway words by W.A. Criswell during the introductory comments to his sermon at the SBC Pastors' Conference in Houston, Texas, on 11 June 1979, brought the house down with cheers and applause. More pessimistic observers might say those words brought the SBC house down! Not really, however.

Dissected sixteen years later with the benefit of hindsight, the words of the famous pastor of First Baptist Church, Dallas, Texas, contained significance unimaginable that night in Houston. In terms of future SBC leadership, those words introduced Adrian Rogers, the person most responsible for the transformation of the Southern Baptist identity over the next decade. Moreover, those words prophetically, if unknowingly, symbolized the passing of the mantle of fundamentalist leadership in Southern Baptist life from Criswell to Rogers.

In terms of future SBC politics, Criswell's words meant that gentlemen's agreements were no longer operative. Heretofore, former SBC presidents, of which Criswell was one, refrained from public endorsements of possible candidates for national SBC offices. Criswell broke that code of conduct. But many rules of SBC civility would be raucously shattered before the decade of the eighties closed, for on that night in Houston Southern Baptists were on the verge of the "mother" and the "father" of all Baptist controversies.

In a historical sense, Criswell's words marked the first installment in the transformation of the SBC from a conservative to a fundamentalist denomination. In terms of the denominational controversy that ensued, Criswell's words are as good as any to signal publicly the firing of the first official salvo in the wrenching and decade-long struggle for the control of the largest Protestant denomination in America.

Criswell proved to be prophetic when he said, "We will have a great time here." Criswell's crowd did indeed have a great time in Houston in

1979. On the first day of the SBC meeting that year messengers to the convention elected Adrian Rogers as president on the first ballot with 51.36% of the vote, over five other candidates. A first-ballot presidential election in the SBC was rare, if not unheard of. Criswell's crowd also had "a great time" for the rest of the decade, successfully electing their fundamentalist presidential candidates for the next eleven years over their moderate rivals. Did these presidential elections change anything in SBC life? Almost everything! They changed almost everything because Southern Baptists during this decade argued about almost everything.

Before exploring the documents of the most serious controversy in the history of the SBC, you need an overview so you can get your bearings.[1] Two factions, fundamentalists and moderates, polarized the SBC from 1979 to 1990. While the war at the national SBC level between the rival parties ended in 1990, fallout persists to the writing of these lines in the spring of 1996. A good bet is that debris will continue to fall at national, state, associational, and local church levels for several years to come.

With numerous antecedents, the conflict began in earnest on 12-14 June 1979, at the annual meeting of the SBC in Houston, Texas. Three fundamentalist leaders emerged prominently at that meeting and skillfully guided the fundamentalists to triumph over moderates for twelve years. Those three were Paige Patterson, then president of Criswell Center for Biblical Studies in Dallas, Texas; Paul Pressler, a layman from Houston, Texas; and Adrian Rogers, pastor of Bellevue Baptist Church in Memphis, Tennessee. Each served a crucial role in the fundamentalist victory. Patterson, a professor, was the theological architect and polemicist; Pressler, a judge, was the political strategist; and Rogers, an effective and popular preacher without whom the fundamentalists probably never would have won, stirred to action mass SBC audiences.

Beginning in the spring of 1979, Pressler and Patterson designed and announced a ten-year plan whereby fundamentalists could gain political control of the SBC. Garnering a following by proclaiming that "liberalism" had invaded the entire denominational system—seminaries, colleges, universities, publication agencies, denominational press, and almost all

---

[1]As indicated in the preface, I draw heavily in this section, the introductory sections, and the conclusion from my previously published chapter in the revised edition of *Not a Silent People* (Macon GA: Smyth & Helwys Publishing, Inc., 1995) 83-112.

of the national boards and agencies—they discovered they could use the appointive powers of the SBC presidency and thereby dominate the denomination. The political focal point of the controversy became, therefore, the struggle for the election of the president of the SBC.

Three previous controversies of the twentieth century rocked the SBC, but in none did political factions struggle for the SBC presidency. These controversies were the Norrisite Controversy of the 1920s, the Genesis Controversy of the 1960s, and the Broadman Controversy of the 1970s. Indeed, the reason why the Fundamentalist-Moderate Controversy has been more serious for Southern Baptists than any of the previous three is that the fundamentalists of the 1980s interpreted the problem to be systemic, not singular or isolated. In contrast, the Norrisite controversy focused on a single issue—evolution; the Genesis Controversy focused on a single person—Ralph Elliott; and the Broadman Controversy focused on a single book—volume one of a commentary series. The Fundamentalist-Moderate Controversy, therefore, was different in its focus on control of the SBC presidency.

Following the 1979 election of Adrian Rogers as SBC president, every one of the seven presidents through 1995 were fundamentalists who used their presidential powers to achieve the fundamentalist agenda by stacking the boards of all trustee agencies, something never done in SBC history. By 1990, hardliners dominated virtually every SBC agency's board of trustees, the control mechanisms of the denomination.

They did not do it, however, without a mighty struggle, as the percentages for the presidential election will verify.[2] A resistance movement to the fundamentalizing of the SBC began on 25 September 1980 in Gatlinburg, Tennessee. Encouraged by Duke K. McCall, SBC patriarch and longtime president of the Southern Baptist Theological Seminary in Louisville, Kentucky, Cecil Sherman, the lanky, slow-talking, fast-thinking pastor of the First Baptist Church in Asheville, North Carolina, called the Gatlinburg meeting, galvanized the resistance movement, and became the single most important moderate leader throughout the conflict. Kenneth Chafin, James Slatton, Daniel Vestal, along with many others, were important to the moderate cause, but Sherman's courageous voice called the movement into being and stayed at the moderate helm for most of the decade. After the controversy ended and the moderates

---

[2]For these percentages, see the chronology below.

organized the Cooperative Baptist Fellowship, moderates called on Cecil Sherman to spearhead the new Baptist organization.

While the political key to the fundamentalist victory throughout the decade was the election of the SBC president and the subsequent trustee appointments, the fundamentalist rallying cry was "the inerrancy of the Bible." The popular name of the controversy became the "Inerrancy Controversy." While the Bible was a central issue, the strife focused on far more than either the nature or interpretation of the Bible. The conflict, therefore, should be known as "The Fundamentalist-Moderate Controversy."

Even the word "controversy" may be too tame and tepid a word for what happened. Everybody asked during the controversy and they continue to ask, "What was the issue? Why the explosion?" Fundamentalists want you to believe that it was simply a matter of the nature of scripture, or, more specifically, that they believed the Bible and moderates did not. That was and is humbug, though there is certainly a difference between the two groups regarding the Bible.

Moderates, on the other hand, interpreted the conflict in the early years almost exclusively as a political grab for power, an exercise in ecclesiastical piracy by people who had never paid their share of the denominational bills, nurtured denominational institutions, or participated in denominational programs. That was shortsighted, though history confirms that it obviously contained an enormous truth. As events unfolded, fundamentalists desired exceedingly more than the "parity" they claimed they wanted in the early years. They wanted tightfisted control of the denomination, without moderates.

Historians and observers of the battle have numerous interpretations of what it was all about. Now that some dust has settled we still have to squint, but maybe we can see a bit more clearly. What happened was a culture clash, a clash of Baptist cultures. And the "Baptist" part of the culture clash is crucial. The SBC fight of the 1980s was not merely a reflection of the larger culture war going on in America at that time. Specific "Baptist" ingredients made the SBC struggle distinct.

For example, some identified with the moderate cause who were theologically comfortable with the fundamentalists. Why then identify with moderates? Because of the "Baptist" ingredients in the struggle. These ingredients included what historians call the "voluntary principle" in religion and the cardinal Baptist distinctives evolving from that princi-

ple: the priesthood of all believers, anticreedalism, congregational autonomy, religious liberty, and separation of church and state.

Make no mistake, however. While it was Baptist, it was a Baptist
"culture clash," a head-on collision between rival ideologies and conflicting visions. Conflicting visions of what? As I said earlier, of almost
everything. Cecil Sherman and Paige Patterson, for example, had
differences which, as Diane Winston accurately said, "began with theology but spilled into worldviews that diverged on everything from political
issues to denominational structures."[3]

Winston, a non-Baptist, has written one of the best, brief, nontechni-
cal, journalistic accounts of the controversy. While a journalistic and not
historically precise account, and while the contrast would have been
better had she used Rogers rather than Patterson, Winston does a good
job of introducing one to the conflicting visions of the fundamentalists
and the moderates. The reader must also understand that Patterson did not
speak for all fundamentalists, nor Sherman for all moderates, but
Winston's contrast of Patterson and Sherman lets one "feel" the
difference in the two groups.

> For Patterson, the Baptist is first and last a soul winner bound to the
> irrefutable word of God. God's word supersedes all else—in fact, it shapes
> all of life. God's word dictates political stands—opposing abortion and the
> ERA, fighting godless communism and strengthening a Christian America;
> it clarifies ecclesiastical choices—building larger churches and bringing in
> more lost souls; it advances theological positions—banning women ministers
> and opting for evangelism, rather than dialogue with other religions. Patter-
> son's is a rigorous system demanding adherence to an all-or-nothing faith.
> It is also an ideology that coincided with the then-reigning sensibility in
> American life. Like Reaganism it vaunted the triumph of the chosen, as evi-
> denced in outward signs of election: bigger, better, richer.
>
> Cecil Sherman's understanding of Baptist life has fewer sharper edges.
> The Baptist is bound to the Bible, but each human being is free to interpret
> Scripture. Denominational life is not undergirded by creed but by freely
> given cooperation in missions and educational work. Religious life is a rich
> weave of faith-driven individuals seeking God in their own way. Moderates
> may not like abortion, but they recognize it may be necessary in some cases.

---

[3]Diane Winston, "The Southern Baptist Story," in *Southern Baptists
Observed: Multiple Perspectives on a Changing Denomination*, ed. Nancy Tatom
Ammerman (Knoxville TN: University of Tennessee Press, 1993) 17-18.

They believe the Baptist way is right, but they will listen to a Jew or Muslim. They can appreciate big and beautiful sanctuaries, but they say teaching believers to live Christian lives is as important as saving souls.[4]

One attitude, generic in character, hung as a colossal canopy over all the contention. That attitude was "control versus freedom," no new conflict in Baptist history. Fundamentalists argued for stricter controls in light of what they believed was too much freedom that had issued in false teachings. Moderates, on the other hand, lobbied for freedom in the face of what they thought was a nonbaptistic and paralyzing control. This central issue may also be described as "conformity versus liberty" or "uniformity versus diversity." Fundamentalists were interested in theological conformity and denominational uniformity. Moderates were interested in liberty of conscience and denominational diversity. The "control versus freedom" war played itself out in seven smaller battles.

Biblically, the two groups disputed the nature and interpretation of the Bible. Fundamentalists argued that the original documents of the Bible contained no scientific, historical, geographical, or theological errors. This is a theory known as "biblical inerrancy." According to fundamentalists, if one were not an "inerrantist," one did not believe the Bible. And this despite the fact that both Paige Patterson and Paul Pressler admitted that we do not have an accurate text of the Bible.[5]

Moderates, on the other hand, contended for the authority of scripture "for faith and practice" but not as an inerrant scientific and historical book, arguing correctly that we have no original documents of the Bible, only copies. Moderates saw the emphasis on inerrancy as bibliolatry, an unnecessary flirting with idolatry because only God is without error. Moreover, moderates interpreted the Bible so as to allow for a symbolic interpretation of Adam and Eve, while fundamentalists viewed this interpretation as denying the truth of the Bible.

Fundamentalists insisted again and again that the central issue in the controversy was the *nature* of scripture, not the *interpretation* of scrip-

---

[4]Ibid., 18.

[5]While maintaining no mistakes in the original autographs of the Bible, Patterson said that grammatical mistakes and "transcribal inadvertencies" exist so that "we can now arrive at a 98% accurate text." See document 8, below. Pressler also spoke of "a few scribal errors which do not effect any doctrine." See document 32, below.

ture. Fundamentalists meant two things when they spoke of the *nature* of scripture. They meant first that they believed that the nonexistent Hebrew and Greek originals of the Bible are without errors. They knew better, of course, than to pursue that argument about the Bible we now have.

Secondly, in contending that the core issue was the *nature* and not the *interpretation* of scripture, fundamentalists really meant the nature of scripture as *they understood it*. The fundamentalist-dominated Peace Committee Report of 1987 and the use of that report by fundamentalist leaders "makes it clear," as theologian Fisher Humphreys says, "that at least part of the problem is different interpretations."[6] In his remarkable little book on how the controversy has affected Southern Baptist theology, Humphreys argues that the belief that the Bible alone is God's Word, a tenet Baptists share with all Protestant Christians, was unaffected by the controversy.[7] Humphreys is amazingly correct! In other words, the authority of the Bible as God's Word is something Southern Baptists—fundamentalists, conservatives, moderates, and liberals—have always believed and still believe. The controversy did not change that. What the controversy changed is the fact that only one understanding of the Bible and one interpretation of the Bible is now permitted.

Theologically, the combatants wrangled over the role of women and pastoral authority. Fundamentalists insisted on a hierarchical model of male-female relationships and denied a woman's right for ordination to the ministry or the diaconate. Moderates, more egalitarian in outlook, advocated equality between women and men and affirmed ordination for women. Fundamentalists embraced pastoral authority in the local church to the point of saying that the pastor was to "rule" the church. Moderates believed any such notion was contrary to the biblical and Baptist heritages and countered with the historic Baptist emphases of the priesthood of all believers and congregational authority.

A clear theological difference, little noticed and without much public debate but maybe at the very root of the controversy, was a conflicting vision of God. I have been carrying a quote around in my files for years, one of those I cannot be sure where it came from, though I think it may have originated with conservative preacher A. W. Tozer. It goes like this,

---

[6]Fisher Humphreys, *The Way We Were: How Southern Baptist Theology Has Changed and What It Means to Us All* (New York: McCracken Press, 1994) 157.
[7]Ibid., 137.

"What comes into our minds when we think about God is the most important thing about us." In the early years of the SBC conflict I was lecturing at Florida State University, trying to explain the nature of the controversy as I understood it. When I finished, a Lutheran campus minister, one who knew well the recent takeover of the Missouri Synod by fundamentalists, said to me, "You moderates are going to be in trouble if you do not take fundamentalists on regarding the core issue." And then he added, "The core issue is neither politics nor the Bible; the core issue is the nature of God and the fundamentalists' usurpation of God with the Bible, theology, and culture."

In his pivotal Pastors' Conference sermon in 1979 fundamentalist Adrian Rogers said, "And if we had to choose one word that would describe God, that would characterize God, that would epitomize God, it would not be the word *love*. It would have to be the word *holy*. Holy, holy, holy, is the Lord God of Hosts."

Alan Neely, a moderate and former professor of Missions at Southeastern Baptist Theological Seminary in Wake Forest, North Carolina, and present professor at Princeton Theological Seminary, was the first Southern Baptist I heard describe the Fundamentalist-Moderate conflict among Southern Baptists as "fundamentally an argument about God." He meant that fundamentalists are mired in a concept of God that is exclusive, intolerant, and legalistic, while moderates stressed God's inclusiveness, forgiveness, and acceptance.

Moderate R. Wayne Stacy, former pastor of the First Baptist Church in Raleigh, North Carolina, in a sermon entitled "Risky Business," makes something of the same point. Stacy said, "While most of what you heard and read suggested that the controversy among Southern Baptists focused on what one has described as 'The Battle for the Bible,' the real battle is taking place on a more basic battleground—*what do you believe about God*?" Stacy argued that only God—"the only uncreated reality in the universe"—can be called "inerrant" or "infallible" and that this God works in the world *incarnationally*, without guarantees or being risk free. Making a different point, Bruce T. Gourley in a recent book also lifts up the conflicting visions of God between fundamentalists and moderates. Arguing that fundamentalists engage in "humanizing God," Gourley makes the same point in more extensive fashion as did the Lutheran campus minister in Florida, Alan Neely, and Wayne Stacy.

Educationally, the two parties argued over almost every facet of theological education—content, parameters, personnel, and methodology.

Much of the heat of the controversy focused on theological seminaries, especially Southeastern Baptist Theological Seminary at Wake Forest, North Carolina, and Southern Baptist Theological Seminary at Louisville, Kentucky. Before the battle was over, both of these institutions were firmly in the grasp of fundamentalist control and undergoing radical transformation under fundamentalist presidents Paige Patterson at Southeastern and Al Mohler at Southern.

Ethically, the combatants disagreed over the implications of religious liberty and separation of church and state, particularly as those principles related to prayer in public schools, abortion, capital punishment and related national issues. Most of the energy in the area of ethics was spent in the fundamentalist opposition to and moderate defense of both the SBC's Christian Life Commission and the Baptist Joint Committee on Public Affairs, a national agency based in Washington, and supported by several Baptist denominations in the United States. Both of these agencies were traditionally strong advocates of religious liberty and strict in their emphasis on the separation of church and state.

Historically and *denominationally*, the two groups disputed the place of creedalism in Baptist life, the intent and purpose of the SBC (whether missional or doctrinal, functional or theological), and the freedom/control of the denominational news agency (Baptist Press) and the denominational publishing agency (Baptist Sunday School Board; Broadman Press). Moderates opposed theological creeds, believed the purpose of the SBC was functional, and wanted the Baptist Press and Baptist Sunday School Board free from excessive control. Fundamentalists, on the other hand, while claiming to be noncreedal, centralized and creedalized the SBC to a degree unheard of in Baptist life, and pressed for rigid boundaries for the work of the Sunday School Board.

Missiologically, they differed over the theological credentials for missionary appointment and the vocational purposes of missionaries. This particular dimension of the contest focused on the SBC Foreign Mission Board and the Home Mission Board, two of the darling agencies of the denomination.

Politically—in terms of national politics—fundamentalists identified with the political right wing and moderates tended to be more centrist. Fundamentalists tended, for example, to support Reagan-Bush Republicans and moderates more generally identified with Carter-Clinton Democrats. To illustrate, after the fundamentalists gained control of the SBC and the moderates had organized the Cooperative Baptist Fellowship, Dan

Quayle and Oliver North, right-wing Republicans, were celebrated speakers at the SBC while Jimmy Carter spoke at a meeting of the CBF.

The two groups were so divided they could not even arrive at mutually acceptable names for the rival parties. Both wanted to be called "conservatives." That term, therefore, has little value in describing the conflict. In fact, both parties wanted the term so much that at one point the Baptist Press, the denominational news agency, dubbed the adversaries, in the name of fairness, with the cumbersome names of "The Fundamentalist-Conservatives" and "The Moderate-Conservatives." The most accurate terminology is "fundamentalists" and "moderates," though neither party likes its appellation. Fundamentalists were sometimes called "inerrantists," "the takeover group," or "the Pressler-Patterson faction," after the name of two of their founders. Moderates were sometimes called "liberals," "denominational loyalists," "Baptists Committed," or "traditionalists," because they maintained that they were the traditional Baptists. Since the fundamentalists gained control of the SBC news agency, the Baptist Press releases always refer to SBC fundamentalists as "conservatives."

Numerous books and articles have now been written detailing the blow-by-blow accounts.[8] "Blow-by-blow" is good terminology, for this was a staggering, twelve-round heavyweight denominational fight. Looking back, one can discern three distinct phases to it. In the initial phase, the first five rounds (1979–1983), the opponents were, in boxing language, "feeling each other out." The fundamentalist challenger, while never tentative, appeared at times awkward and uncertain of triumph. Likewise, the moderates, especially denominational agency heads, while exhibiting severe apprehension, believed in the early years that the upstart could be "handled." The second phase lasted from 1984 to 1987. During this period a precise momentum swing occurred, the decisive momentum change coming in the fifth round in 1984 and intensifying until the SBC meeting in 1988. The third phase, the knockout rounds, came during 1988–1990. While the bell rang to end the major battle in 1990, "bleacher fights" have occurred almost every year since and still continue.

---

[8]See the For Further Reading list, below.

For Further Reading

(The list is chronological, from 1986 to 1996.)

James Carl Hefley, *The Truth in Crisis*, five volumes (Dallas: Clarion Publications, and Hannibal MO: Hannibal Books, 1986–1990). Hefley's work, eventually consisting of five volumes, may be considered the "official" fundamentalist interpretation of the conflict. There is now a sixth and summary volume available from Hannibal Books.

Joe Edward Barnhart, *The Southern Baptist Holy War* (Austin TX: Texas Monthly Press, 1986), a very important book for understanding the philosophical and theological dimensions of the conflict.

Ellen M. Rosenberg, *The Southern Baptists: A Subculture in Transition* (Knoxville: University of Tennessee Press, 1989), a narrowly sociological interpretation of the conflict that nevertheless contains important insights.

Claude L. Howe, Jr., "From Houston to Dallas: Recent Controversy in the Southern Baptist Convention," and "From Dallas to New Orleans: The Controversy Continues," *The Theological Educator* (Spring 1990), an excellent year-by-year chronological portrayal of the controversy and one of the best with which to begin a study of the struggle.

Nancy Tatom Ammerman, *Baptist Battles: Social Change and Religious Conflict in the Southern Baptist Convention* (New Brunswick NJ: Rutgers University Press, 1990), a very important work, heavily cultural and sociological in approach, written by a moderate but praised by fundamentalist Paige Patterson.

Bill J. Leonard, *God's Last and Only Hope: The Fragmentation of the Southern Baptist Convention* (Grand Rapids MI: Eerdmans Publishing Company, 1990), one of the best overall treatments of the controversy in book form.

Ralph H. Elliott, *The Genesis Controversy and Continuity in Southern Baptist Chaos: A Eulogy for a Great Tradition* (Macon GA: Mercer University Press, 1992), a blistering indictment of what he calls SBC "doublespeak" and a very important book for understanding previous controversies as antecedent to the Fundamentalist-Moderate Controversy.

Grady C. Cothen, *What Happened to the Southern Baptist Convention?* (Macon GA: Smyth & Helwys, 1993), subtitled "A Memoir of the Controversy," is written by one of the most important denominational leaders in the last half of the twentieth century, and it and Leonard's work were the best entries into the controversy for the novice until the publication of David T. Morgan's in 1996 (see below).

Nancy Tatom Ammerman, ed., *Southern Baptists Observed: Multiple Perspectives on a Changing Denomination* (Knoxville: University of Tennessee Press, 1993), contains the article mentioned above by Diane Winston and other excellent articles, especially the one by Samuel S. Hill.

Walter B. Shurden, ed., *The Struggle for the Soul of the SBC: Moderate Responses to the Fundamentalist Movement* (Macon GA: Mercer University Press, 1993), includes extremely valuable chapters by some of the major moderate voices during the controversy such as Cecil Sherman, Daniel Vestal, Duke McCall, Glenn Hinson, Alan Neely, James Slatton, and others.

William S. Stone, Jr., "The Southern Baptist Convention Reformation, 1979–1990" (Ph.D. diss., Louisiana State University, Baton Rouge LA, May 1993), describes the controversy by highlighting the overlooked dimension of the role of rhetoric.

Grady C. Cothen, *The New SBC: Fundamentalism's Impact on the Southern Baptist Convention* (Macon GA: Smyth & Helwys Publishing, Inc., 1995), an extremely valuable sequel to Cothen's 1993 book noted above.

Fisher Humphreys, *The Way We Were: How Southern Baptist Theology Has Changed and What It Means to Us All* (New York: McCracken Press, 1994), a simply written, superbly presented account of the theological dimensions of the controversy; very important.

Bruce T. Gourley, *The Godmakers: A Legacy of the Southern Baptist Convention?* (Franklin TN: Providence House Publishers, 1996), a hard-hitting appraisal of how the new SBC fundamentalism and the twisted threads of Southern Baptist history (regionalism, racism, Landmarkism, anti-intellectualism, fundamentalism, etc.) have created some denominational golden calves.

David T. Morgan, *The New Crusades, The New Holy Land: Conflict in the Southern Baptist Convention, 1969–1991* (Tuscaloosa: University of Alabama Press, 1996), the most recent, the most chronological, the most comprehensive, the most copiously documented, and the best one-volume introduction to date; Morgan's book is now the best place to begin in understanding the background and general developments of the controversy.

Part I
1979–1983

Introduction to Part I

Even though fundamentalists won every presidential election during the initial five-year period of the controversy, partisans on both sides during this initial phase had good reason to be unsure of the long-range outcome. Why? For one thing, history was on the side of the moderates. Extremists in Southern Baptist history such as J. R. Graves and J. Frank Norris[1] had never been successful. Many people among traditional Southern Baptists, therefore, naively took an "it-can't-happen-here" approach to the Patterson-Pressler assault in the spring of 1979.

Experienced sages of the denomination, such as Duke McCall, warned otherwise. Speaking before the annual meeting of the SBC Historical Commission in spring 1980, McCall urged Southern Baptists to avoid thinking "it couldn't happen here." Confronting one of the old and persisting myths of Southern Baptists, McCall predicted the SBC takeover even though many thought "the stability of the Southern Baptist Convention is self-righting and that it always comes back, and that our leaders, once in places of power, become the leaders representing the total fellowship."[2]

As one reviews the early months and years of the controversy, however, a lull definitely appeared in the fundamentalist attack. The first sign of this lull came in early May 1980 when Adrian Rogers announced he would not seek a second presidential term because of his church responsibilities in Memphis. While heavy church work may in fact have been the case, those responsibilities obviously slackened in the mid-1980s when Rogers accepted the SBC presidency two more times during the intensifying fundamentalist juggernaut. One wonders if Rogers genuinely believed the takeover was a possibility early on. Maybe Rogers, recog-

---

[1]For a brief introduction to these individuals and their movements see Walter B. Shurden, *Not a Silent People*, rev. ed. (Macon GA: Smyth & Helwys Publishing Inc., 1995) 40-51, 53-67.

[2]As cited in James Lee Young, "McCall Concerned about Published Takeover Plans," *Baptist Press*, 1 May 1980, 3.

nizing the potential for a major denominational wreck, had second thoughts about the entire enterprise.

A second signal of "lull" in fundamentalist momentum came in May 1980. Fundamentalist patriarch W. A. Criswell, Paige Patterson's pastor and "supervisor" at First Baptist Church in Dallas, announced that Patterson would withdraw from the fundamentalist effort at electing SBC presidents. The methods adopted by Patterson and others, Criswell said, are "those of a different world" that Baptists traditionally disdain. Everybody in the Southern Baptist Convention should have known that something new was in the mix when Criswell could not rein in his younger associate and Paul Pressler.[3]

A third signal of fundamentalist tentativeness came from Rogers in May 1982. In an interview with Jack Harwell, editor of the *Christian Index*, Rogers voiced grave doubt that the SBC would ever adopt a "moderately narrow theology,"[4] the theology that Rogers believed the SBC began with in 1845. Historically, the SBC carried out its work within a philosophical framework of "theological diversity and functional unity." In other words, Southern Baptists cooperated in ministry endeavors while not requiring doctrinal uniformity.

What Rogers and other fundamentalists said they wanted was "Doctrinal Unity, Functional Diversity," the theme of Rogers's 1987 presidential address in St. Louis. In the end, as their attitude toward the Cooperative Baptist Fellowship demonstrated, they wanted and achieved even more. When the controversy ended, fundamentalists had "doctrinal uniformity *and* functional uniformity." The point here, however, is that in the spring of 1980 Rogers doubted that the SBC could be moved away from its commitment to theological diversity. In that same interview Rogers, in pleading for functional diversity, said that Southern Baptists had "made a golden calf" out of the Cooperative Program, by which he meant the entire functional and programmatic work of the denomination. This last statement aroused so much ire that Rogers took the platform at the Southern Baptist Convention in New Orleans in June to issue a word of explanation and apology.

---

[3]As quoted in "Criswell Says Patterson Won't Lead Inerrantists," *Baptist Press*, 9 May 1980, 6.

[4]See "Doctrinal Unity, Program Unity Rise, Fall Together, Rogers Says," *Baptist Press*, 14 May 1982, 6.

In addition to Rogers's "golden calf" statement, fundamentalists committed other major gaffes which under normal circumstances would have sabotaged their cause. Paul Pressler registered for the meeting of the SBC in Houston in 1979 as a messenger of a church of which he was not a member, clearly a violation of the SBC constitution. Wayne Dehoney, a former president of the SBC, took the SBC platform, waved at the sky boxes where Pressler and Patterson were sitting, and verbally eviscerated Pressler for his unethical registration. Additionally, in the spring of 1980 Paige Patterson created a backlash when he called the names of seven Southern Baptists, some of whom were quite popular, who represented for him the nature and extent of liberalism in Southern Baptist life. Fundamentalists always fared better with general accusations than with specific name calling.

In August 1980, after he had been elected SBC president in June, Bailey Smith, one of the more unguarded but colorful of the fundamentalists, created something of a national religious furor when he said that "God Almighty does not hear the prayer of a Jew." Moderates, wondering where this left Jesus, showcased this sentence for what it was: authentic fundamentalist intolerance. The very next month, in September, Paul Pressler announced to a group of Baptists in Virginia that the fundamentalists were "going for the jugular," by which he meant the control of the trustees of the various SBC agencies and, therefore, the domination of the SBC. His language left little to the imagination as to the fundamentalist agenda, although such agenda was then and has continued to be denied.

One can point to other signs of uncertainty of a fundamentalist victory in these early years. During two of the four years from 1980 to 1983, two "unaligned" preachers were elected to the coveted position of president of the SBC Pastors' Conference. These were Jim Henry and Ed Young, both of whom had not yet identified with the fundamentalist movement. Later, however, as the Pressler-Patterson movement picked up steam, Henry would endorse the fundamentalist cause and Young would join it outright. The other two presidents of the Pastors' Conference during this period were Fred Wolfe and Charles Stanley, unequivocating fundamentalists. The point is, however, that the fundamentalists were not yet at the swaggering stage, not yet winning everything up for vote.

Moderates, moreover, had enough victories in the early years to offer some encouragement to their side. At the 1979 SBC meeting where Dehoney publicly embarrassed Pressler, moderates also adopted a resolution in appreciation of their seminaries, defeated a constitutional amendment which would have prevented ordained women from serving on the home or foreign mission field, and reaffirmed a restrained 1976 resolution on abortion. Five years later such action would be unheard of.

What appeared to some as a major moderate victory in 1981 turned out not to be so. Herschel H. Hobbs, former SBC president, primary author of the 1963 SBC confessional statement, and the nearest person to a "pope" Southern Baptists had at the time, tried to squash the inerrancy brouhaha with a motion that missed its mark. At the Los Angeles convention Hobbs called upon the SBC to reaffirm its 1963 confessional statement, including the preface which, as Hobbs said, "protects the individual and guards us from a creedal faith." The apparent intent of the motion was to reaffirm the noncreedal and voluntary nature of the confessional statement while appeasing the fundamentalist insistence on inerrancy. Wayne Dehoney had made something of the same motion as early as 1979, but it did not get written into the record appropriately.

Moderates were slow learners. One does not appease fundamentalists. During later debate on Herschel Hobbs's motion, Adrian Rogers deftly requested that some of Hobbs's comments that reflected the inerrantist tendency be read into the record. Later in the controversy, Hobbs's comments would be cited by fundamentalists as case history that *The Baptist Faith and Message* article on the Bible was an inerrantist statement. Fundamentalists used Hobbs's statements that "leaned" toward inerrancy to better effect than moderates used Hobbs's statement about the noncreedal and voluntary nature of *The Baptist Faith and Message*. Again however, in 1979 and 1981, many erroneously thought Dehoney's and Hobbs's effort at peacekeeping would do the trick for moderates. It did not.

In this earliest phase of the struggle almost every Baptist state editor editorialized against the fundamentalists while the denominational bureaucracy was solidly but silently against the Patterson-Pressler efforts. If you add to this the early fundamentalist goofs and the not unimpressive moderate victories recounted above, you may wonder why things turned out as they did. One must not forget, however, that fundamentalists experienced enough victories in these early years to keep them charging, even if cautiously and while taking a step back every now and then. They impressively won every year the SBC presidency, with its enormous appointive powers for implementing the inerrancy strategy. Moreover, they kept predominant control of the Pastors' Conference.

In 1980 fundamentalists successfully presented and persuaded the SBC to adopt a resolution entitled "On Doctrinal Integrity." That resolution admonished SBC trustees to "only employ, and continue the employment of, faculty members and professional staff who believe in the divine inspiration of the whole Bible, infallibility of the original manuscripts, and that the Bible is truth without any error." Again in 1981, fundamentalist power defeated a moderate motion that would have limited the appointive powers of the SBC president, the control button in the convention. In 1982, SBC resolutions engineered by fundamentalists endorsed scientific creationism, a federal constitutional amendment prohibiting abortion, and an amendment regarding voluntary prayer in public schools. These resolutions marked a deviation from past SBC actions regarding government involvement in religious matters, and indicated a clear turn to the right in SBC life. Fundamentalists landed some huge blows in the first phase of the conflict.

Forced to select a single event in the years 1979–1983 that profiled the future conflict within the SBC, one would do well to point to the 1979 SBC Pastors' Conference in Houston, Texas. The name could be misleading. It is a "Preaching Conference," a preaching conference for pastors, and it meets immediately prior to the annual meeting of the SBC. It became in the decade of the controversy an orchestrated political rally for SBC fundamentalism. Bill Leonard was correct when he said that "1979 was the culmination of a century of doctrinal debate and the beginning of a new denominational coalition."[5] That new denominational coalition's first public manifestation, however, appeared at the Pastors' Conference in Houston in 1979.

The SBC Pastors' Conference that year contained several ingredients of the future fundamentalist agenda. One was the denominational agenda of control, reflected not only in the preconvention politicking of Patterson and Pressler, but also in the announcement by Criswell at the Pastors' Conference that Baptists had gathered to elect Rogers as SBC president. Also, James Robison expressed the control agenda in his vitriolic Pastors' Conference sermon. Robison said:

> I believe we must not only elect a president who believes the Bible is the infallible, inerrant word of the living God, but we must elect a president who is totally committed to the removal from this denomination of any teacher, any educator who does not believe the Bible is the infallible, inerrant word of the living God.[6]

---

[5]Bill J. Leonard, *God's Last and Only Hope* (Grand Rapids MI: Eerdmans, 1990) 138.

[6]See document 3.

The entire fundamentalist worldview, including the inerrancy formula and the control agenda, would be used in the future to purge SBC institutions of nonfundamentalists and thus to transform the SBC.

The theological agenda of inerrancy and its straw man "liberalism" also constituted a major thrust of sermons at the Pastors' Conference, especially those by Robison, as illustrated above, and by Adrian Rogers. With broad swipes at "liberals," "humanists," "entrenched denominational bureaucrats," and "professors," Rogers and Robison brought the vast majority of the audience to its feet again and again. "Have you ever noticed how many of these instructors of higher learning," Robison sarcastically asked, "look like they've been embalmed with the fluid of higher education? I don't know why they think they have to come out and sit on the platform and look like a God-forsaking corpse." Cleverly, Rogers reported a fictional conversation between two demons where one said, "If those liberal theologians ever really discover the power of the cross, hell help us, all heaven will break loose."

Rogers launched his sermon by stressing that a successful ministry was rooted in Rogers's type of theological orthodoxy. "You look and you see the churches that are reaching and winning and baptizing people in this day of sagging statistics," he proclaimed, "and every one of them, and I say every one of them, is a conservative fundamental Bible believer. Every one of them!" A variation of this theme often used by fundamentalists throughout the controversy was that mainline denominations declined because they deserted fundamentalist-type theological orthodoxy.

In addition, Rogers raised the issue of the role of women, speaking of "Satan's fib about women's lib." Describing the women's drive for equality as "this unisex movement," the gifted preacher said it "has been belched out of hell." Rogers's attitude toward women's role in society and the church triumphed in the infamous 1984 SBC resolution on the role of women.

Probably more of a characteristic than a theme, the militancy of the fundamentalist drive is clearly evident in Rogers's sermon in 1979. In 1984 fundamentalists rebuked moderate Roy L. Honeycutt vigorously and mercilessly for his "Holy War" sermon. However, Rogers closed his 1979 Pastor's Conference sermon with a Holy War rhetoric that predated Honeycutt's. At one point Rogers said,

> I want to tell you it's time we stopped trying to save our ministries. It's time we stopped trying to save our reputations, it's time we stopped trying to

save our organizations, it's time that we get out of the boat with both feet and let the devil take the hindmost, live or die, sink or swim, every inch, every ounce, and go for God. I believe that. We've not yet resisted unto the blood. Don't let Satan cause you to back up, let up, shut up, until you're taken up.

Brother, it's time to love not our lives unto the death. Now listen, I don't have to live. They've come out with a new statistic on death recently. One out of one people die. I don't have to live. I don't even have to be liked. I want to love everybody and I want to be loved. But the man who tries to please everybody will please the devil most of all. It's time that God's people stood up.[7]

Finally, the national agenda of right-wing politics, which became so apparent in the SBC fundamentalist movement, manifested itself explicitly in Charles Stanley's Pastors' Conference sermon entitled "Stand Up America." While never alluding to Jerry Falwell or his "Moral Majority" movement, Stanley's sermon called upon Southern Baptist preachers and laity to unite with this extremist ideology.

The entire fundamentalist agenda came packaged in passionate, incendiary, and inflammatory preaching. Preachers became provocateurs, fomenters of dissatisfaction with what was going on both within the denomination and the nation. Anyone who doubts the power of the pulpit to bring about radical change should revisit the tapes of SBC fundamentalist preachers during the decade of the 80s. The political organizing of Pressler and Patterson, left to itself, never would have changed the SBC. Without the bombastic rhetoric of Rogers, Robison, Stanley, and other preachers like them at national SBC gatherings, the fundamentalist political machine might still be on the runway. Because of that rhetoric, however, the takeoff occurred at Houston in 1979.[8]

---

[7]See document 2.

[8]I am indebted to William S. Stone, Jr. and his study of the controversy for stressing the importance of the 1979 SBC Pastors' Conference, especially the rhetorical dimension of the fundamentalist success. Anyone present at that meeting realizes the truth of Stone's contention. The rhetoric of the controversy has been too little noted as a crucial ingredient in the struggle. See William S. Stone, Jr., "The Southern Baptist Convention Reformation, 1979–1990: A Social Drama" (Ph.D. diss., Louisiana State University, 1993).

1979

Chronology

<u>February 22.</u> The *Christian Index*. Names of those to preach at the SBC Pastors' Conference in Houston are released, and read like a Who's Who of future fundamentalist leaders of the next decade: Homer Lindsay, Jr., president, Adrian Rogers, W. A. Criswell, Jerry Vines, Charles Stanley, and others.

<u>May 10.</u> *Baptist Press* news release by Toby Druin in which Paige Patterson and Paul Pressler confirm reports that meetings had been held in at least fifteen states to encourage messengers to attend the SBC in Houston to elect a president committed to biblical inerrancy. Patterson said the meetings grew out of a concern that every resolution in recent years aimed at underscoring Southern Baptist belief in biblical inerrancy "has come back toothless." No particular candidate was named but Patterson said Jerry Vines, Richard Jackson, Adrian Rogers, Bailey Smith, Homer Lindsay, and John Bisagno would be acceptable. See document 1.

<u>May 24.</u> The *Christian Index* reports that Harold Lindsell, president of the Baptist Faith and Message Fellowship, said in an interview with the Memphis *Commercial Appeal* that it is time for Southern Baptists to face the issue of inerrancy even if it meant the loss of 500,000 members. Lindsell also announced he would be speaking in several cities across the nation before the SBC in Houston, promoting sales of his new book entitled *The Bible in the Balance*. Lindsell denied the Baptist Faith and Message Fellowship had been involved in the Pressler-Patterson meetings across the nation.

<u>June 12–14.</u> SBC, Houston, 15,760 messengers, Jimmy Allen presiding.
—At the Pastors' Conference preceding the SBC, fundamentalist Homer Lindsay, Jr. presides over a parade of preachers who lash out at alleged "liberals" within the SBC. Moments after Adrian Rogers blasted liberalism, implying SBC scholars were among them, W. A. Criswell endorses him to be the next president of the SBC. Several elements of the future fundamentalist agenda manifest themselves in Pastors' Conference sermons, especially Rogers's, Robison's, and Stanley's. See documents 2 and 3. Fundamentalist James T. Draper becomes president of the Pastors' Conference.
—Fundamentalist Adrian Rogers elected as president on the first ballot with 51.36% of the vote, over five independent candidates. In a news conference

following election, Rogers said he was not part of the Pressler-Patterson political machine and that he hoped the kind of political organization that led to his election would not be a pattern for future elections of SBC presidents.

—Resolution ironically adopted at the beginning of an intensely political twelve-year-long fight "On Disavowing Political Activity in Selecting Officers." See document 5.

—Paul Pressler, one of the architects of the fundamentalist movement, registered as SBC messenger from a church to which he did not belong, a violation of the SBC constitution.

—Wayne Dehoney, former SBC president, drew warm applause when he went to the microphone, pointed to a "sky room" at the top of the convention hall as being campaign headquarters for Paul Pressler. Dehoney also accused Pressler of being an "illegal messenger" who was not properly certified.

—Motion by Wayne Dehoney and approved by the Convention reaffirming the section of the 1963 Baptist Faith and Message (BFM) dealing with the Bible and the purpose of the BFM to "serve as information to the churches, and which may serve as guidelines to the various agencies of the Southern Baptist Convention." At Adrian Rogers's call for specificity regarding the Bible, Dehoney interpreted the BFMs statement that the "The Bible is truth, without any mixture of error" in a way that unintentionally advanced the fundamentalist movement. See document 4.

—A constitutional amendment to prevent ordained women from serving on the home or foreign mission field was defeated. The attitude toward ordained women underwent radical change in the decade ahead.

—Reaffirm temperate 1976 abortion resolution. See document 6. A more extreme antiabortion amendment of the whole failed but would pass in 1980 and in future conventions.

July 31. Porter W. Routh retires and is succeeded by Harold C. Bennett as executive secretary-treasurer of the SBC executive committee. This begins a series of significant retirements with the loss of established and influential leadership in the SBC.

Document 1
News Story: Announcement of Inerrancy Movement
Baptist Press, 9 May 1979

"Groups Meet in 15 States to Push SBC President"
by Toby Druin

DALLAS (BP)—Paige Patterson of Dallas has confirmed reports that meetings have been held in at least 15 states in recent months to encourage messengers to attend the Southern Baptist Convention in Houston, June 12-14, to elect a president committed to biblical inerrancy.

Patterson, president of the Criswell Center for Biblical Studies operated by First Baptist Church, Dallas, acknowledged that he and Houston appeals court judge Paul Pressler have attended many of the meetings, according to a report in the May 9 issue of the *Baptist Standard*, Texas Baptist newspaper. Patterson has attended a half dozen or more of the "spontaneous meetings" and Pressler at least three or four.

The Dallas preacher-educator denied that the meetings radically depart from the procedure usually followed in the electing of a convention president. They are "unique but not different," he told *Baptist Standard* Editor Presnall Wood, who said in a separate editorial in the May 9 issue: "It is fine for an individual or group to meet as many times as they desire prior to a convention, but it is the wrong direction when an attempt is made to turn the Southern Baptist Convention into something like a national political convention of block voting of messengers, favorite son candidates and messenger demonstration for nominees."

The established practice over the years has been for friends of a particular nominee, with his encouragement or simple consent, to contact others and urge them to vote for him. Occasionally someone is nominated spontaneously. But most of the nominees know well ahead of time that letters are being written and calls made in their behalf. However, meetings to organize such an effort are believed to be new to the process.

Both Patterson and Pressler previously have been linked to the ultraconservative Baptist Faith and Message Fellowship, although Patterson said he had never been a member of it and that the organization, in his opinion, had exercised "poor judgment" in the past. The BFMF has sought to ferret so-called "liberals" in the SBC.

Pressler said he had been a member of the fellowship but had let his membership lapse several months ago.

The meetings, Patterson said, have had two priorities:

"1. To meet together with fellow Baptists who were greatly concerned about some things happening in the Southern Baptist Convention with a view to discussing how we could help those in leadership to know what we feel the majority viewpoint really is and especially as it concerns the reliability of the Scriptures.

"2. To discuss ways by which we might be able to secure the elected leadership of the convention from among those who we know are committed to biblical inerrancy."

The meetings, he said, grew out of a concern over the fact that every resolution offered in recent years aimed at underscoring Southern Baptist belief in biblical inerrancy "has come back toothless."

He said he feels there is a growing feeling of frustration among Southern Baptists, and, saying he was borrowing a quote from radio commentator Paul Harvey, added, "I certainly would hate to see an uncivil war break out in Houston."

Both Patterson and Pressler cited "liberal" teachings in Southern Baptist seminaries such as Southern and Southeastern and in state Baptist colleges such as Wake Forest University and the University of Richmond as cause for alarm.

The president of the convention could be strategic in ferreting out so-called "liberals" through appointments, in conference with the vice presidents, to the Committee on Committees, which could in turn appoint persons to other committees. The president also names the Committee on Resolutions in conference with the vice presidents.

Both Patterson and Pressler stressed they were pushing no particular person for president at the time, although Patterson said there were several men who would be acceptable—Jerry Vines, pastor of Dauphin Way Baptist Church, Mobile, Ala.; Bailey Smith, pastor of First Southern Baptist Church, Del City, Okla.; Richard Jackson, pastor of North Phoenix Baptist Church; Adrian Rogers, pastor of Bellevue Baptist Church, Memphis, Tenn.; Homer Lindsay Jr., pastor of First Baptist Church, Jacksonville, Fla.; and John Bisagno, pastor of First Baptist Church, Houston.

Pressler is a member of First Church, Houston, which he admitted joining after Second Baptist Church, Houston, last year failed to elect him a messenger to the convention in Atlanta.

Smith told the *Baptist Standard* that he has not encouraged a nomination but that calls from "quite a few" people indicate "I may well be (nominated)." Vines said he would have to pray about it if someone asked permission to nominate him, and Rogers, Lindsay, and Bisagno have already ruled out their nomination, although Patterson said he feels Rogers is "draftable." Jackson could not be reached for comment.

(In another interview dealing with potential SBC presidents, the *Standard*'s May 9 issue reported that four other persons—not related to the meetings attended by Patterson and Pressler—have been mentioned as possibilities. They are Abner McCall, president of Baylor University, Waco, Texas, Douglas Watterson, SBC first vice president and pastor of First Baptist Church, Knoxville,

Tenn.; William L. Self, pastor of the Wieuca Road Baptist Church, Atlanta; and Porter W. Routh, who is retiring after 28 years as executive secretary-treasurer of the SBC Executive Committee.

(Routh told the *Standard* he has not been approached and that it would "be just impossible for me this year to even consider letting my name be presented." McCall and Watterson, who said they were not campaigning for the job, said they have been contacted by a number of persons and will likely be nominated. Self said he is not seeking the job and has not decided whether to allow his name to be placed in nomination.)

Document 2
Adrian Rogers's Pastors' Conference Sermon
10 June 1979

"The Great Deceiver"
by Adrian Rogers

And we say tonight Praise the Lord, Dr. Lindsay, for the music from the First Baptist Church of Jacksonville, Florida. I don't know whether that's going to help me preach or if it just took all of the preach out of me. But what a blessing to hear that music tonight. And the statistics at the First Baptist Church of Jacksonville, Florida, are phenomenal. They've just built a big auditorium that seats somewhere between 3,000 and 4,000 people in downtown Jacksonville. Now you just can't have a church anymore in downtown, you know! And Brother Homer told me the other day, he said, "Adrian, I don't know what I'm going to do. It's filled up, it's running over, and we're praying about a brand new auditorium." Can you believe that? I tell you, it's just amazing and a blessing.

And when you're talking about statistics in the First Baptist Church in Jacksonville, you don't have to lie. But I heard about one preacher who was lying about his Sunday school statistics. And so the other preacher remonstrated with him about it and he said, now wait a minute. He said if I lie about my Sunday school to you, and you know that I'm lying to you, and I know that you know that I'm lying to you, isn't that like telling the truth?

Now, I want to talk about a bigger liar than a preacher tonight who exaggerates his Sunday school attendance. And that liar is Satan. And the title of this message tonight is "The Great Deceiver." Jesus was talking about Satan in John 8:44. Actually he was talking to the unsaved Pharisees, and he said, "You are of your father, the devil, and the lusts of your father, ye will do. He was a murderer from the beginning and abode not in the truth, because there is no truth in him. When he speaketh a lie, he speaketh of his own, for he is a liar, and the father of it."

Two things we learn about Satan from the Lord Jesus Christ. 1. He is a murderer. 2. He is a liar. Never forget this about the devil. His motive is murder. His method is the lie. And he is the father of all liars. And he is the best liar. He is the master liar. And because he is the master liar he tells the cleverest lies. And the cleverest lies sound the most like the truth. And every good lie has just a little truth in it. We had a clock that wouldn't even run that was right twice a day. And any lie has some truth in it.

But I want to say, dear friend, that a clock that is five minutes wrong is more dangerous than a clock that is five hours wrong. You see a clock that is five hours wrong, and you say, "Ha, that's wrong, what time is it? Somebody tell me." But a clock five minutes wrong could have caused you to miss your plane to come to Houston to the Southern Baptist Convention. And so the devil wants you to believe the wrong thing. And there are seducing spirits with doctrines of devils. And the devil is not primarily a pusher of dope, though he is; he is primarily a pusher of lies.

And I want to talk about that great deceiver, the devil tonight.

You see, the devil had rather have you believe a wrong thing than to do a wrong thing. Because the thought is the father of the deed. The Bible says, as a man thinketh, so is he. You sow a thought, you reap a deed; you sow a deed, you reap a habit; sow a habit, you reap a character; sow a character and you reap a destiny. And it all begins with a thought. As a man thinketh, so is he.

And so if the devil can get lies implanted in your mind, then he has you. And conversely, dear friend, you're not going to do anything right until you begin to think right. Now I've read something amazing in some of our Baptist papers lately. Do you know what they're saying? They're saying forget orthodoxy and go on with evangelism. That's ridiculous! Absolutely ridiculous. My friend, what you believe has so much to do with what you do that it's even almost absurd to talk about it.

Now, I went to a meeting that was called by some of our Southern Baptist leaders to talk about evangelism, and the leader whom I respect who was up there said this, and he's a very fine man, and I love him. But these were his first statements, or this was his first statement. He said, "Now gentlemen, we are not here to discuss theology, we are here to discuss evangelism." I said, that's your first mistake, right there.

Friend, let me tell you something. Your zeal is never any greater than your conviction. And your convictions come out of the Word of God. Now, don't you let anybody tell you that what I'm saying is not true because you mark it down. You look and you see the churches that are reaching and winning and baptizing people in this day of sagging statistics, and every one of them, and I say every one of them is a conservative fundamental Bible believer. Every one of them!

[Applause]

Homer Lindsay believes the Bible. John Bisagno believes the Bible. Richard Jackson, Bailey Smith, they all believe the Bible. Dr. W. A. Criswell, I think he believes it. Stan Coffey believes the Word of God. Jerry Vines, Bobby Moore, Harold O'Chester, Jim Henry, O. S. Hawkins, Tom Ellif. These boys say, "I believe that the book, the Bible, is the inerrant, infallible Word of God." And because they believe it, and because when they preach the trumpet gives no uncertain sound, God is using those churches.

Now, granted there are some churches who believe the same thing who are not baptizing people. And so that's not the only way, I mean, that's not the only ingredient. But it is a basic ingredient. Now you can believe just as straight as a gun barrel and be just as empty. But let me tell you something, friend. You cannot win souls and you cannot have a great evangelistic church divorced from biblical orthodoxy and rock-ribbed convictions about the Word of God. And if you don't believe it you go out and look at these guys who pussyfoot about the Bible and check the baptismal records. I don't care what they say, they can give all this palaver about let's forget orthodoxy and let's get on with evangelism and missions, but mister, it won't wash.

Now, there are two books in the Bible that the devil especially hates. So I'm going to use them tonight. One is the book of Genesis and the other is the book of Revelation. I'll tell you why he hates these two books. Because in the book of Genesis his doom is pronounced and in the book of Revelation his doom is executed. And so he hates these two books.

Someone has well said there is no devil in the first two chapters of the Bible nor the last two chapters of the Bible. And I say "Praise God for that." But the devil hates Genesis, and he would tell us that Genesis is myth. He hates Revelation and he would tell us that Revelation is mystery. But I want to use these two books tonight to talk on this message that we're going to entitle "The Great Deceiver." And it's going to be, after all of this talk about orthodoxy, an unorthodox sermon, because it's going to have two points. Number one, I want us to look in the book of Genesis, the third chapter, and see what I call tonight "Satan's Deceit." And then I want us to look in the book of Revelation and see what we call "Satan's Defeat."

I. Satan's Deceit

In Genesis the third chapter, beginning in verse one, I read these words: "Now the serpent was more subtle than any beast of the field, which the Lord God had made. And he said unto the woman, Yea, hath God said ye shall not eat of every tree of the garden." Now what was the devil doing, first of all? Now remember, he's the master liar. And being the master liar, he tells lies about the biggest subject. And the biggest subject is God.

Satan Discredits God's Lavish Provisions

And what he's trying to do now is discredit God in the eyes of Eve and the first thing that he does, number one, he discredits God's lavish provisions. Have you got that? He discredits God's lavish provisions. "Hath God said ye shall not eat of every tree of the garden?" Did God say you couldn't have that? Now what he was trying to do is to get Eve to think negatively about God. To make Eve believe that God was some sort of a spoil sport. That God was some sort of a cosmic killjoy. That God was so straightlaced and cruel that he was forbidding them any enjoyment and any pleasure, and that anything good is a no-no. It's either illegal, immoral, or fattening, and God says, you can't have it. And any time he sees anybody having fun he moves in to break up the game.

Had God said that? That isn't what God said. Now notice what Satan said that God said in Genesis 3:1. "Now the serpent was more subtle than any beast of the field which the Lord God had made, and he said unto the woman, yea, hath God said ye shall not eat of every tree of every tree of the garden."

What did God say? Here's what God did say, and how terrible it is to tamper with the Word of God. Here's what God did say in Genesis 2:16. "And the Lord God commanded the man saying, of every tree of the garden, thou mayest freely eat." God says, listen, I made it for you, Adam; I made it for you, Eve. Help yourself. God is a good God. And don't forget that. You cannot imagine how gloriously and splendorously beautiful was the Garden of Eden. And it wasn't God primarily that put man out of the garden, it was sin that put man out of the garden. God made it for man.

I heard one time about Cain and Abel crawled up and looked over a wall and they saw the Garden of Eden, they hotfooted it back to Adam, and they said, Daddy, we've seen the most beautiful place, and they described it to him, and they said, Dad, do you think we could ever live in a place like that? Adam said, we did once, boys, before your mother ate us out of house and home.

Now friends, it wasn't God, it was sin. You know, the devil wants you to think negatively about God. The devil wants you to think that God is some sort of a cruel deity up there making a lot of laws and hurling them down like thunderbolts to try to make you squirm like a worm in hot ashes, trying to keep them. Don't get that idea of God. God is so good. And every time God says "Thou shalt not," God is just saying, don't hurt yourself. And every time God says "Thou shalt," God is saying help yourself to happiness.

I don't buy everything Oral Roberts has to say by any means. But he says something good. He says God is a good God. That's right. God is a good God. Listen to these verses. Psalm 37:4, "Delight thyself in the Lord, and he shall give thee the desires of thine heart." Psalm 84:11, "For the Lord God is a sun and shield, the Lord will give grace and glory. No good thing will he withhold from them that walk uprightly." First Timothy 6:17, "God giveth us richly all things to enjoy."

And I've been preaching for some time now, but there's two things I've never heard. Number one, I've never heard any spirit-filled Christian say I'm sorry I gave my heart to Jesus Christ. And the second thing I've never heard is, I've never heard anybody say I want to tell you how much the dear sweet old devil means to me. And I don't expect to hear it either. Oh friends, God is a good God, and so the first thing the devil did, in satan's deceit, he discredits God's lavish provisions. And if he can get you to thinking negatively about God, he has you.

Satan Denies God's Lawful Punishments

The second thing he did, not only did he discredit God's lavish provisions, but he denied God's lawful punishments. And we read here where Eve said to the serpent, "you know God said we're not to eat it," and she added a little bit, neither shall we touch it lest we die. And then the serpent says in Genesis 3:4, "Ye shall not surely die." Now here's the second lie. He's denying God's lawful punishment. Since God is not good, it follows that he is not to be trusted. And so the devil now moves from doubt to denial. First of all, "hath God said," and then "ye shall not surely die."

Now dear friends, the devil's gospel is still out around today that God does not punish sin, but I want to tell you with all of the unction and function and emotion of my soul that God, in spite of how holy and how loving he is, that God does punish sin. It's not that God is too good to let a man go to hell, it is that God is too good not to let a man go to hell, who breaks his law, and tramples under his dirty feet the precious blood of the Lord Jesus Christ. And if we had to choose one word that would describe God, that would characterize God, that would epitomize God, it would not be the word love. It would have to be the word, holy. "Holy, holy, holy, is the Lord God of Hosts."

And if God were to let one half of one sin ever go unpunished, God would topple from his throne of holiness. No longer would he be a holy God. They say in a courtroom that when a guilty man is acquitted, the judge is condemned. And my dear friend, God will never be condemned for his lack of righteousness and holiness.

Satan Distorts God's Loving Purpose

Now the third thing the devil does, not only does he discredit God's lavish provisions, and not only does he deny God's lawful punishments, but he distorts God's loving purpose. He distorts God's loving purpose. The devil went on to say to Eve, "Ha, God does know. That in the day that you eat thereof, then your eyes will be opened. And you will be like God." "You will be as God," really is what he said, "knowing good and evil."

And, let me tell you, I said, the cleverest lie sounds the most like the truth.

Friend, listen, it's not a sin to want to be like God. That's what all of life is all about. We want to be godly. If God had not wanted us to be like him, why did he make us in his image? And listen, that's what he's doing. He is right now working to conform me to the image of his son, who is God himself. And it's not a crime to want to be like God. But satan said, "Eve, you disobey, Eve, you do your own thing, and you will be as God." That is, you'll be a little old cheap tin god of your own making. And right here and now we see Satan's fib about women's lib. It started right at this point. Satan says to Eve, "Eve, I'm going to liberate you. You see, what God said you ought to do and ought not to do is cramping your style. You have not had the fulfillment that you ought to have.

And Eve, listen, there are great vistas out there, there are marvelous things that you can do. And after all, Eve, you only go through life once, grab all the gusto you can."

And so Eve now is listening to the devil when she ought to be rebuking the devil. And she is now about to get liberated. Now let me say something about women's liberation, lest you think I'm a chauvinist. Huh. Anybody knows that a woman is infinitely superior to a man at being a woman. And everybody knows that a man is infinitely superior to a woman at being a man. And God made us different that he might make us one. Don't ever forget that it was God that made them in the beginning male and female, and God said "That is good" and this unisex movement has been belched out of hell.

Brother, listen, my wife Joyce may be equal with me but thank God she's not the same as me. It's the difference that attracted me and *viva la difference*. God made us different that he might make us one. But here satan says to Eve, "Now Eve, you're just a babe in the woods. Why, Eve, your eyes are not even open. Try it, you might like it. And if you don't like it you don't have to do it anymore. But how are you going to know whether it's right, or how are you going to know whether it's wrong until you try it. After all, experience is the best teacher."

Not when it comes to sin! The Word of God is the best teacher. And the deeper a person goes into sin the less they know about sin. You know, this thing of try it and experience it, that's as old as the Garden of Eden. One young lady who had sold her purity, one young lady who had played the harlot and had become the dirty plaything of even dirtier men who had the devil's initials carved in her heart was speaking to a young pure beautiful virgin girl and tried to get that girl to sacrifice her purity on the altar of some man's lust. And you know what that young virgin girl said to that fallen girl, she said "Let me tell you something. Anytime I want to become like you are, I can, but anytime you would again like to be like I am you never can." Let me tell you something friend, experience is not the best teacher.

But here's the ironical thing, Satan talked about being as God. When God does have a divine destiny for us, to make us one with His Son, the Lord Jesus Christ, conformed to His image for all eternity. Now that's Satan's deceit and Satan is a liar, and he is a master liar.

II. Satan's Defeat

But now I want us to turn to the book of the Revelation for the last part of this message. I want us to see Satan's defeat. Because the book of the Revelation still is speaking about the old serpent that we see as he crawled his slimy corroding path unto the pages of history. I read here in Revelation 12:9 these words: "And the great dragon was cast out, that old serpent." Yes we've already met him, that old serpent, called the Devil and Satan who deceiveth the whole world, he was cast out into the earth and his angels were cast out with him.

Now we know who we're talking about in Revelation 12:9 and now I want you to listen to Revelation 12:11. It's speaking about the serpent, the great deceiver. And the Bible says, "And they overcame him by the blood of the lamb, by the word of their testimony; and they loved not their lives unto the death."

Now I want to speak to you just a little bit about Satan's defeat. Incidentally, I was sitting on an airplane going somewhere and I happened to land in Tulsa, Oklahoma, and I prayed, the seat next to me was vacant, and I prayed for the person whomever it might be who would sit in that seat, and I said, Lord send the right person and help me to witness to whoever comes in, and I just prayed for the vacant seat, and who would occupy it. After awhile a beautiful young lady, about twenty-six years of age, with a big armful of bundles came, and just plopped herself down. I had just been reading my Bible, and I had been studying Revelation 12:11, "And they overcame him by the blood of the lamb, and by the word of their testimony; and they loved not their lives unto the death." And I had a brown Bible and I put it in my briefcase, and closed it. She came and sat down and reached down and got a brown Bible and started to read from it. I said, "That's a good opener" (to myself) and I turned and said to her, "Say, I like your Bible, and I have one like it." She said "You do." She said, "I was looking for a verse on overcoming." I said, "Well, let's try Revelation 12:11: 'And they overcame him by the blood of the lamb, and the word of the testimony, and they loved not their lives unto death'." She said, "Oh praise the Lord. That's just the verse I need. You know, before I got on this airplane, I prayed that God would put me by the right person."

Well, you can call that circumstances if you want. Oh, dear friend, satan's defeat, "They overcame him by the blood of the lamb, by the word of their testimony, and they loved not their lives unto the death." I want to give you the three c's of victory, and here they are: Calvary: the blood of the lamb; Confession: the word of their testimony; and Commitment: they loved not their lives unto the death.

Calvary: the Blood of the Lamb

How are you going to overcome the great deceiver? Number one: through Calvary, through the blood of the lamb. And, dear friend, there is no victory in this place, in your church, in my church, in your life, in my life, apart from the precious blood of the Lord Jesus Christ. Now somebody might say, "Now, Bro. Rogers, that's a truism." But it's not a truism anymore. I had a tape played to me from some boy who questioned his professor in one of our Baptist schools and that professor said, "Of course, I don't believe that it was necessary for Jesus to die for man to be forgiven." Now you think I'm lying, you come to me and I'll give you his name, but it's not polite to call names in public. You know, listen, if we speak in glittering generalities, they say now, don't do that. You name his name. Or keep quiet. And if you name his name, they say, "Don't do that. Don't pick on personalities. Just deal with principles." You know. That's right.

Let me tell you something friend, apart from the blood of Jesus, there is no overcoming. There is no power, and thank God the blood has never lost it's power. They overcame him by the blood of the lamb. Billy Graham said when he first started preaching a college professor from Cornell came to him and said, "Young man, you are a very good speaker, and you have the potentiality to go places but you're going to have to leave out that blood stuff." Billy said I made up my mind right then to preach on the blood of Jesus more than ever. More than ever. "They overcame him by the blood of the lamb."

You might as well throw snowballs at the rock of Gibraltar as to try to remove Satan apart from pleading the blood. He hopes you don't learn this. Two demons were heard talking, someone says, and one of them said to the other one: "If those liberal theologians ever really discover the power of the cross, hell help us, all heaven will break loose." Jesus Christ, before He went to that cross, anticipating the cross, said "No. Is the prince of the world cast out, the cross, Satan sneers at my endeavors, he laughs at my intentions, he mocks my organization, but he fears the blood of Jesus Christ." He does, he does, and you can call that superstition, but you'd better go back to the Word of God. They overcame him by the blood of the lamb. Let me tell you something. Satan was defeated at that cross. He hopes you don't learn it. We don't pray for victory, we pray from victory. The victory's already won. It's about time we stopped fighting a battle already lost and started enjoying a victory already won. They overcame him by the blood of the lamb.

And you'll never overcome him until you confess your sins and put them under the blood, and until you're clean. And as I stand before you tonight there is no unconfessed, unrepented of sin in my life. You say, big deal. I don't say big deal, that's what it ought to be. That's the way we all ought to live. I cannot preach with the power until the blood of Jesus Christ, God's Son has made me clean, and it keeps me clean. They overcame him by the blood of the lamb. Now if you say that I said I never sinned, or that I'm sinlessly perfect, you misunderstood me. The only way you could live above sin would be to have a room over a pool hall. But I want to tell you something. There is no overcoming the devil apart from the blood of Jesus Christ.

Confession: The Word of Their Testimony

Now secondly, not only did they overcome him through Calvary, but they overcame him through confession. "And the word of their testimony." The Bible says, let the redeemed of the Lord say so. And I tell you that it is high time that we as God's children open our mouths. The greatest sin in my estimation of the twentieth century church is silence. And I for one am going to refuse to be cowarded down and let somebody shut me up!

It is Satan's plan to silence good people in desperate days. And to get us intimidated. And I want to serve notice to all of those who would like to intimidate those who believe the Bible, they can hang it on their feet. Let me say something else. I'm not talking about being arrogant, I'm not talking about being nasty. But I'm saying it's time that God's people stood up and overcame him by the word of their testimony. And when you give your testimony, don't forget to give it to the devil.

Listen, the Bible says resist the devil and he will flee from you. When your sin it is under the blood and Satan gets on your case you speak out loud to him and say, "Satan, in the name of Jesus Christ, whose I am and who I serve and in the power of His shed blood, I resist you, and I rebuke you, you're trespassing on my Father's property. Be gone!" And he will flee from you. You say isn't that like praying to the devil. You're not praying to a cat when you're saying "scat."

Commitment: They Loved Not Their Lives Unto Death

Listen, they overcame him through Calvary, they overcame him through confession and finally they overcame him through commitment. "They loved not their lives unto the death." I want to tell you it's time we stopped trying to save our ministries. It's time we stopped trying to save our reputations, it's time we stopped trying to save our organizations, it's time that we get out of the boat with both feet and let the devil take the hindmost, live or die, sink or swim, every inch, every ounce, and go for God. I believe that. We've not yet resisted unto the blood. Don't let satan cause you to back up, let up, shut up, until you're taken up.

Brother, it's time to love not our lives unto the death. Now listen, I don't have to live. They've come out with a new statistic on death recently. One out of one people die. I don't have to live. I don't even have to be liked. I want to love everybody and I want to be loved. But the man who tries to please everybody will please the devil most of all. It's time that God's people stood up. Jim Elliott said he is no fool who gives what he cannot keep to gain what he cannot lose. They overcame him by commitment.

Conclusion

This story, and I'm finished. Some of Caesar's soldiers came against a little island off the coast of Great Britain and they were going to take that island. The villager's were just a peaceful, pacific sort of a people. But when they saw these soldiers, they got their hoe handles, they got their pitchforks, they got the few weapons that they had to go down and do battle, and to defend the little island. But they saw Caesar's soldiers do a strange thing. When they got out of the ship they turned around and put a torch to them and set them on fire, and pushed them out to sink and burn. And when the people saw that, and they saw that these soldiers had not come to retreat, they had come to win, conquer or die, the people laid down their pitchforks, they laid down their hoe handles, and they surrendered. I think it's time that all of us said, Oh, God, I'm gonna burn those boats. I'm not gonna leave them pulled up on the beach. No matter what it costs. I've only got a few years left. And God, live or die, sink or swim, I love not my life unto the death. Oh God, give us revival.

> I saw the martyr at the stake.
> The flames could not his courage shake,
> nor death his soul appall.
> I asked from whence his strength was given.
> He looked triumphantly to heaven
> and answered "Christ is all."

And he is! Bless his holy name.

Document 3
James Robison's Pastors' Conference Sermon
10 June 1979

"Satan's Subtle Attacks"
by James Robison

[Introductory remarks. . . .]

I'm speaking tonight on "Satan's Subtle Attacks." I appreciate Dr. Rogers reading my text. And Dr. Criswell preaching my second point. And since I'm speaking on satan and his work, I thought I would begin on making some comments on Southern Baptists. I sincerely thank God for Southern Baptists. What I am about to say I mean from the very bottom of my heart, as I will mean everything that I say tonight from the bottom of my heart.

I was led to Christ in a Southern Baptist church in this city, by a Southern Baptist pastor and his wife in this city, and they happen to be here tonight to hear me speak at a Southern Baptist meeting for I guess the first time, because most of them where I've spoken have been so far away that they have been unable to attend. I'd like you to meet the lady and the man that led me to Christ. Rev. and Mrs. Hale, would you stand, Mom and Pop Hale, would you stand? This precious pastor and his wife led me to Christ right here in this city. I was baptized in a Southern Baptist church.

I was called to preach in a Southern Baptist church. I was married in a Southern Baptist church, and I left there and went to a Southern Baptist College. Southern Baptists taught me to trust Jesus only. Southern Baptists taught me to believe that the Bible is the infallible, inerrant word of the living God. Southern Baptists taught me to pledge allegiance to no one other than the Lord God almighty. I was never taught to pledge allegiance to a denomination, to its program, or to its philosophy, but to love the Lord my God with all my heart, soul, mind, and strength. And I thank God for that heritage, and for the Southern Baptists who taught me that. And I learned that lesson well. And I thank you.

I would also like to say on the positive side before we move on to more important things, I thank God for the great seminary professors, college professors, and pastors who teach the Bible, preach the Bible, live the Bible, and demonstrate the power of the Bible. I thank God for seminary professors who love souls, who inspire young people, who fill the minds with knowledge but also wisdom and who put a fire in the hearts of young men and inspire them so they are able to overcome the subtle attacks of satan. Thank God for those college professors and seminary professors who instill that into the hearts of our young people. Praise God for them, and may God increase their number.

I encourage you tonight to pledge your allegiance to the Lord God and to never be guilty of following a denomination for the sake of following a denomination, or follow a preacher for the sake of following a preacher. If we do that, then we are more foolish than those who followed Jim Jones to a suicidal death in the jungles of Guyana.

My friends, if we as Southern Baptists forsake the truth of God's word and if we as a denomination tolerate liberalism in any form and continue to support it we will be guilty of the suicidal death of countless millions of people throughout the world. We must not tolerate anyone who does not teach and preach that the Bible is the word of Almighty God.

And I pray that every person in this assembly will make up your mind that we are going to stand for God's word without apology and without compromise. My friends, we are in a battle. And we are in a battle with satan. And satan is subtle. As Dr. Rogers read a moment ago, satan was more subtle than any beast of the field. My friend, our enemy is the devil. Most of us spend most of our time fighting one another. It is my sincere prayer that we will give our undivided and earnest attention to proclaiming the word of God and fighting satan, his powers, and his principalities.

We find a description of satan and I preach tonight three points. And I pray my outline doesn't get in the way. I have preached for seventeen years and I have always been more concerned about an outcome than an outline. I have always walked to the pulpit with a goal in my heart rather than a guide in my mind. And although I have a guide and I have an outline, you pray that it will not get in the way of what the Lord might want to do tonight. I want to speak on our subtle enemy and satan's subtle attacks.

The Opponent

First of all we'll consider the opponent. If you want a description of the attitude and the character of satan, read Isaiah 14 beginning with the twelfth verse. And you will find the pride of satan, as he says, I will, I will, I will. I will be as God without God. The beginning of the rapid descent into destruction for all humanity begins with the rejection of God as God in an individual's life. When they knew God, they glorified, neither were thankful, but became vain in their imaginations. The first catastrophic step toward calamity and disaster is the rejection of God as God. And Lucifer did that and he was cast out of heaven.

In Ezekiel chapter 28 beginning at the eleventh verse, you will find a description of satan, that he was full of wisdom, that he was perfect in beauty, that he was a created being, for the scripture says, you were created. You will find that he was perfect in all of his ways. Created in his fashion. Until iniquity was found in him and God said I'm going to destroy thee, and I will cast thee to the ground. Satan is referred to in the scripture by the name satan fifty-four times. Satan is called the devil thirty-eight times in the New Testament. He is called Beelzebub, ruler of the demons. Satan is called the liar, the worthlessness, and the lawless one. Satan is referred to as the wicked one and the evil one, as the great dragon, the old serpent, the destroyer, as the prince of the power of the air, as the enemy, the murderer, the accuser, the father of lies, the adversary, the roaring lion, and the ruler of darkness. Let no one deceive you friend, we have a real enemy, a real adversary.

And satan is attacking. Satan is powerful, but he is not omnipotent. Satan is free to travel the universe, but he is not omnipresent. Satan is wise, but he is not omniscient. We are in a war and many of our friends and many in our family are not even aware there's a battle. Many of them do not care. Some have defected and have turned to the other side.

Satan is attacking us today. He attacks the unsaved. He attacks them with darkness, procrastination, materialism, and worldliness. He attacks the saints of God. He uses disturbance and doubt, disobedience and discouragement, and despair and defeat. He attacks the church with worldliness, pride, division, and bitterness, and pettiness and selfishness, independence, and also doubt.

With the nations he uses apathy, apostasy, anarchy, and ultimately alienation. Satan is powerful, but greater is he that is in us than he that is in the world. And I believe, as Dr. Rogers preached, we have the power within us through the blood of the lamb, by the word of our testimony through the power of the Holy Spirit to overcome satan.

The Objects of Satan's Subtle Attacks

Now I want us to consider what I believe to be the most important part of my message tonight. I want us to consider the objects of satan's subtle attacks. Who is satan attacking? Satan attacks everything God made. He attacks the total creation of Almighty God. He attacks men, women, marriages, homes, families, nations, churches, and yes, satan attacks denominations.

And my friend, he also attacks Southern Baptists. Satan is subtle. He does not always make a frontal attack. Most often it's very, very subtle and secretive. Satan's major attack is on the Word of God. His attack is on Jesus. When Satan saw Jesus Christ dying on that cross, what he thought to be his greatest victory turned out to be his most awful defeat. But satan has unleased all of the powers belonging to him against the Son of God, against the Word of God.

Jesus said I am the way; He is salvation. When satan attacks him, he attacks salvation. Jesus said I am truth. When satan attacks Jesus, he attacks truth. Jesus said I am light. When he attacks Jesus, he attacks the spirit of God who breathes into us the breath of redemptive life because of the blood shed on Calvary's cross. Satan attacks scripture. He not only attacks scripture, he attacks with scripture.

Please listen to me. When satan wishes to destroy the thinking of a denomination he will begin by influencing the thinking of those who teach the minds of others. He will attack in the places of learning, the places of instruction. And he will seek to sow seeds of doubt in the minds of those who are instructing others.

He doesn't ever want them to stand up and say the Bible is not the Word of God. He simply wants to create in the minds and the hearts of the hearers and the learners a seed of skepticism. . . .

He wants to destroy a spirit of revival and a desire for evangelism. He wants to make man believe he's an island to himself. That all there is to life is higher learning, and more learning, and more learning, until we're ever learning, but never able to come to the knowledge of the truth. . . . We will be led aside, seduced by men who teach devil doctrine.

It is happening, it is happening continually. Do you realize that evangelists and evangelism have been made a mockery of in our institutions of higher learning, for decades, for decades. As I have traveled across this land I've listened and I've heard, and I've heard well. The mockery of those who instruct our young people concerning those who dare to defy satan, who dare to defy denominationalism, and proclaim the message of God and go out after the lost with a burning compassion for souls. They'll make a mockery of them. I know it's so.

In my room tonight there's a tape that makes me nauseous. As I listen to a seminary president tear down one of the men on this platform and make a mockery of him, and a mockery of what he believes. I'll say more about it later as he talked about fighting dirty. When in God's name do you need to fight a man of God dirty? When in God's name do you ever want to attribute a man who loves souls and loves God and loves his word as being dirty? God have mercy on us.

You want to know what my savior said about those of you who sow one seed of doubt in the mind of a precious little believer? If I understand our brilliant teachers and scholars, one is referred to as young when he is very mature in years as Timothy was referred to as a child, and I was told by our instructors in college that he was probably a mature man. Let me tell you what my savior said to any teacher and any preacher and any evangelist who sows a seed of doubt in the mind of a young person. He said it's better for you that you had a millstone tied around your neck and you were cast into the sea than that you ever hindered one of these, the least of these my little children.

I tell you the minds of our young people are important. And we'd better not poison them. Don't tell me we can't have a Christian school, a Christian university, and a seminary that does more than fill the minds of our students with knowledge. Why can't we build a fire in their soul that all hell can't put out! We can do it. We must do it. If you can't inspire those young people, resign, send them to me. I can inspire them. . . .

Jesus Christ spent his life inspiring people. Not simply instructing them. There's got to be inspiration along with the information brother, or you've got deadness. You'll become walking corpses. Have you ever noticed how many of these instructors of higher learning look like they've been embalmed with the fluid of higher education? I don't know why they think they have to come out and sit on the platform and look like a God-forsaking corpse. Pickle! An intellectual skepticism. God forgive them. Let me tell you satan not only attacks scripture, he attacks with scripture. And I declare to you that when satan makes an attack on a spiritual man he will always use scripture to attack him.

Example: Jesus Christ. How did satan attack Jesus? All three counts, scripture: it is written, it is written, it is written. Satan is the most masterful user of scripture in the universe apart from the spirit-filled Christian. And a man not spirit filled is never insulated from satanic attack. You cannot isolate your children from satanic attack, but you can insulate them with your prayers and the power of the Holy Spirit. And we need to do that. But satan always uses scripture. And the way he uses scripture is by overemphasizing one scriptural truth to the exclusion of other scriptural truths. He will get you to go to seed on one aspect of the faith. He will tell you that one truth is all truth. And when one truth is presented as all the truth, it becomes untruth.

Example: God is love. Is that truth? Some of you are afraid to say. See, you're getting gun shy already. Let me ask Dr. Criswell, he's not afraid. God is love, is that truth. That's truth. Dr. Rogers, God is love, is that truth. Dr. Rogers? Is that, is that, be still now, don't get all upset, is that all the truth? No it is not. But satan has convinced the American people that that is the sum total of the truth of God. God is love. That's truth. But it is not all the truth.

And satan has so emphasized the truth, God is love, that if you ever hear a preacher stand up and say, God is holy, and God is a God of anger, and God is a God of wrath, and God is a God of judgment, you draw back. You resist. For we've been brainwashed by satan's subtle attack. I was at one of our colleges recently where the head of the religion department says you can believe what the Bible says about wrath if you want to, you can believe what the Bible says about judgment if you want to, and anger, but I believe that God is a God of love and I don't believe that other stuff. And he's the head of the religion department of one of the largest schools and they handed a list to those students who said they loved God this year, and said this list are those who cannot appear on campus. And Dr. Criswell's name was on there, but my name was at the top of the list. But I appeared on that campus, during chapel. And I got to meet with the students in the basement, while they had chapel upstairs. Praise God, I'll take the basement anytime if I can just have the Bible in the basement. That's all I care about. I'd rather have it.

God is love. But God is also a God of wrath. God is also a God of judgment. Do you believe that? If you don't believe that, don't claim to believe the Bible. Do you preach it? God said preach it. Well, one of our prominent denominational leaders recently said, and I quote, "My only apprehension is creating an atmosphere in the convention resulting in an erosion of trust in denominational leadership, and shifting the denomination's priority from evangelism and missions to biblical inerrancy." Let me sum up what he's saying. He's saying, let's get back to evangelism and forget the battle for the Bible. That's what he's saying. I heard about some boys the other day having a wonderful baseball game. Suddenly one of them hit the ball out into the weeds. Frantically, the boys rushed out into the weeds and began to search for the ball. They searched for many moments, and finally for hours until they were exhausted, they dug, pushed, pulled weeds, and plowed. They couldn't find the ball. Finally one of the sharp fellows in the crowd said, ah, let's forget the ball and get back to the game.

Friend, without the Bible you haven't got a game. Just in case you don't know it, without the Bible you have no message. Without the Bible you have no mission. Without your Bible you have no evangelism. And brother, it's not the Bible plus something and it's not the Bible minus something. And it does make a difference which Bible you read.

Somebody says, well, we just got to trust them all to make it out alright. Then why don't we give them Joseph Smith's Bible? He said that was a golden Bible. May I impress upon your mind that these who attack God's word will be suave, sophisticated, educated, smooth. Jesus said they are wolves in sheep's clothing. Paul said they are masquerading as angels of light. But Jesus also said, "By their fruit ye shall know them." I don't care if a seminary president stands up and tells me, "I believe the Bible. I believe it from cover to cover. I believe it's the inerrant, infallible word of God." I want to know what those professors under him believe about the Bible. I don't just care what they believe, what are they teaching? Dr. Criswell says, "I believe the Bible," and he's got a staff full of people who make a mockery of the Bible. I say that man's a deceiver. Don't believe what they say, Jesus said. Ye shall know them by the fruit of their life.

How many of them are coming out of our seminaries and our colleges today aflame for souls? How many of them are coming out of our schools ready to fight hell and all of his demons for the word of God? How many are coming out for a burning passion for souls? Many are, yes. But oftentimes it's in spite of what they hear, and in spite of what they learn. My friend, I wouldn't tolerate a rattlesnake in my house. I wouldn't tolerate a snake of any kind in my house, I wouldn't care how pretty he is. And I wouldn't tolerate a cancer in my body. I want you to know that anyone who casts doubt on the word of God is worse than cancer and worse than snakes.

But that old serpent satan was more subtle than any other. Somebody says, I believe the Bible, I believe it's the inerrant, infallible word of the living God. Friend, that doesn't make you a great man. How many of you will stand up tonight and say I believe the Bible's the infallible, inerrant word of God, that doesn't mean anything. Some of the sorriest characters I've met in my life, and the most un-Christlike people I've ever met in my life claim to believe the Bible is the inerrant, infallible word of God. It's not simply a matter of saying I believe the Bible is the inerrant, infallible word of God, are you living the Bible as the inerrant, infallible word of God? Are you obeying the Bible? You may say I believe the Bible, and not be a great man because you don't live the Bible. And

I'll assure you of this one thing, there will never be a great man in the sight of God who does not believe the Bible, and believe it is the inerrant, infallible word of God.

I'd like to make another point concerning some of the criticism that's been flowing throughout the land in some of our papers. It seems that if you're not a Southern Baptist you have no right to say a word to Southern Baptists. I frankly think it's below the dignity of any seminary professor, president, or any educator in the Southern Baptist Convention to refer to the dedicated, disciplined work of a great man like Harold Lindsell as poppycock. I think it's a rotten shame. I'd like to inform you tonight in case you don't know, you don't have to be a Southern Baptist to know the truth. You don't even have to be a Baptist to know the truth. And it's high time we Southern Baptists and Baptists wake up to realize there's some other people who may be telling us a word of truth, and we're too near the forest to see it for the trees. And you'd better listen.

My dear friend, John the Baptist was not a Pharisee, nor a Sadducee, neither was Jesus a Pharisee, but they preached unto those men the truth. Paul was not a Gentile, but to the Gentiles he delivered truth. It may be that God will raise someone up outside Southern Baptist ranks to call us back, and you'd better not thumb your nose to someone delivering the word of God to you Southern Baptists. You'd best not pledge your allegiance to Southern Baptists, but pledge them to God.

Wise is the man who recognizes truth and responds to it. Truth is the word of God. The Bible is truth. The Bible is the standard by which any society may be accurately measured. It is the only standard by which any man or any society may be accurately measured. The Bible is truth. I am not truth. The Bible is truth. Dr. Criswell is not truth. The Bible is truth. A truth is determined truth by the measure of truth. That which is false is determined false by the measure of truth. If I make a true statement, it is determined true by the measure of truth, the Bible. If I make a false statement, it is determined false by the measure of truth, the Bible.

There is such a thing as truth. The Bible says in Proverbs 23:23, buy the truth and sell it not. The Bible says in John 14:6, Jesus speaking, I am the truth. The Bible is truth. John 17:17, thy word is truth. If you want freedom in America, if you want freedom in your life, remember this, apart from truth, there is no freedom. Jesus said, "Ye shall know the truth, and the truth shall make you free."

The departure from God, and the rejection of God as God leads to the second step in our rapid descent to destruction. And the second step God says, is changing my truth into a lie. And then God says, I will give you up to lust, and to vile affections, and you will defile your bodies in lustful living and in unnatural vile affections. And that's exactly what's happening in our land today. Because we have forsaken the word of truth.

And God knows we must uphold truth at all costs. We must fight satan if it costs us our life, and stand for the purity of the word of God. I believe that it is imperative at this point in Southern Baptist history, and I think this is the most critical convention we have ever had as Southern Baptist people. I believe it is imperative this year, that we elect a president who believes that the Bible is the infallible, inerrant word of the living God. But I believe more than that. I believe we must not only elect a president who believes the Bible is the inerrant, infallible word of God, but we must elect a president who is totally committed to the removal from this denomination any teacher, any educator, who does not believe that the Bible is the inerrant, infallible word of the living God.

If you tolerate any form of liberalism, any form of skepticism of the word of God, any belittling of the importance of the word of God and its doctrines, if you belittle the importance of biblical New Testament evangelism, you are the enemy of God. Satan, my friend, is attacking the word of God. Satan will never concede that the Bible is the divine, inspired, infallible, inerrant word of God.

Satan denies the doctrine of verbal plenary inspiration of the Bible which gives authority and inerrancy to the Bible. This is the doctrine that he hates and despises. Listen closely, when we say that the Bible is verbally inspired, we mean that God's supervision of what was written extended to the individual words in the original text. As given in the scriptures, God did not give men ideas that they were then permitted to record in any way that pleased them. God's inspiration extended to the individual words.

When we say that the Bible is plenary inspired, we mean that it is inspired in its entirety from Genesis right through Revelation. Some scripture may seem to some more important or more valuable than others but the scripture is inspired in its entirety. No scripture is more or less inspired than any other scripture. All of the Bible is inspired. It is the infallible, inspired, inerrant, in all of its content. Because God inspired the Bible, the scriptures are without error. There is no geographical error, no historical error, no scientific error, no religious error, no doctrinal error to be found in the word of God because God would not be party to deception by propagating error.

The Bible is the word of God. And because the word of God is inspired and inerrant, it is absolute, the absolute in the final authority in all matters of life and doctrine what we do, what we think, what we believe, how we live, must conform to the word of God or we are following the deception of satan. It is the doctrine of the inspiration of the word of God that satan hates.

Much is taught today in the name of what is called academic freedom. Let me give you the definition of the word academic freedom. From the latest edition of the American Political Dictionary. Academic freedom is the principle that teachers and students have the right and the duty to pursue the search for truth wherever the inquiry may lead, free of political, religious, or other restrictions except those of accepted standards of scholarship.

My friends, I have an announcement to make tonight. The search for truth has ended. I hold truth in my hand and it is the word of God. It is the Bible. We have found the truth. You need search no more. Zero in on it, hide it in your heart that you might not sin against God. That which is not of faith is sin.

Let us not ask again, did God really create the universe and the world as we know it? Did God really create Adam and Eve and breathe into them the breath of life? Creating them from the dust of the ground? Never ask it again. Never ask again, was Jesus really born of a virgin? Did Moses really write all five of the books of the law, the Peneteuch? Did the sun really stand still? Did God really inspire the first twelve chapters of Genesis, or are they a myth or a fable? Never ask it again.

Never ask did the axe head really swim? Did the fish swallow Jonah? Did Jesus do the miracle? Was Adam a man or did he look like him and become a race? How many Isaiah's wrote the book? Is the Bible dependable? Is God still on the throne? Is Jesus coming back to earth? Is there a hell? Did Abraham really offer Isaac? Quit asking those silly questions. Forget it and preach the fact of it. They're all true. Every bit of it.

I can't help but wonder what would happen if someone was courageous enough to read these statements. What if someone made this statement at this convention? "We accept the scripture as the all-sufficient and infallible rule of faith and practice and insist upon the absolute inerrancy and sole authority of the word of God. We recognize at this point no room for division, either of practice or belief, or even sentiment. More and more we must come to feel as the deepest and mightiest power of our conviction, that of 'thus saith the Lord,' is the end of the controversy. Any controversy. With this definitely settled and fixed, all else comes into line as regards our belief and our practice." Good statement.

What about this quote? "Baptists would have schools of their own and make them positively Christian. What does this mean? It means that the teachers should be godly men. No unbeliever should fill a chair in a Christian institution. He must be discrete, not a violent man, nor an enemy of Jesus, and yet he is unfit for the place when he cannot insert a positive Christian influence. We can get godly Christian teachers, we can get them if we will, and we will if we understand our business. Sometimes even professing Christian leaders and teachers depart from the faith and teach things that subvert the faith they once possessed or professed. If we control the schools, we can remove him. Of course, they will howl about liberty, all of them do when they are forced to go their own way and join their own kind. We should not mind that, however, we are conducting a Christian school and this is understood when we employ teachers, and we do not intend to pay men to pull down what we employed them to build up. They should have the manhood to withdraw. But if they should not, we should have the courage to ask them to leave. The trustees have a sacred trust to God which must be honored."

These statements are verbatim from a book called *Baptists: Why and Why Not*. The first statement was printed by the Sunday School Board in Nashville, in 1900, and was made by Mr. Sunday School, Mr. J. M. Frost, who at that time was secretary for the Sunday School Board of the Southern Baptist Convention. The second quote was by Dr. J. P. Greene, president of William Jewell College back in 1900. Boy, would he ever like to see that school now! Both quotes are from the same book that contain twenty-five papers, all about the same.

Now I know some of you are feeling a deep note of compassion in your heart as you look here upon this poor stammering soul. I know that you are very sensitive. And you are saying, "James, don't you know that what you're saying tonight about the problems of Southern Baptists is hurting your ministry?" Friend, I'm not here tonight representing my ministry. I'm not here tonight on behalf of my ministry. I'm here tonight representing the word of God, the Bible. I'm here representing Jesus Christ, my Lord and my Savior. I'm here representing God himself, God Almighty. He gave his life for me.

I must be willing to sacrifice my life, my ministry and my reputation for the upholding and the building of his truth and his word. I'm not here in defense of my reputation. I'm here to proclaim the word of God. I'm not here to win a popularity contest, but to preach what God's word says.

Friend, if you worship your minister, if you worship your denomination, you're bowing to a golden calf. You're an idol worshipper. I know there will be papers that will come out saying I get so tired of going to pastors' conferences and hearing them giving us up the creek, and talking about what all is wrong with Southern Baptists.

Let me tell you what our denominational leaders in many senses of the word want. Not all of them. Some of them are such great men of God, I'm not worthy of walking in their presence. I want you to know some of them are just like the government bureaucrats, brother, they're ingrained, and they're worse than cancer. Now listen to what I'm saying. You want to know what our leadership wants? That tries to turn their back on the truth? They want somebody to stand up at these meetings and put another coat of paint on the house. And they want us to make the house look as good as it can but the truth is friends, the house has a foundation that's eaten up with termites. And I don't care how much paint you put on the house, when the foundation is infested with termites, you'd better pray to God for him to send someone with enough courage to get in there and root those little devils out. I'll guarantee you, they'll destroy the house.

Frankly I'm getting tired of reading about the conservative bunch as being the bad guys. Why don't they ever do some editorials on the liberals? Why don't they do some editorials on the garbage? Why do they always bust the good guys? I can just hear you now, somebody out there saying, "That's just James Robison, he's just taking a cheap shot." I wonder if it was a cheap shot from Charles Spurgeon that cost him his affiliation with this denomination. I wonder if it was a cheap shot that put the Wesley brothers out of the churches and into the fields. Was it a cheap shot that made the life of Roger Williams a life of suffering and rejection? A cheap shot that brought great suffering to William Penn? Was it a cheap shot that severed the head of John the Baptist from his body? A cheap shot that led Peter to be crucified upside down? A cheap shot that exiled John the beloved to Patmos agony? Was it a cheap shot that kept John Bunyan in prison for years, writer of *Pilgrim's Progress*? Was it a cheap shot that crushed the life's blood out of Stephen? Was it a cheap shot that caused Martin Luther to become an outcast when he nailed his theses to the door? Was it a cheap shot that finally ended the life of the Apostle Paul? Was it a cheap shot that sent Elijah running for his life? Was it a cheap shot that nailed Jesus Christ, the Son of God to the cross? Friend, if those were cheap shots then just let me join the ranks of the cheap-shot artists.

I'm telling you, my dear friend, the day has come for every one of us that turn our back on anything that has defiled the name of the Lord God and his blessed word. Ezekiel chapter 13, through the prophet Ezekiel, has a hard word to say to the prophets, or teachers, or instructors who do what the Bible said: "Seduce my people by crying peace when there is no peace, who build the wall with untempered mortar." God says, "I'm going to send a storm, and I'm going to tear down the walls, and I'm going to reveal the foundation that you built upon." You'll find that those prophets were building with vain visions and building upon vanity, not upon the word of God.

I wonder how much has been erected in our denomination and across our land in the name of some preacher's ego. It's a shame when any one of our convention papers, and I happen to have it right here in front of me, because I wouldn't want you to get a good enough look at it to see which one it is, but I think it's a crying shame, brother, when somebody refers to a man of God like Paige Patterson, and I want to tell you he's more Southern Baptist than the bird that wrote this article. I declare to you brothers, he's Southern Baptist blood, bought and born. Born again by the power of God, filled with the Holy Spirit, believes the word of God. His dad, executive secretary of the state of Texas, a great man of God, thank the Lord for him, called this the work of the devil. Brother if that's the work of the devil, let me just call your writing something. It's the writing of the devil. I think it's a pity.

Somebody says, "Well, it's a dirty bunch." I guess that makes the disciples the dirty dozen. What's wrong with these men who believe the Bible? What's wrong with the people across this land of ours who believe the Bible, wanting to stand up and stand together for what God said is "My word"? A very important convention!

Our Opportunity

I want to close tonight by talking about our opportunity. I've talked about our opponent, I've talked about the objects of his attack. Let me talk about the opportunity that we have, please. Matthew 28:[18]19-20, Jesus spoke unto them saying, "All power is given unto me in heaven and earth. Go ye, therefore, and teach all nations, baptizing them in the name of the Father, and of the Son, and of the Holy Spirit. Teaching them to observe all things whatsoever I have commanded you; and, lo, I am with you always, even unto the end of the age." The last words of Jesus before he departed into heaven is: "It is not for you to know the times or the seasons which the Father hath put into his own power, but you shall receive power. After that the Holy Ghost is come upon you, you shall receive power, and you shall be witnesses unto me, both in Jerusalem, and in all Judea and in Samaria, and unto the uttermost part of the earth."

My friend, I believe the last words of someone we love are held dearest to us for as long as we may live. We're talking about getting back to missions and to evangelism, and until we make up our minds what our message is, and that the Bible is the word of God, and that we won't tolerate any attack upon God's word, we're not going to be mission minded, and we're not going to be evangelistic.

We can talk about how we can get more money, friends, but I can guarantee you it'll be because of schemes and not because of the power of God on people. I promise you this, if our people would come back to God, if our schools would commit themselves to God, and our teachers would commit themselves to God, and our people would commit themselves to winning souls and preaching the word of God, you wouldn't be able to count the money God would send us for this denomination.

I mean, our people are so anxious for us to preach the truth, teach the truth, and live the truth. All over this land there are people praying, ready to die for the truth. I'm meeting an unusual breed of Christians today. They're willing to march through hell for heavenly causes. But they won't tolerate hellish doctrines taught in our schools in the name of the Lord. We need to get back to our only power. And that's the power and the authority given to us through the Holy Spirit and the word of God. We need to get back to our only purpose, and that's making disciples as we go and present the gospel of Jesus. We need to get back to the only person, that's Jesus Christ, as our Lord and our Savior. And we need to deliver his message to the world.

I don't know how long it's been since you've led anyone to Christ, how long it's been since you've wept over a soul. You know, as I travel about the land, I meet many people that have never had the joy of leading a soul to Christ. I wonder tonight if I asked you to stand up, how many of you have led someone to Jesus in the last three months, I wonder how many could stand up. I wonder how many could stand up if I asked you how many of you put forth an honest effort to tell somebody about Jesus.

Do you realize that last year we had 8,000 Southern Baptist Churches, I mean 6,000 Southern Baptist Churches who baptized no one. Over 6,000! Do you know that we've had more people saved in the kitchens of motels across this land than the leading church has baptized? I've been traveling about the land raising money to lead people to Christ on nationwide television to pay for the time in advance.

We've got a man on our staff named Sam M[???], last Thursday night in Knoxville, Tennessee, he led eleven precious souls to Jesus in the kitchen. The next day he led seven to Christ in the kitchen. Week before that he led twenty-two people to Christ in the kitchen. You say, I'd bet they're not getting saved. Oh, I just wish you'd give them to me and let me start a church with them. I'm telling you, their hearts are so full of glow in the love of God. Friend, if you're full of Jesus, and you're full of God's word, you'll be telling his story. You'll not only tell his story, you'll demonstrate his story. Would you make a commitment of your life and take advantage of the opportunity, yes, even an obligation that God has given us to fulfill this great commission?

Do you know that if we would make a commitment to God's word and come back to him totally, I believe that we could triple the number of people we baptized last year this year. Baptism is not the issue. The issue is the word of God, and obedience to it. But in the word of God, Jesus said, "Go, tell." In the word of God, he said, "Go, tell." In the word of God he said you shall be witnesses unto me—not some of you—all of you.

And until we preach it and we demonstrate it, it won't happen. If you place little importance upon the word of God, you don't believe it, you'll not believe that hell is hot and heaven is real. And you'll not believe that the only way to heaven is through Jesus. Till we stand up and preach the word of God with urgency and with conviction our people will not be motivated to action. God help every one of us as preachers, and every one of us as laypeople to get on our knees and pray that God will bring us back to a total commitment to his word of God and to the proclamation of it and the demonstration of it.

A fundamentalist was talking about having me there the other day to preach, and he wrote me a letter and said, "I can't have you preach in our church because you're a Southern Baptist." And then I got a letter from a group of Southern Baptists who had invited me for a crusade, and said, "Well, we're afraid to have you for our crusade because you've preached in fundamentalist churches, so we can't afford to have you." And then the word got out on me, last week I spoke to the Assembly of God Convention in north Texas and I thought, "Oh my!" And I found myself wondering, what am I? I'm not a Southern Baptist, and I'm not an Independent, and I—what am I? I finally realized what I am. I'll tell you what I am. I'm a *dependent* Baptist.

And you know what I'd like to recommend that we do in our hearts, I wish we could do it in writing, but nobody would ever pass on that. On July 4, 1776, they met to sign the Declaration of Independence. I wish we could sign through our hearts a commitment, a declaration of *dependence*. I wish we could sign a declaration of dependence upon the sovereignty of God, of heaven, and of God for our creation. And say that we're dependent upon the Son of God only for our conversion, dependent upon the Spirit of God for our convictions and our correction. Dependent upon the Bible as the inerrant, infallible word of God as our absolute and final authority. Dependent upon the church of God for our place of service. Dependent upon God's people for our fellowship. Dependent on the blood of the spotless lamb for our cleansing. Dependent on the gospel of Jesus Christ for our message. Dependent on the word of God for our methods. Dependent on the Holy Spirit for our power. Dependent on the seal of God for our security. Dependent on the grace of God for what we do not deserve, the mercy of God to give us what we don't deserve. Dependent on the second coming of Jesus as our blessed hope. Dependent on God's twenty-four hour provision. Dependent upon God's power for our protection, and God's wisdom for our direction.

Why couldn't we sign a declaration of dependence in our hearts like that? I believe God would send us out of here to revolutionize the world. Friend, when satan attacks, he will attack from within.

. . . .

Friend, the enemy will spring up from among us. It is up to us to make certain that we do not lose the faith, nor depart from the faith, for Paul said grievous wolves will spring up among you, not sparing the flock. Satan wishes to slaughter the flock and scatter the flock. God does not want us to be divided. He does not want us to fight among ourselves. I'm not here as an enemy of Southern Baptists. I'm here as the enemy of the enemy of Southern Baptists. I'm here as the enemy of the enemy of God. And we must be his enemies.

God has blessed our ministry. He really has. And you want to know why? You say, I guess it's just because you're such a good leader. No. I really am not. I'm very weak. You say, I guess because you think you're a good preacher. No I really don't think I am. I think God has used me in spite of my weaknesses. Yes, God has blessed us. My how he has blessed. We've had the joy of seeing hundreds of thousands of people come to Jesus Christ. Tens of thousands of these people have come into Southern Baptist churches. Hundreds of them are in our schools and in our seminaries. That's why I'm so concerned. I love them.

Please hear me. God has blessed our ministry. Do you know that all over America people are supporting our work? We're talking about bold missions. We're talking about bold mission thrust. We're talking about raising money to win people to Christ. Praise God! Brother, God wants to give the money to win people to Christ. Do you know that people have supported our work? God's given us over nine million dollars over the last twenty months, and I praise God for that.

But now you hear what I'm saying, friends. I want you to know that God did not give me the support of people because of who I am. God gave me the support of people and the prayers of people because of the message I preach. Brother, I preach the Bible to be the truth of God. The people that follow us are not following me. The people that follow our ministry are not dedicated to me. I have the joy of being a part of a committed people. They're not committed to me, they're not committed to our ministry. They're committed to the proclamation of the truth. The truth at all costs. I declare to you that those who support my ministry, the day I cease to preach the truth, the day I cease to preach it fearlessly, without compromise, without favor, without pledging allegiance to men, movements, mobs, or money, the day I begin to preach to please any denomination, is the day those blessed people withdraw their support. They will not support me, for they weren't supporting me in the first place. They were supporting the word of God and the truth of God, and the message of God. And as long as I preach that, their support will be there, because God's support is there. But the day I fail to do it, they're gone.

You think I could lead our followers into the jungles of Guyana, to commit suicide? Not a one of them. If I had said to our crowd, come on down to Guyana, we're all going to go down there and commit suicide. You'd have read in the newspaper, there's one dead dude in Guyana. Not one other person would have followed me. I say to you, friend, if you are leading people to follow you, if you're seeking to get people committed to the denomination, you are a part of satan's subtle attack on the word and the preaching of God.

Get them to pledge their allegiance to God and if the denomination turns away from God, don't support those that turn away from God. I don't care who they are. If you sit there with even a tinge of devotion to that which is not dedicated to God you've been possessed by satan. You've been defeated by satan's subtle attack. I want to challenge you my dear friends, to preach Jesus, nothing less. Jesus, nothing more, and Jesus, nothing else. God bless you and thank you.

Document 4
Wayne Dehoney's Motion to Defuse Controversy
SBC Annual 1979, 31

Wayne Dehoney (Ky.) moved that this Convention reaffirm the 1963 Baptist Faith and Message Statement on the Scriptures which was overwhelmingly adopted "to serve as information to the churches, and which may serve as guidelines to the various agencies of the Southern Baptist Convention" and which reads as follows: "The Holy Bible was written by men divinely inspired and is the record of God's revelation of Himself to man. It is a perfect treasure of divine instruction. It has God for its author, salvation for its end, and truth, without any mixture of error, for its matter. It reveals the principles by which God judges us; and therefore is, and will remain to the end of the world, the true center of Christian union, and the supreme standard by which all human conduct, creeds, and religious opinions should be tried. The criterion by which the Bible is to be interpreted is Jesus Christ."

The Truth in Crisis, 1:69-70

Adrian Rogers came to the podium where Jimmy Allen was presiding and asked that Dehoney be "more specific in what he means by the 'the Bible is truth, without any mixture of error,'. . . If [he] means the truth of the Bible is true, that's nonsensical. The truth of everything is true."

Dehoney pulled Rogers aside for a brief conference, then returned to the podium and asked Allen again for permission to speak. "My interpretation and Adrian's," Dehoney said, "is that in the original autographs God's revelation was perfect and without error—doctrinally, historically, scientifically, and philosophically. . . . I bring that and ask you to support it." . . .

Herschel Hobbs, who had chaired the Baptist Faith and Message Committee, supported "the Dehoney motion and the position of our president-elect Adrian Rogers." Hobbs then said,

> I've received many letters asking what the committee meant by the Bible is truth, without any mixture of error—if that included the entire Bible or just the part that is truth. Obviously we had reference to the original manuscripts, but we accept [them] by faith, not by sight. . . . The committee understood and so recommended to this convention [in 1963], and the convention adopted it understanding [truth without any mixture of error] to include the whole Bible.

SBC Annual 1979, 45

The Chair opened the floor for consideration of motions previously scheduled for this time. Wayne Dehoney (Ky.) spoke to his motion concerning reaffirmation of the section on the Scriptures in the 1963 Baptist Faith and Message Statement. (See item 23.) Those discussing the motion were: Larry Lewis (Mo.), for: Bill Brock (Fla.), against: Herschel H. Hobbs (Okla.), for. The motion was passed.

Document 5
Resolution Decrying Political Activity
SBC Annual 1979, 58

"Resolution No. 21—On Disavowing Political Activity
in Selecting Officers"

WHEREAS, This is a Convention of Christians serving as messengers from Christ's churches under the leadership of the Holy Spirit, and

WHEREAS, There have been numerous public reports of political-type meetings and materials for the purpose of predetermining the election of the officers of this Convention;

Be it therefore Resolved, that this Convention go on record as disavowing overt political activity and organization as a method of selection of its officers; and

Be it further Resolved, that this Convention urge its messengers and churches to pray for guidance in the priesthood of the believer in all matters of decision and to exercise distinctly Christian actions in all deliberations.

Document 6
Tempered Resolution on Abortion
SBC Annual 1979, 50-51

"Resolution No.10—On Abortion"

WHEREAS, Abortion is a matter of serious concern to the American people in general and to Christians in particular, and

WHEREAS, Messengers to the Southern Baptist Convention have spoken clearly to this issue in 1976 as follows:

> WHEREAS, Southern Baptists have historically held a biblical view of the sanctity of human life, and

> WHEREAS, Abortion is a very serious moral and spiritual problem of continuing concern to the American people, and

> WHEREAS, Christians have a responsibility to deal with all moral and spiritual issues which affect society, including the problems of abortion, and

> WHEREAS, The practice of abortion for selfish nontherapeutic reasons wantonly destroys fetal life, dulls our society's moral sensitivity, and leads to a cheapening of all human life, and

> Therefore be it *Resolved*, that the messengers to the Southern Baptist Convention meeting in Norfolk in June, 1976 reaffirm the biblical sacredness and dignity of all human life, including fetal life, and

> Be it further *Resolved*, that we call on Southern Baptists and all citizens of the nation to work to change those attitudes and conditions which encourage people to turn to abortion as a means of birth control, and

> Be it further *Resolved*, that in the best interest of our society, we reject any indiscriminate attitude toward abortion, as contrary to the biblical view, and

> Be it further *Resolved*, that we also affirm our conviction about the limited role of government in dealing with matters relating to abortion, and support the right of expectant mothers to the full range of medical services and personal counseling for the preservation of life and health.

WHEREAS, This resolution was reaffirmed in 1978,

Therefore be it *Resolved*, that we affirm the positions taken by these Conventions, and

Be it further *Resolved*, that we urge all Southern Baptists to pray earnestly and work faithfully in dealing with this issue.

Document 7
Baptist Press News Wrapup of 1979 Convention
Baptist Press, 14 June 1979, 10-11

"Overt Political Action Angers SBC Messengers"
by Dan Martin and Jim Newton

HOUSTON, Texas (BP)—Anger over doctrinal integrity and convention political organization erupted into charges and countercharges here as messengers to the Southern Baptist Convention debated a resolution on overt political action.

The prime controversy centered around Wayne Dehoney, pastor of Walnut Street Baptist Church in Louisville, Ky., and Paul Pressler, a Houston appeals court judge, who helped lead a coalition of conservatives to elect Adrian Rogers of Memphis, Tenn., as convention president.

The motion, proposed by Ernie White of St. Joseph, Mo., called on the convention to "disavow overt political activity and organization as a method of selection of its officers." Messengers approved the resolution.

In debate on the issue, Dehoney, without mentioning Pressler by name, leveled charges of overt political activity in Pressler's use of the controversial skyboxes (executive suites) at the Summit as political headquarters and referred to Pressler (although not by name) as being an illegal messenger to the convention.

Others chimed in such as Sid Peterson of Bakersfield, Calif., who accused Dehoney of "overt political activity" in past conventions, and especially during Dehoney's presidency of the SBC in 1965–1967.

After the short but rancorous debate, outgoing SBC President Jimmy Allen of San Antonio said he was "grieved by the spirit that is now moving in this room."

After messengers approved the resolution disavowing overt political action, Pressler made an impassioned and tearful personal privilege speech to messengers, defending himself on use of the skyboxes and charges he was an illegal messenger, since he came accredited from a church of which he is an "honorary" member.

Pressler, who is highly respected in the Houston legal community, told messengers that for the first time in his life he is being put in the place where people doubt my word. I am a loyal Southern Baptist. I love the convention and I love the Lord, but I don't like remarks being made about my character.

In an interview afterwards, Pressler denied unconfirmed reports that he and others had encouraged local churches to bus "messengers" to the convention for the election, and that some churches had more than the permissible maximum of 10 messengers.

"It would be absolutely ridiculous, immoral, unethical and wrong to do this," Pressler said.

"I'm against power politics, but I'm for greater participation of laymen in the convention." Pressler said. "I'm absolutely appalled by the reaction that it is wrong to encourage more participation of laymen in the convention."

"All we did was to inform other Baptists about the problem of parking and transportation, and suggest that some churches might want to form transportation pools and more than one church come in buses or cars," Pressler said. He said he did not know of any specific church which brought messengers to the convention by bus.

Earlier, convention registration secretary Lee Porter said that at least 100 ballots had been turned in voluntarily by messengers from churches which had more than the maximum of 10 elected messengers per church.

Porter acknowledged that Pressler had attempted to turn in his credentials, but said he had no authority to accept them since no challenge had been made against the validity of his credentials.

Porter added that in his personal opinion, there is no provision in the constitution for "dual" membership, but there is strict prohibition against a messenger being named by a church where he is not a member.

"In my opinion," Porter said, "Pressler is not a bona fide messenger to the convention."

The angry exchange on political activity caught most messengers by surprise. It came at the end of a long session on the report of the resolutions committee. When the report of the committee failed to act on the overt political activity resolution, White moved that the convention take action.

However, the eruption was only part of the spillover from the doctrinal integrity debate which has embroiled the entire convention.

Other elements of the dispute which occurred Thursday morning, June 14, included a debate on a resolution expressing gratitude to the seminaries, confusion over a proposed bylaw which would have established a "loyalty oath" to conservative principles by future convention officers, and a motion which implied irregularities have occurred in the registration of messengers.

The resolution, a combination of documents proposed by Charles Inman of Monahans, Texas, and David Medley of Tyronza, Ark., both expressed appreciation to staff and faculty members of seminaries "who have persistently and sacrificially taught the truth with love," and called on persons who question the doctrinal integrity of seminary staffers to follow established procedures.

Kenneth Burnett of Alamogordo, N.M., Opposed the resolution, noting there "is a question about some seminary professors," and saying he does not believe in blanket condemnation or exoneration.

Charles Inman, who favored the rewritten proposal, said some men have "crisscrossed this country crying wolf, wolf" about liberals teaching in the seminaries, but have never visited with seminary presidents to discuss their charges.

"It simply calls on them to put up or shut up," he said.

Messengers approved the resolution.

Messengers were braced to debate a motion which would have required establishing a "loyalty oath" for future convention office nominees before messengers balloted on them.

Eli Sheldon, of Oklahoma City, who made the motion, had included a provision that if it was necessary to become a bylaw, it would take effect in 1982.

By oversight, the motion was not printed in the *Convention Bulletin* Wednesday, and debate was postponed until Thursday. President Jimmy Allen apologized to Sheldon, noting he did not realize the bylaw provision was included when debate was postponed.

The convention constitution prohibits bylaws from being debated on the final day of a convention.

Allen told Sheldon that messengers would be allowed to debate the issue Thursday, but it could not be included as a bylaw. He offered Sheldon the opportunity of withdrawing the motion and entering it again next year.

Sheldon withdrew it.

1980

Chronology

<u>January.</u> SBC president Adrian Rogers, Charles Stanley, and Paige Patterson join with Pat Robertson, Jerry Falwell, Jim Bakker, and others in urging removal of the issue of prayer in schools from jurisdiction of federal courts.

<u>April.</u> Fundamentalist publication the *Southern Baptist Journal* moves from Buchanan GA, where William A. Powell was editor to Columbia SC, where Russell Kaemmerling, Paige Patterson's brother-in-law, becomes editor.

<u>April 21.</u> Baptist Press reports Paige Patterson and Paul Pressler had revealed a plan for long-range control of SBC. See document 8.

<u>April 28.</u> Responding to an editorial of April 23 in the *Baptist Standard*, Patterson sent "A Reply of Concern," identifying six professors and one pastor as liberals. The six were Glenn Hinson and Eric Rust of Southern Seminary, Temp Sparkman of Midwestern Seminary, C. W. Christian of Baylor, Fisher Humphreys of New Orleans Seminary, and Frank Eakin of the University of Richmond; the pastor was George Balentine of First Baptist Church, Augusta GA.

<u>May.</u> SBC president Adrian Rogers announces he will not seek a second one-year term because of local church responsibilities.

<u>May 9.</u> Baptist Press reports that W. A. Criswell, pastor, First Baptist Church, Dallas, had announced that Paige Patterson, president of Criswell Center for Biblical Studies, would withdraw from fundamentalist effort to control SBC by electing presidents. Criswell said the methods used by Patterson and others are "those of a different world," that Baptists traditionally disdain. See document 9.

<u>May 14.</u> Article appears in the *Baptist Standard* detailing both Patterson's charges in "A Reply of Concern," and the responses of the seven accused.

<u>June 10–12.</u> SBC, St. Louis, 13,844 messengers, Adrian Rogers presiding.

—SBC Pastors' Conference elects Jim Henry, pastor of First Baptist Church, Orlando, president.

—Fundamentalist Bailey Smith elected president with 51.67% of the vote on first ballot over five independent candidates.

—Resolution 16 adopted "On Doctrinal Integrity" which foretells much of what was to come for the next decade. See document 10.

—Resolution 10 "On Abortion" represented a marked difference from the 1979 Houston convention. This resolution favored governmental interference in the form of a constitutional amendment and made no allowance for abortion except to save the life of the mother.

—Resolution 21 "On Women" declared that the biblical role "stresses the equal worth but not always the sameness of function of women," and opposed the Equal Rights Amendment.

August. SBC President Bailey Smith creates a furor with his statement that "God Almighty does not hear the prayer of a Jew."

September 1. R. Keith Parks succeeds Baker James Cauthen as executive director of the Foreign Mission Board.

September 12–13. In a speech at the Old Forest Road Baptist Church in Lynchburg VA, Paul Pressler announces that the fundamentalists need to go for the jugular. Said Pressler, "We are going for having knowledgeable, Bible-centered, Christ-honoring trustees of all of our institutions who are not going to sit there like a bunch of dummies and rubber-stamp everything that's presented to them." In answer to a question about giving to the Cooperative Program, Pressler said, "Work within the framework of the Cooperative Program." He added, "Give at least enough to have the maximum number of messengers [to the SBC]." See document 11.

September 25, 26. Moderate Movement begins in Gatlinburg TN, when Cecil Sherman calls together a group of seventeen ministers to counter the fundamentalist assault on the SBC. Sherman and Kenneth Chafin become spokespersons for the moderate cause. See document 12.

October. James M. Dunn elected as executive director of the Baptist Joint Committee on Public Affairs to succeed James Wood.

Document 8
News Story: Patterson-Pressler's Long-Range Goals
Baptist Press, 21 April 1980, 1-5

"Patterson Group Seeks Long Range Control of SBC"
by Toby Druin

DALLAS (BP)—The organization that last year pushed the inerrancy question at the Southern Baptist Convention is active again, this time seeking lay participation from every association and state convention.

Its goal is to determine who is elected SBC president for at least four consecutive years and maybe as many as 10, and, through presidential committee appointments, try to control nomination of trustees of SBC agencies.

Lay involvement is being sought because "many pastors lack the courage to deal with the problem," it was charged, and because lay church members control the money going to denominational agencies and can ultimately determine the paths those agencies follow.

Paige Patterson, president of Criswell Center for Biblical Studies in Dallas, revealed the plan and made the charges in a meeting April 3 seeking lay volunteers to organize the effort. He reiterated them in an interview with the Baptist Standard, Texas Baptist state newspaper, on April 14.

A year ago Patterson and Houston appeals court judge Paul Pressler were the key figures in a plan to elect an SBC president committed to biblical inerrancy and to ending an alleged drift toward "liberalism." They organized meetings in most state conventions and then supported Adrian P. Rogers for president. The Memphis pastor was elected on the first ballot.

This year, it was revealed at the meeting April 3 at the Spurgeon-Harris Building which houses the Criswell Center in Dallas, that Pressler has organizations in all state conventions. He is attempting to enlist laymen in every association.

Dallas attorney Edward J. Drake, a former chairman of deacons at First Baptist Church, Dallas, presided over the April 3 meeting, explaining that Pressler had requested he serve as North Texas organizer, responsible for seven Texas counties. Drake also has been named to the SBC committee on resolutions by Rogers, who disavowed knowledge of current political plans.

Two other Dallas men, attorney August Boto and accountant J. Keet Lewis, were presented at the meeting as being responsible for organizing laymen in Dallas Association. Fourteen attended, including three pastors, although at least 50 "concerned laymen" had been invited.

The object is to enlist laymen from each Southern Baptist church, encouraging them to become more involved in their associations, state conventions and the SBC, especially attending the upcoming meeting of the SBC in St. Louis.

The organization is offering assistance in getting rooms at Ramada Inn South or at Concordia Seminary, Patterson said.

Drake said the object was to enlist laymen to help stem, as he charged, the drift away from the Bible which had resulted in the evangelistic ineffectiveness of other denominations.

Patterson, principal speaker at the meeting, said, "The issue still is truth—is the Bible in fact totally and completely true? Are we really in substance reduplicating the faith of our founding fathers—are we true to the Anabaptist vision? Do we believe today what Hubmaier, Marpeck, Helwys, Smith, Richard Furman, Judge R. E. B. Baylor, B. H. Carroll, J. B. Tidwell . . . believed?"

"I am of the persuasion that most Baptists do" still hold such beliefs, he said in his office at the Criswell Center. "But I am also of the persuasion that a very large contingency in significant denominational posts do not in fact believe that any longer."

In the interview he declined to identify those "in significant denominational posts" or any of the seminary or college professors he charges are not teaching according to his "historic" Baptist beliefs.

"Our objective has never been to get anybody fired," he said. But he acknowledged that has happened in the past when similar charges have been made.

Their "preference" is twofold, he said—first to see genuine revival sweep all SBC agencies so the "historical" beliefs that have characterized Southern Baptists could "manifest" themselves and second that those who hold views contrary to those beliefs voluntarily go elsewhere.

For now, he said, the matter is in the hands of the trustees of the SBC institutions and agencies.

He quoted B. H. Carroll, president of Southwestern Baptist Theological Seminary, who before his death in 1914, Patterson said, told his successor, L. R. Scarborough, that Southwestern was the "last bastion of orthodoxy left."

"He told Scarborough he was to keep Southwestern in its orthodox position and he said, 'If liberalism develops on the faculty take it to the faculty. If the faculty won't hear you, then take it to the trustees. If the trustees won't hear you, take it to the convention that appointed them. And if the convention that appointed them won't hear you, then take it to the people—the people will always hear you'."

Even though "a number of months have gone by" since his organization first leveled its charges, Patterson said, "We do not feel we have given sufficient time yet to various boards of trustees involved to go beyond that and take it to the convention itself or again beyond that to the people themselves."

But the effort to determine election of the SBC president is aimed at ensuring that future boards of trustees agree with the Patterson position. The SBC president appoints not only the committee on resolutions but also the committee on committees which names the committee on boards, which nominates trustees. The trustees then are elected by the convention.

Patterson told the April 3 meeting that they could depend on Adrian Rogers naming a committee on committees sympathetic to their views. Explaining that statement in the April 14 interview, he said he was referring to Rogers' reply to a reporter shortly after his election that he would not knowingly appoint anybody to any committee who was not completely solid in his confidence in the Scriptures, the infallibility of the Bible.

He said he had not seen Rogers' nominations and has tried to avoid discussing convention matters with him, because he didn't want to place an "albatross around his neck in me and whatever I was doing."

Rogers, contacted in Memphis, said he knew nothing of the current political moves, dissociated himself with them, and said he was "amazed and mildly disappointed" at the news.

He said he was almost through with his committee nominations, and that he would always try to name persons to committees who believed in the integrity of the Scriptures. "That is where I have been all my life, Paige Patterson notwithstanding. And I don't think anybody would want me to be otherwise," he added.

He said he was unaware of Drake's involvement with the organization effort, that his only knowledge of him was that he was a member of First Baptist Church, Dallas, was a former chairman of deacons there and "loved the Lord."

Patterson also told the April 3 meeting that Harold C. Bennett, SBC Executive Committee executive secretary-treasurer, could "be depended on." He explained he had met with Bennett to explain what they were doing, seeking whatever advice or warning Bennett might have.

"By 'he could be depended on,' I meant he could be depended on theologically," Patterson said later. "Dr. Bennett has reaffirmed not only to me personally but also on television and elsewhere his total confidence in the Scriptures. He is a man of absolute and undying integrity. I have never seen anything in him that would give any reason to suspect anything other than total integrity."

It would be erroneous to imply Bennett had encouraged him or his efforts, he said. "He was very neutral, as a good executive probably should have been."

Bennett confirmed he had met on March 6 with Patterson in Bennett's office in Nashville. It was his understanding that Patterson had meant his group intended to elect an SBC president for five consecutive two-year terms, he said, but he tried to be neutral in the matter, giving neither encouragement nor warning.

"I have tried to listen to whoever calls and wants to talk to me," he said.

Patterson said he would favor no change in the 1963 statement of Baptist Faith and Message and knew of no movement among his friends or followers to accomplish it.

"I wouldn't change the 1963 statement myself," he said. "I am perfectly happy with it because, as you know, it says the Bible contains truth without mixture of error."

"Whether you say inerrant or truth without mixture of error for its matter is inconsequential. In fact, our whole deal is not the necessity for changing the statement of faith. Our whole concern is to not continue to make a mockery of it. Let's admit what it means, which, of course, was done by both Herschel Hobbs and Wayne Dehoney at the Houston convention. They said what was meant by the writers."

Hobbs, chairman of the committee that drafted the statement, and Dehoney, pastor of Walnut Street Baptist Church in Louisville, Ky., both stated in Houston they felt the writers of the statement held to the inerrancy of the original autographs—the actual writings of the prophets and apostles—when they drafted the "truth without any mixture of error for its matter" portion of the statement on Scriptures.

At that time, Hobbs and Dehoney said the Bible was "without error doctrinally, historically, scientifically and philosophically." That wording was not officially adopted by the convention, and some are saying an effort will take place in St. Louis to make it official.

Patterson said his definition of inerrancy would be that there was no mistake in the original autographs of the Scriptures. There are grammatical mistakes and "transcribal inadvertencies or whatever you want to call them" in Bibles today, he said, but "we can now arrive at a 98 percent accurate text." The remaining two percent in question are "scribal problems that can be worked out gradually," he said.

The current controversy is not new, he insisted, citing others in the past, and saying the present move was brought on "as much as anything else by the willingness of certain groups to really deal with the Broadman Commentary issue."

The commentary issue erupted at the SBC meeting in Denver in 1970 over interpretation of Genesis. Volume 1 subsequently was revised in 1973.

Patterson said emphatically he felt what he is doing is not divisive and should not be branded as "politics."

Liberal tendencies have emasculated other previously orthodox denominations, he said, when they ignored warnings. "I think the real question is do you help anybody by pretending that serious disease is not present," he said.

"What we are doing is not politics," he said, responding to the mention of the convention action last year decrying overt political activity.

"And I just wonder how some other people feel about it who are on the other side. It is no secret Jimmy Allen publicly politicked for the office of president. He called a meeting in St. Louis (before his election in 1977) and one of our St. Louis brethren was at a microphone in Houston asking for permission to speak to remind the president of that fact and that he was at the meeting. But he was not recognized.

"That is one of the great injustices. We were labeled with politicking and calling meetings. Nobody else calls meetings? It's just not true."

Allen, contacted in Richmond where he was involved in a "Follow Christ Crusade," said he had spoken to a regular pastors' conference at the invitation of St. Louis pastor Cleveland Horne who said in introducing Allen that he would be nominated to succeed James L. Sullivan who had recently indicated he would not serve a second term. "There was a lot of discussion about the SBC there that day," Allen said, "but no political strategizing."

The big difference, Patterson said, was that his group did not have a candidate. "We do not have a candidate; we shall not have candidates. Our whole thing has been issue-oriented, not candidate-oriented."

Drake said, however, to the laymen April 3 that Judge Pressler would remain in contact before the convention with his association and state organizers and during the sessions in St. Louis, determining the issues and keeping them informed about them.

But Patterson, insisting "eternal vigilance" is the price of a "God-honoring denomination," said such maneuvers are not "politics." "I don't see any difference in that and in what B. H. Carroll instructed Lee Scarborough to do when he said he should be sure the people know what's going on.

"We are not running a candidate. We are concerned Baptists, and if that is politics then what state paper editors do when they write is also politics. Any time an editor editorializes he is in politics. He is giving his viewpoint and he has an entree to the people that even pastors don't have," Patterson said.

Of those pastors, he said at the April 3 meeting, "Let's face it, most lack the courage to deal with the problem."

In the interview later he said he probably should have said "many pastors" instead of "most pastors," however. "When you are talking to a group you don't always say exactly what you want to say," he explained.

But he said that his investigations over the last few months had led him to believe that in the eyes of many pastors the convention has become "big brother."

"And I would not hesitate to say that many pastors fall into one of two categories. Either they have not investigated for themselves and out of a false sort of loyalty refused to investigate, do not want to know or don't want to be bothered with it.

"Or they know it and understand it and have admitted to us they see it and understand and yet do not have the courage to stand up for it."

He doesn't find such problems among laymen, he said.

"We have found that when a layman has it put in front of him and he looks at it, he says, 'Oh, my goodness.' He is not trying to go to a new pastorate. He is going to be right where he is from now on," Patterson said.

The laymen also control the money, he noted, "And apparently that is the only thing some folks understand," implying laymen who support SBC programs, especially those who are big givers, can get things done when others cannot.

Patterson expressed his love for the convention and said he intends to stay with it.

"I love our Southern Baptist people and think we are—as far as I can tell—the best opportunity this old world has for hearing the gospel before Jesus comes.

"My commitment is to stay and to love it and work for it and I will do that whether or not I am accepted by leadership or rejected by leadership. It won't make any difference.

"I have done what I have done without antagonism and with love for everybody. And if God will help me I intend to keep it that way."

Document 9
News Story: Criswell's Announcement
That Patterson Would Withdraw from Political Movement
Baptist Press, 9 May 1980, 6

"Criswell Says Patterson Won't Lead Inerrantists"

DALLAS (BP) — Pastor W. A. Criswell of the First Baptist Church, Dallas, said May 8, that his associate, Paige Patterson, will withdraw from the leadership of a movement aimed at electing presidents of the Southern Baptist Convention and controlling nominations of the trustees of SBC agencies.

Although the Dallas pastor praised Patterson's commitment to the effort and his zeal to keep SBC institutions "true to the Word of God in its credibility, infallibility and inerrancy," he said the methods used by Patterson are "those of a different world" that Baptists traditionally disdain.

For the last two years, Patterson, president of Criswell Center for Biblical Studies in Dallas, and others have led a convention-wide organizational effort to insure election of an SBC president committed to biblical inerrancy. They have charged that the denomination is drifting toward "liberalism."

Patterson recently unveiled the latest plan to attempt to elect the SBC president for at least four consecutive years, possibly as many as ten.

He told the *Baptist Standard*, Texas Baptist state newspaper, in an interview, April 14, that he had kept Criswell "fully" informed about his organization's efforts.

But the hue and cry over the news accounts of those efforts and Patterson's naming of seven persons he accused of liberal teachings prompted a meeting, Tuesday night, May 6, at First Baptist Church, Dallas, which sponsors the Criswell Center.

The meeting was of the present chairman and six former chairmen of deacons at the church, who have been something of an executive committee since Criswell's heart attack in January.

No formal vote was taken, but the expression of the men was reportedly 4 to 3 in favor of Patterson withdrawing from his political involvement.

Criswell said Patterson's future involvement would be "resolved" and Patterson "will be a part of the resolving. After a little while you will never hear of it again."

Patterson was hospitalized with a pneumonia-like ailment at Baylor University Medical Center and was unavailable for comment.

Document 10
SBC Resolution on Doctrinal Integrity
SBC Annual 1980, 51

"Resolution No. 16—On Doctrinal Integrity"

WHEREAS, Southern Baptists cherish our abiding conviction that the Bible is a perfect treasure of divine instruction which has God for its author, salvation for its end, and truth, without any mixture of error, for its matter, and

WHEREAS, We believe freedom should be balanced with responsibility and doctrinal integrity, and

WHEREAS, We acknowledge not only the right but the responsibility of this Convention to give explicit guidelines to the governing bodies of our various institutions,

Therefore be it *Resolved*. That the Southern Baptist Convention express its profound appreciation to the staff and faculty members of our seminaries and other institutions who have persistently and sacrificially taught the truth with love—enriching our appreciation for the Bible as God's Holy Word and enhancing our ministry in Christ's name, and

Be it further *Resolved*, That we exhort the trustees of seminaries and other institutions affiliated with or supported by the Southern Baptist Convention to faithfully discharge their responsibility to carefully preserve the doctrinal integrity of our institutions and to assure that seminaries and other institutions receiving our support only employ, and continue the employment of, faculty members and professional staff who believe in the divine inspiration of the whole Bible, infallibility of the original manuscripts, and that the Bible is truth without any error.

Document 11
News Story: Pressler's "Going for the Jugular" Statement
The Religious Herald, 18 September 1980, 8-10

"Committee Appointments the Key"
by Tom Miller

Pressler Sees Control of All Boards after Pittsburgh Convention

"We are going for the jugular," Houston Judge Paul Pressler said of Southern Baptist institutions. "We are going for having knowledgeable, Bible-centered, Christ-honoring trustees of all of our institutions, who are not going to sit there like a bunch of dummies and rubber stamp everything that's presented to them, but who are going to inquire why this is being done, what is being taught, what is the finished product of our young people who come out of our institutions going to be."

Pressler, a layman who has gained national denominational prominence in the past two years, says the direction is firmly set and a shift in control is certain in three years.

The judge was joined by Paige Patterson in a Lynchburg conference September 12 and 13.

Billed as "A Conference on the Conservative Move in Our State and Our Convention," the meeting was sponsored by Old Forest Road Church and its pastor Arthur B. Ballard.

About 175 persons, including a choir of more than 50, were present for the first session Friday evening. Attendance Saturday morning, without the choir, dropped to less than 40.

"The Bottom Line Is Trustees"

Pressler said of the 1980 SBC resolution on doctrinal integrity, "the bottom line is trustees, not resolutions."

"I'm going to be in Los Angeles to vote for the nominees of the Committee on Boards as a result of Adrian Rogers's Committee on Committees, because that's gonna make the difference.

"And I'm going to be in New Orleans and I'm going to be in Pittsburgh to vote for the nominees that come out of the Committee on Committees and the Committee on Boards because that's going to make the difference.

"By the time those three committees have gotten their trustees elected—and they will be—then we've got 60 percent good, reliable trustees on our institutions. Then they'll pay attention."

Rogers Decision Called "Blessing"

Pressler said the surprise decision of Adrian Rogers not to serve a second term turned out to be a blessing, since Bailey Smith is not likely to face opposition in Los Angeles.

Pressler said Los Angeles and Pittsburgh were cities where "grass roots Southern Baptists could not go" and control of the election of a president might not be possible.

If tradition holds, a new president will be elected in New Orleans in 1982 and Kansas City in 1984.

But Pressler and Patterson are not assuming victories.

In a question and answer period the two speakers were asked "Are Texans as organized for this crucial one [the Los Angeles convention] as St. Louis?" Patterson answered, "There are eight more crucial ones. Don't think the so-called moderate element will lie down and play dead."

Patterson said there probably would be no effort to unseat Bailey Smith as president, but he has heard there will be an alternate slate of nominees for the Committee on Boards report.

Patterson suggested budgeting money "to take your messengers to the convention," adding that was one of the few things on which he and Southern Seminary president Duke McCall agreed.

Judge Pressler said a "great contribution to the cause of Christ is redeeming of Southern Baptist institutions even if it takes hurting some place else in the church budget to send every possible messenger to the convention."

Pressler did, however, take a firm stand for supporting the Cooperative Program.

In answer to a question from his host pastor, Pressler advised not cutting the Cooperative Program from the budget.

"Work within the framework of the Cooperative Program," Pressler said. "Give at least enough to have the maximum number of messengers."

Old Forest Road Church, which sponsored the meeting, makes no contribution through the Cooperative Program, electing to designate to selected Virginia and Southern Baptist causes.

The church has not been reluctant, however, to apply for Cooperative Program funds. In 1980 they have received $5,000 in a Bold Mission grant and been approved for a $25,000 Extension Board loan for the black Jericho Mission sponsored by the church and Lynchburg Association.

BGAV Leaders met Ballard Group September 5

Friday evening a conferee raised a question that brought public disclosure of a September 5 meeting in Richmond between elected officers of the Baptist

General Association of Virginia and its executive staff and Arthur Ballard and persons chosen by him.

At that meeting, which the editor of the *Religious Herald* attended as an observer, Ballard indicated there was discussion of a recommended amendment to article III, section B, of the BGAV Constitution.

The proposed amendment, reported May 1, 1980, in the *Religious Herald*, would change the formula for qualification of messengers to require greater contributions for the maximum number of messengers. Also, a church would qualify for messengers on the basis of contributions "through the Cooperative Program funds of the General Association" instead of the present "to the funds of the General Association."

A conferee at the Lynchburg meeting, whose church apparently does not contribute through the Cooperative Program, said of the proposed amendment, "We would have to go against our convictions to have messengers."

Patterson observed, "Clearly, this is taxation without representation," and said if such a proposal were made in Texas there would "be a scrap about it."

The Texas Baptist Constitution qualifies messengers solely on church membership, with four messengers for the first 100 members and one additional messenger (to a maximum of 25) for each additional 100.

Patterson said the proposed Virginia change is an attempt to "force a minimal doctrinal position by giving to things you don't really believe in." "That is extremely unbaptistic and contrary to everything that has been done heretofore in Southern Baptist life." he added.

Pressler said "I want to remind you the tide is moving in the right direction. Our seminaries are going to be ones we are proud to support before too long. Hang in there and don't let them disenfranchise you while we're winning the vote and winning the victory. The day will probably come in not too many years when they will be urging repeal of that because they won't be happy with the good, solid Bible teaching that will be coming out of our institutions."

Another conferee questioned Ballard about the proposed constitutional amendment, saying, "I find no one who knows anything about it. I'm wondering if we're not being frightened by something that is not there."

Ballard Unsure of Committee Report

Ballard responded, "I have some information that it is from a subcommittee of the By-laws Committee that supposedly has brought this to the attention of the main committee of the state and we have looked into it and know it has been brought up and even have discussed it, but whether or not it will be presented by the General Board is yet to be seen in November."

A third person said, "We confronted the issue and I believe we've been heard. We have gone through proper channels."

The "proper channels" apparently referred to the September 5 meeting requested by Allen Gaines, president of the BGAV.

At this point in the discussion, Ballard said, "I remember both Executive Secretary Stephenson and President Gaines saying they had no problem with people knowing the meeting was held, it was just that information not be shared as to what went on."

Patterson Was the Preacher

Patterson, president of the Criswell Institute of Biblical Studies in Dallas, delivered two sermons in Lynchburg.

Except for responding to questions, he confined himself to preaching and left the organizational work to Pressler.

Last spring, when Patterson revealed his intention to lead an effort to control elections at the SBC for ten years, W. A. Criswell announced Patterson would withdraw from leadership, then followed that with another statement of strong endorsement of Patterson's doctrinal position and leadership of the Criswell institute.

Judge Pressler accused "the Baptist press" of distorting the issue and failure to report vicious attacks on Patterson by two deacons in First Church, Dallas, one of whom, Pressler said, left the church and joined Park Cities Church within ten days.

Of the reports on Criswell's curbing Patterson's activities, Pressler said, "The Baptist press orchestrated a story that Dr. Criswell had muzzled Paige. They don't know Paige Patterson. Nobody ever muzzles Paige Patterson."

Pressler said Criswell, SBC president in 1969–1970, told him, "If I had known the powers I had as president of the Southern Baptist Convention, things would have been different. I didn't know I had the ability to appoint anybody I wanted to the Committee on Committees."

"So," Pressler quoted Criswell, "the first thing you've got to do is inform a president of the powers which he has. The second problem I had was that I did not know who the knowledgeable conservatives were throughout each state in the convention, and you need to know who your conservatives are."

Pressler suggested for Virginia an organized chain of communication, including the *Concerned Baptist Messenger*, a publication occasionally issued by Arthur Ballard.

The chain of communication, said Pressler, should include someone in each association and a layman in each church. This is necessary, said Pressler, because "The press is not, has not been fair."

Pressler was not specific in several references to "The Baptist press," whether he was referring to Baptist Press, the news service of the Southern Baptist Convention, or to the 34 state Baptist papers supported by the Cooperative Programs in each state.

"Because we had good chains of communication, we could correct the false reports of a manipulated press," he said of the articles appearing last May when Adrian Rogers announced the end of his service as president.

The judge said the Baptist press "seeks to destroy that which they oppose," but "Because we had a good chain of communication we were able to let people know what was actually going on."

Expenses Said Exaggerated by Press

The judge singled out North Carolina Editor Marse Grant for criticism for reports on expenditures by himself in his activities. Pressler said Grant reported he had spent $50,000 to $100,000, figures he categorically denied.

He said his only expense has been "a plane ticket here or there and a telephone bill which sometimes upsets my wife."

Citing the Houston Convention resolution against "overt political activity" within the convention, Pressler said, "It's all coming from the other side," and cited as leaders Southern Seminary President Duke McCall, Pastors Wayne Dehoney, Kenneth Chafin, "and others."

Judge Pressler said, "The question today is what the Bible is, not the methodology of transmission."

He identified a liberal as one "who believes the Bible does or could contain any kind of error."

Admitting "I am not a theologian," Pressler told the audience, "I believe everything the Bible says, but I'm not sure what it says."

In Patterson's first sermon, based on Jeremiah 6, he compared the condition of Israel in the fifth and sixth centuries B.C. to America and the Southern Baptist Convention in the twentieth century.

Verses 10 and 15 were singled out for comments on the denomination. Patterson quoted three unnamed Southern Baptist theologians, saying they "look at the Word of God and have no delight in it."

Interpreting verse 15, the Dallas preacher said, "The saddest part about our denomination is there is no shame that we've lost Wake Forest University completely. There's no shame that we have virtually lost the University of Richmond; no shame that in the institutions and even the pulpits of our Lord the Word of God is not honored and magnified, but rather, we talk about sociology and psychology and the events of the day."

Patterson said the "threat of (God's) judgment is on our denomination."

Bold Mission Thrust "Was Already Failing"

Referring to the denomination's Bold Mission Thrust, he said, "They're blaming the failure on us but it was already failing before the Bible issue ever came up."

During a prayer following an invitation, Patterson said he did not ask for seminary professors to be removed from their positions, but that a revival occur in their hearts.

Patterson's second sermon was a defense of plenary, verbal inspiration, and inerrancy and infallibility of the Bible.

Citing words of Jesus in the gospels, Patterson said Jesus believed in verbal inspiration (Matt. 22:29-32); plenary inspiration (Luke 24:25-27); infallibility of scripture (John 5:39-47); and inerrancy of scripture (Matt. 5:18).

Booklet Series Tells Patterson Beliefs

The sermon included portions of Patterson's booklet "The Issue Is Truth," first of a projected series of 12 under the title "The Shophar Papers."

In a question and answer period, Patterson emphasized that when using the terms inerrant and infallible, he is always talking about the nonexistent autograph (original) writings.

"But," he declared, "in 98 to 99 percent we know exactly what the original was."

KJV Translators Said to Be "Lost"

He deprecated the King James Version of the Bible as a 1611 translation "by a bunch of Anglicans most of whom were lost," and cited "tragic translation" in the King James Version.

Quizzed on "variant readings" in ancient copies of scriptures, Patterson said, "We know that are copiest errors, but we are able to establish beyond shadow of doubt the original text."

The Dallas educator said he does not preach on John 8:3-11, the account of Jesus' treatment of the woman accused of adultery. He believes the passage to be a spurious text, "not of the hand of John," but believes it is a true record of John's preaching, added by a follower.

Regarding Mark 16:9-20, almost universally accepted as a spurious passage, Patterson said, "In my opinion, God saw that the ending of it (Mark's Gospel) got lost. I don't think the ending of it, as Mark wrote it, properly was inspired and inerrant. That's only a theory. But the point is we don't have the right ending of Mark's Gospel. It's lost somewhere."

Of Old Testament books that scholars agree were produced by an editor, Patterson said, "If there was an editor, he was fully inspired, so that what we have is inerrant and infallible."

Document 12
News Story: Beginning of Moderate Movement
by Cecil Sherman in Gatlinburg, Tennessee
Baptist Press, 3 October 1980, 1-3

" 'Concerned' Pastors Discuss Future; Deny Forming Faction"
by Dan Martin

GATLINBURG, Tenn. (BP)—An informal group of 15 to 20 "concerned" pastors met here to discuss the issues and future of the Southern Baptist Convention, but deny they are forming a political faction within the denomination.

The meeting was held in reaction to a group which has set as its goal capturing control of the Southern Baptist Convention, its agencies and institutions.

"We are taking them at their word," said Cecil Sherman, pastor of First Baptist Church of Asheville, N.C., who organized the meeting. "I regret this has come to pass, but I feel we have no choice (but to fight back)."

The catalyst which set off the meeting was a published report which quoted Texas Judge Paul Pressler outlining a plan to capture control of the convention through appointment of trustees to the agencies, boards and institutions.

Sherman, who also is president of the Baptist State Convention of North Carolina, said no formalized organization was planned, but that participants "have returned to our states to try to gather some friends to go to the convention," referring to the 1981 Southern Baptist Convention, to be held in June in Los Angeles.

Sherman added: "Somebody is going to have to stay after this for several years, continuing as long as our convention is in this broken condition."

Sherman declined to identify other participants, saying all would "tell the truth" if asked about their own participation, but had agreed not to reveal the identities of the other participants.

However, Baptist Press has learned the participants included at least one former president of the Southern Baptist Convention, Carl Bates, pastor of First Baptist Church of Charlotte, N.C. Also, all of the participants were pastors; no denominational worker attended.

"I would not presume to tell you whether we have any clout," Sherman said. "We are just people who think the stated objectives of Judge Pressler and Dr. (Paige) Patterson mean harm to the convention. . . . We reluctantly assembled to work to change the leadership of the convention. We did not turn this corner, we were jerked around it by events in Houston and St. Louis (the 1979 and 1980 meetings of the SBC)."

Welton Gaddy, pastor of Broadway Baptist Church of Fort Worth, Texas, said: "the only clout we have is in influencing people around us. This (the

Gatlinburg meeting) is a diverse group, with concerns for the convention which transcend our diversity. That is indication of some clout."

Although the controversy within the 13.4 million-member denomination swirls around the "inerrancy and infallibility" of the Bible, Sherman and his brother Bill, pastor of Woodmont Baptist Church in Nashville, claim the real issue is "not theology or the Bible," but an "overt power grab." Bill Sherman adds: "Never in the SBC have we had a group who has come out with the stated purpose—the transparent purpose—of taking command. Our system is built on mutual trust and cooperation, so we have been vulnerable to this."

Another participant, Kenneth Chafin, pastor of South Main Baptist Church in Houston, adds: "They have taken a theological word (inerrancy) and have used it to confuse the issue. The issue is really power."

Several of the participants claim the "inerrancy" faction really is composed of noncooperating Baptists, rather than cooperating Southern Baptists.

"The difference between a noncooperating Baptist and a Southern Baptist is how much they give to support the work of missions we are about," said Bill Sherman.

He maintained a majority of the inerrancy supporters give minimally to the Cooperative Program. "We have a group among us who want complete control of the convention, yet are giving $1 a week. They want to tell us how to run it, how to spend the money, what to believe. But they are not paying for it."

Adds Cecil Sherman: "The real Southern Baptists have been outflanked by the clever, political work of a minority. I think that I and my kind are the real Southern Baptists, friends and supporters of missions. Missions is what called this convention together and what will hold us together rather than doctrinal issues.

"If they (the inerrantists) believe the Bible so much, why don't they put their money where their mouth is? The real contributors to Southern Baptist life ought to determine the policies."

Another participant, Vernon Davis, pastor of First Baptist Church, Alexandria, Va., said the inerrancy debate puts the SBC "in danger of being sidetracked from the basic support of missions and evangelism and the strengthening of our institutions. The people who have been supportive of the institutions and missions should be heard from."

All of those interviewed by Baptist Press see the possibility of a split, although none want one to occur. "We are not interested in a split," said Lavonn Brown, pastor of First Baptist Church of Norman, Okla. "We are simply interested in knowing what we can do to move the convention to a more moderate direction than some of the extremism that has come of late."

Brown, a former trustee of Southern Baptist Theological Seminary, added: "Our question is does anyone, regardless of theological position, have the right to seek to control the SBC?"

Chafin, chairman of trustees at Southwestern Baptist Theological Seminary, noted his reluctance to form a "counter machine" to the Pressler-Patterson coalition.

"I hate to see it, because then it becomes a power struggle, where you don't have trust levels, good communications. It is just an effort to see which group can haul the most warm bodies in to vote," Chafin said.

"I am not really interested in creating a 'political' party, but I also am not going to roll over and let a group of Frank Norrisite fundamentalists steal the institutions of my denomination," he added.

1981

Chronology

<u>June.</u> Fifteen Southern Baptist historians appeal for defense and protection of denominational heritage relating to Baptist distinctives, the purpose of the SBC, the centrality of the Bible, and the Baptist aversion to creedalism.

<u>June 9–11.</u> SBC, Los Angeles, 13,529 messengers, Bailey Smith presiding.

—Ed Young, pastor of Second Baptist Church, Houston, elected president of the Pastors' Conference. Unaligned with either moderates or fundamentalists at this time, Young would eventually embrace the fundamentalist movement and be elected SBC president.

—Bailey Smith reelected SBC president with 60.24% of the vote over moderate Abner McCall with 39.30%.

—Motion of Moderates to limit SBC president's power in the appointment of the Committee on Committees fails. The failure of the motion highlights the power of the presidency in the fundamentalist strategy to dominate the boards and agencies of the SBC. See recommendation 9 regarding bylaw 21 in *SBC Annual 1982*, 24.

—Motion by Herschel H. Hobbs, former SBC president and primary author of the 1963 "Baptist Faith and Message," to reaffirm both the voluntary nature of *The Baptist Faith and Message* and its statement on the Bible. See document 13.

—Passed resolution 10, a strong traditional Baptist statement on religious liberty and separation of church and state that praised both the Baptist Joint Committee and the Christian Life Commission. The stance of this resolution as well as that of the BJC and the CLC come under increasing criticism. See document 14.

—Moderates successfully amend the Committee on Boards report.

Document 13
Hobbs's Motion to Reaffirm the Baptist Faith and Message and Its Statement on the Bible
SBC Annual 1981, 35, 45

Herschel H. Hobbs (Okla.) moved that, in light of the marvelous and challenging president's address, "We reaffirm our historic Baptist position that the Holy Bible, which has truth without any mixture of error for its matter, is our adequate rule of faith and practice, and that we reaffirm our belief in The Baptist Faith and Message adopted in 1963, including all seventeen articles, plus the preamble which protects the conscience of the individual and guards us from a creedal faith." The motion was referred to the Committee on Order of Business for scheduling in a later session.

. . . .

President Smith announced the time for considering scheduled motions and recognized Herschel H. Hobbs (Okla.) to discuss his previously offered motion. . . . [Adrian Rogers (Tenn.) subsequently asked, just before the vote, that the body request the recording secretary to place in the record the preceding remarks by Hobbs. The request was sustained by common consent.] The pertinent (last) portion of Hobbs' statement: "This motion is designed to emphasize that the preamble is as much a part of the statement voted by the Convention as any other part. When the Convention voted to set up a committee to do the study that resulted in this statement, it said that the product *shall* serve as information to the churches and *may*—notice the difference—not shall, *may* serve as guidelines for agencies of the Convention. Now the other one thing that I want to say is this. I was asked a question many times—I was asked it this morning—concerning the first paragraph [of the motion] that defines the Holy Bible: 'which has truth without any mixture of error for its matter.' Now I'm reading from the King James Version—2 Timothy 3:16—'all scripture is given by inspiration of God.' The Greek New Testament reads, 'all'—without the definite article—and that means every single part of the whole is God-breathed. And a God of truth does not breathe error." Larry Lewis (Mo.) raised points for clarification regarding the motion's intent and its effect on resolution no. 16 (Doctrinal Integrity) adopted by the 1980 Convention; the president and Hobbs responded. The Hobbs motion passed by an enthusiastic standing vote.

Document 14
Traditional SBC Resolution on Religious Liberty and Church and State
SBC Annual 1981, 56

"Resolution No.10—On Affirming Religious Liberty
and Separation of Church and State"

WHEREAS, The United States Constitutional principle of religious liberty has given freedom for expression of the separation of the church and state; and

WHEREAS, This precious principle is under constant attack by those who would serve sectarian purposes; and

WHEREAS, The growth of government poses a constant threat of intrusion upon this indispensable principle; and

WHEREAS, The Baptist Joint Committee on Public Affairs, the Christian Life Commission, and other agencies are deeply committed to the principles of religious liberty and separation of church and state; and

WHEREAS, These agencies have repeatedly given leadership and assistance to Southern Baptists involved in problems regarding religious liberty and the separation of church and state; and

WHEREAS, The need is evident for continued vigilance and determination to preserve religious liberty;

Be it therefore *Resolved*, That we express our gratitude to the Baptist Joint Committee on Public Affairs, the Christian Life Commission, and other agencies for their efforts in defending Christian morality and ethics; and

Be it further *Resolved*, That we affirm our belief that religion flourishes best without government's interference or tax support; and

Be it further *Resolved*, That we caution schools directly or indirectly connected with this Convention to give serious study to the high price which government usually exacts for its favors; and

Be it further *Resolved*, That we call on our people to support the institutions which serve our religious objectives; and

Be it further *Resolved*, That we voice our earnest protest against tax proposals which would finance educational and other activities of churches or religious groups; and

Be it further *Resolved*, That the Southern Baptist Convention, in accordance with and in commitment to the First Amendment to the Constitution of the United States, and to the historic Baptist principle of church and state separation, deplore and reject the arrogation of the right of any group to define and pronounce for all people what is the Christian faith, and to seek through political means to impose this faith upon the American people under a government which is mandated to safeguard and respect the people of all religions and no religion.

Be it finally *Resolved*, That we express our thanks to God for courts which uphold the First Amendment against the enormous pressures of our time.

1982

Chronology

<u>February.</u> Moderate Roy L. Honeycutt succeeds Duke K. McCall as president of the Southern Baptist Theological Seminary.

<u>May 14.</u> Fundamentalist Adrian Rogers stated in an interview with moderate Jack Harwell, editor of the *Christian Index,* that the point of tension in Southern Baptist life was "the Cooperative Program: we're trying to get everybody to support everything the same way." As fundamentalists gain increasing power in the SBC, they will affirm the CP; conversely moderates will echo Rogers's earlier criticism of the way CP is used. See document 15.

<u>May 27.</u> The *Christian Index* reports that Duke K. McCall would be nominated for the presidency of the SBC in New Orleans.

<u>June 15–17.</u> SBC, New Orleans, 20,456 messengers, Bailey Smith presiding.
—Fundamentalist Fred Wolfe, Mobile pastor, elected president of the Pastors' Conference.
—Fundamentalist Jimmy Draper elected president on second ballot with 56.97% of the vote over moderate Duke McCall with 43.03%.
—Fundamentalist Bailey Smith preaches strident and controversial sermon, unlike his presidential address at Los Angeles. See document 16.
—Moderates successfully amend and replace three nominees on the Committee on Boards report.
—Resolutions approved endorsing scientific creationism, supporting a constitutional amendment prohibiting abortion, and sanctioning an amendment regarding voluntary prayer in public schools. See documents 17, 18, and 19. These resolutions mark a deviation from past SBC actions regarding government involvement in religious matters, and reflect a sharp ideological turn to the right in SBC life.

<u>November 17.</u> Arkansas Baptist Convention adopts resolution opposing the views on apostasy of Dale Moody, longtime professor of theology at Southern Seminary. Moody is terminated at Southern.

<u>November 29.</u> Moderate group meeting at Atlanta airport decides to launch newspaper (*SBC Today,* later *Baptists Today*).

Document 15
News Story: Adrian Rogers's "Golden Calf" Statement
Baptist Press, 14 May 1982, 6-7

"Doctrinal Unity, Program Unity Rise, Fall Together, Rogers Says"
by Dan Martin

ROME GA (BP)—Doctrinal unity and program unity in the Southern Baptist Convention rise and fall together, former SBC President Adrian Rogers says.

"You can't have one without the other," said Rogers, immediate past president of the 13.8-million member denomination and pastor of Bellevue Baptist Church in Memphis, Tenn., at a press conference in Rome, where he was preaching at West Rome Baptist Church.

Rogers, however, noted he is in favor of the denomination's cooperative missions, education and evangelism efforts, but feels it is "not only illogical, it is immoral to ask a man to support with his money and with his influence . . . things that are theologically repugnant to him."

Baptist Press obtained a tape recording of the press conference from West Rome church pastor Jerry Vines, who called the meeting.

The Memphis pastor told the press conference—attended by only one newsperson, Jack U. Harwell, editor of the *Christian Index*, journal of the Georgia Baptist Convention—that Southern Baptists "have made a golden calf of the program. . . . It's almost easier to be against the Virgin Birth than the program."

By program, he said he meant the entire work of the denomination, of which the Cooperative Program is a major part.

The Cooperative Program is the denomination's unified giving plan, through which the 36,000-plus churches support missions, education, evangelism and other efforts, including state and national conventions, missionaries at home and abroad, theological education, colleges and universities, hospitals, child care facilities and other activities.

In 1981, according to the SBC Stewardship Commission, the churches contributed $229,471,751, of which $81,685,873, was channeled through the national convention.

For Rogers, an outspoken proponent of biblical inerrancy (belief that the Bible, in its original autographs, is without error), denominational support is linked to conservative theology.

He said Southern Baptists started out "with a moderately narrow theology," and while the denomination "always refused a written down, finely honed creed," there were common beliefs, such as "the inerrancy of the scriptures, salvation by grace through faith, the priesthood of the believer, autonomy of the local church, baptism by immersion of believers only, the security of the believer. . . . "

Alongside that narrow theology, the denomination "had a broad program. Well, then somebody said about 1925, we need to narrow the program. So we got the Cooperative Program. So not only could we more or less believe the same things, but correspondingly and logically, we could support the same things."

After the "golden years" of a narrow theology and a narrow program, Rogers claimed that what we have now is a broad theology where everybody is saying we have unity in diversity. But the unity in diversity is only theological, not program wise. And so now the sin . . . in the Southern Baptist Convention is not that you be aberrant in your theology; but the sin in the Southern Baptist Convention today is that you be aberrant in your program, that you don't do the program just right, that you fail to support everything."

He added the question revolves around "what we believe about the word of God. If we can't settle that, I believe it is the ultimate cancer that will destroy the organism. There are two different schools of thought; there is a continental divide; there is an east is east and a west is west. Either the word of God is infallible or it's fallible; it is inerrant or it is errant."

He charged the denomination has "many professors who do not believe the Bible is historically, philosophically, scientifically and theologically without error," a point inerrantists stress, maintaining the Bible is without error in all of these dimensions.

He said he would "fight, really, for the right of every man to believe as he wants," and added: "I don't want to talk too bravely, but I'd be willing to die for . . . the freedom . . . for you to believe what you believe. But don't you realize that when you're asking me to pay your salary or else be thought of as a bad boy, that you are forcing your beliefs on me . . . ?"

He commented there are some within the denomination "who would like to put a steel band around our dollars. They say you do not have room to wiggle program-wise, but we've got plenty of room on the other side to wiggle theologically. And, again, I say, what is sauce for the goose is sauce for the gander."

Rogers said if he could prescribe a solution "the best . . . would be to go back and narrow up this again, so we can say everybody more or less believes alike, everybody more or less supports alike. . . . Nobody's in a straitjacket."

But, he added, "I sincerely doubt that will ever happen."

Rogers' "next best thing," is "that we have widened the theology, correspondingly we widen the program," to allow freedom of belief but also freedom to support or decline to support the component parts of the denomination.

"I would say that perhaps we could remove tension from our Southern Baptist Convention if we would relax our insistency of Southern Baptists walking in lockstep program-wise," Rogers said. "We cannot put people in a straitjacket program-wise and have an unlimited freedom theologically."

He said he knows his proposal "strikes at the very vitals of what we are trying to do because someone says the genius of our Southern Baptist work is the concentration of our efforts in our programs," but adds, "First best is to have a commonality of beliefs and a commonality of program."

While Rogers says he does not advocate changing the wording of the 1963 Baptist Faith and Message statement in regards to the Scripture, he did say the problem could be solved if the statement were amended and "just simply said the Bible not 'has' but 'is' truth without any mixture of error, period." The average layman wouldn't see the difference, he added, but "that is where the theological fur would begin to fly."

He claimed that when denominationally employed persons sign the statement and still believe the Bible is fallible, the "problem (is) not theological but ethical."

Rogers commented that the 1981 annual meeting of the denomination in Los Angeles "was the biggest head on collision we've ever had in the Southern Baptist Convention. I do think that we came away agreeing to disagree."

He added he was "grieved, strongly grieved" that SBC President Bailey Smith was opposed for reelection to a traditional second term, but added he thinks "a lot of the spirit of conviviality was due to Bailey's spirit of grace."

While participants came out of the convention "without being all bristled up," Rogers says he does not think "that the issues were dissolved just because we came out in sort of a nice feeling. The gut level issues were not resolved, and I don't think that they will be for a long time."

He predicted a large attendance for the 1982 annual meeting in New Orleans (June 15-17) and said: "I don't feel the conservatives are going to be asleep, or that they are not going to be interested, that they are not going to be there. They will be."

Document 16
Excerpts from Bailey Smith's 1982 Presidential Sermon

"Southern Baptists' Most Serious Question"
by Bailey E. Smith, 15 June 1982

. . . .

If Southern Baptists ever try to escape the absolute priority of evangelism and the authority of the infallible, inerrant Word of God, we will not be able to escape the mediocrity of other mainline denominations. I asked a former preacher who had graduated from seminary what his non-Baptist seminary did for him. He said to me, "It made me an atheist." Many of their edifices are no longer churches to proclaim the unsearchable riches of Christ. They are country clubs with steeples on top. They are conservatories of culture instead of lighthouses of Gospel truth.

I heard of a family who was having a very particular preacher to dinner. This preacher could not stand slang phrases at all. The father told his two sons that if they used one slang phrase he would work them over. As the preacher was eating with the family, one of the sons said, "Pass me those cotton-pickin' potatoes." That father grabbed that boy, jerked him outside, dragged him behind the barn and beat him within an inch of his life. The boy's cries could have been heard for miles. The father got back into the house, sat down at the table, looked at his other son and said, "Now, what do you want?" I'll tell you one thing, I don't want any of them cotton-pickin' potatoes." We don't want the cotton-pickin' potatoes that made the other denominations die.

To the degree that Southern Baptists move from this great salvation it shall move toward such mediocrity. We will not escape.

We will not escape the deadness of the so-called social gospel that has done very little good for society and has no gospel. They speak of race relations, world hunger, temperance, and human ethics, but it has always been the evangelistic Bible-honoring church that has opened its doors to all races and put food on the table of the hungry.

. . . .

We of Bold Mission Thrust commitment need to understand that there are some marriages that will not work. We cannot wed missions to liberalism; evangelism to liturgical worship; spiritual power to high church music; Holy Ghost unction to sleepy sermons; or transformed lives to skeptical preachers. We must preach the Bible, live the Bible, and obey the Bible. We must not be bland, benign, bickering Baptists, but Bold, Believing, Bible Baptists.

Document 17
SBC Resolution on School Prayer
SBC Annual 1982, 58

"Resolution No. 9—On Prayer in Schools"

WHEREAS, The first amendment to the Constitution of the United States of America clearly states that the Congress shall pass no law prohibiting the free exercise of religion, and

WHEREAS, The same first amendment protects us against the establishment of religion, and

WHEREAS, A constitutional amendment is pending wherein there is no violation of either of those ideals inherent in the separation of church and state, and

WHEREAS, This proposed amendment neither requires nor restricts the vocal expression of individual or group prayer in public schools, and

WHEREAS, Considerable confusion as to the rights and privileges guaranteed by the Constitution with regard to prayer in schools has been engendered by the Supreme Court decisions of 1962 and 1963, and

WHEREAS, Public school officials and lower courts have frequently misinterpreted these Supreme Court decisions as a ban on voluntary prayer, and

WHEREAS, For 170 years following the writing of the First Amendment, the right of prayer in public schools was a time-honored exercise and a cherished privilege, and

WHEREAS, Southern Baptists historically have affirmed the right of voluntary prayer in public places, and

WHEREAS, The proposed constitutional amendment reads simply, "Nothing in this Constitution shall be construed to prohibit individual or group prayer in public schools or other public institutions. No person shall be required by the United States or by any state to participate in prayer," and

WHEREAS, This proposed amendment does not constitute a call for government-written or government-mandated prayer.

Therefore, be it *Resolved*, That we the messengers of the Southern Baptist Convention in session, June 1982, New Orleans, Louisiana, declare our support of the aforementioned proposed constitutional amendment.

Be it further *Resolved*, That we shall work continually to hold fast to our faith and to the freedoms in which we believe and by which we live.

Document 18
SBC Resolution on Scientific Creationism
SBC Annual 1982, 59

"Resolution No. 14—On Scientific Creationism"

WHEREAS, The theory of evolution has never been proven to be a scientific fact, and

WHEREAS, Public school students are now being indoctrinated in evolution-science, and

WHEREAS, Creation-science can be presented solely in terms of scientific evidence without any religious doctrines or concepts, and

WHEREAS, Public school students should be taught all the scientific evidence on the subject of the origin of the world and life, and

WHEREAS, Academic freedom and free speech should be encouraged rather than inhibited.

Therefore, be it *Resolved*, That the Southern Baptist Convention in session in New Orleans, Louisiana, June 1982, express our support for the teaching of Scientific Creationism in our public schools.

Document 19
SBC Resolution on Abortion
SBC Annual 1982, 65

"Resolution No. 11—On Abortion and Infanticide"

WHEREAS, Both medical science and biblical references indicate that human life begins at conception, and

WHEREAS, Southern Baptists have traditionally upheld the sanctity and worth of all human life, both born and preborn, as being created in the image of God, and

WHEREAS, Current judicial opinion gives no guarantee of protection of pre-born persons, thus permitting the widespread practice of abortion on demand, which has led to the killing of an estimated four thousand developing human beings daily in the United States, and

WHEREAS, Social acceptance of abortion has begun to dull society's respect for all human life, leading to growing occurrences of infanticide, child abuse, and active euthanasia.

Therefore, be it *Resolved*, That the messengers to the 1982 Southern Baptist Convention affirm that all human life, both born and preborn is sacred, bearing the image of God, and is not subject to personal judgments as to "quality of life" based on such subjective criteria as stage of development, abnormality, intelligence level, degree of dependency, cost of medical treatment, or inconvenience to parents.

Be it further *Resolved*, That we abhor the use of federal, state or local tax money; public, tax-supported medical facilities; or Southern Baptist supported medical facilities for the practice of selfish, medically unnecessary abortions and/or the practice of withholding treatment from unwanted or defective newly born infants.

Be it finally *Resolved*, That we support and will work for appropriate legislation and/or constitutional amendment which will prohibit abortions except to save the physical life of the mother, and that we also support and will work for legislation which will prohibit the practice of infanticide.

Document 20
News Wrapup of the 1982 SBC
Baptist Press, 8 July 1982, 3-4

"New Orleans SBC Viewed by Editors"
by Dan Martin

NASHVILLE, TN (BP)—Editors of 20 state Baptist newspapers used terms such as uneasy, hostile, volatile, polarized, uncertain and tug-of-war to describe the 1982 annual meeting of the Southern Baptist Convention.

The editorials, while commenting on a variety of things, generally spoke of the atmosphere of the convention, the emergence of political parties, the performance of the outgoing president, and speculations about the new president.

David Simpson of the *Indiana Baptist*, one of the newest editors, wrote: "Baptists from around the world had an opportunity to say something positive about Christ, the church and brotherly love. The statement, to say the least, was garbled."

Edgar Cooper of the *Florida Baptist Witness*, described the 125th annual meeting: "From the welcoming address . . . to the final amen, there was a feeling of tension and a noticeable division of the messengers. The so-called conservatives and moderates were at it again."

J. B. Fowler of the *Baptist New Mexican* said the "lack of trust that has developed across the denomination the last three or four years made this the most divisive convention I have attended since 1950 when I went to my first one in Houston."

Presnall W. Wood, of the *Baptist Standard* in Texas, wrote that Southern Baptists "left Los Angeles in 1981 thinking they had turned the corner on a wearisome controversy, but they left New Orleans still standing on the corner."

C. R. Daley of the *Western Recorder* in Kentucky, said the meeting "is history and we are still together with no formal split in sight. . . . There were no clear winners but there were clearly some losers. They were Bold Mission Thrust, mutual trust among Southern Baptists and the 'sweet, sweet spirit in this place' which we often sing about."

Jack U. Harwell of the Georgia *Christian Index*, was encouraged, writing that the "mixed signals" say "Southern Baptists are going to stay somewhere near the middle of the road on most issues, but always on the 'right' side of that middle line, never on the left."

Many of the editors wrote of the division of the denomination, with John Roberts of the *Baptist Courier* in South Carolina, writing that the convention is "divided, with strong feeling on each side of the division. This division is deeper than it was last year, or the year before, or five or 10 years ago. It goes much deeper than rallying around an individual and opposing another. At the core of each side is commitment to an ideology and determination to see that ideology prevail."

Al Shackleford, editor of the *Tennessee Baptist and Reflector*, said: "It is now evident that our convention has evolved into two political parties. . . . It was distressing . . . to see that on almost every issue faced the votes—and the debaters—were predictable, right down the party line."

He added that if the two parties remain equal, "our future conventions will be dominated by bitter debates," and that if one gains sufficient strength to domi-nate the convention "our beloved SBC would face the likely possibility of a split."

Larry High of the *Maryland Baptist*, wrote that if political activities are esca-lated, "our convention will make the Republican and Democratic conventions look like amateur night."

Lynn Clayton of the *Louisiana Baptist Message* wrote that the convention "is held together by the glue of trust—trust in God and trust in fellow Baptists," adding that "present internal conditions of charges, countercharges and partisan politics are weakening our glue."

Wood of Texas wrote that the "division was there and it was not over the Bible. Nor is the issue over being liberal or conservative. Southern Baptists are conservatives and finding a label to describe differing Baptists is difficult. But whatever the label, the conservative messengers were divided and it was over control of the institutions."

"The struggle . . . is control," Shackleford wrote, adding that the political plums in the SBC are the control of the trustees of the SBC agencies and institu-tions. The key to that system is to control the presidency and its power to name the Committee on Committees which nominates the Committee on Boards which nominates the trustees."

The presidency of the 13.8 million member denomination drew much atten-tion, a situation which Marse Grant, of the *Biblical Recorder* in North Carolina criticized, writing that the politicking—before the convention and during it—has overshadowed everything else. Time was when Foreign Missions night or a great message dominated the memories of those attending. Not so any longer. Now it's the presidency."

The new president, Jimmy Draper, pastor of First Baptist Church of Euless, Texas, did not draw unanimous approval.

Dick McCartney of the *Oklahoma Baptist Messenger* said questions about Draper are hard to answer "without qualifications. It depends on a number of things. Who will be his advisers and confidants? How does he perceive the office? What personal agenda does he have? Few people beyond the president can answer them."

He added that "time will tell" but commented he is "optimistic. . . . What Southern Baptists desperately need right now is a new commitment to openness. I believe we may have the beginning of that in Jimmy Draper."

New Mexico's Fowler noted he "has no quarrel" with Draper, but advised him to remember "that the Southern Baptist Convention belongs to all of us—conservatives, ultraconservatives and the not-so-conservatives. It is ours and we love it. We will rebuke it when it is wrong and fight for it when it is right and do battle with anyone who tries to steal it."

Julian Pentecost of the *Religious Herald* in Virginia, said Draper "is on record to the effect he wants his presidency to be one of healing and bringing us together. . . . This desperately needs to be done and we hope and pray he will be equal to the challenge. If he is to achieve his objective, it is imperative he accept the reality of our diversity."

Outgoing president Bailey E. Smith, pastor of First Southern Baptist Church of Del City, Okla., got praise and criticism. Several editors lauded him for presiding with "sincerity, fairness and wit." He was criticized for his appointments.

Georgia's Harwell said Smith's presidential message was "one of the most strident rightist messages we have heard in years." Kentucky's Daley said the message was "appropriate in theme but its tone was inflammatory and accusatory."

Daley said Smith's appointments to the key committees "constituted an abuse of office and betrayed any claim he ever made for a healing role as president."

A number of editors criticized the resolutions committee, with Fowler saying it was "heavily orchestrated . . . by members of America's religious right movement." He said the solutions on prayer and scientific creationism were "tragically unfortunate."

Oklahoma's McCartney said the SBC "deserves more than it got" from the resolutions committee, adding that if the conventions "must have a committee on resolutions, we should make them broadly representative of Southern Baptists or we should limit the scope of their work to the routine resolutions of appreciation and acknowledgement."

Missouri's Terry spelled out that the committee chairman, Norris Sydnor Jr., was advised by Ed McAteer, founder of the Religious Roundtable, a right-wing political organization, and said: "In retrospect, one cannot help but wonder why Smith appointed a person chairman of the resolutions committee who had never before attended a session of the Southern Baptist Convention. . . . One also wonders who directed the committee, Sydnor or McAteer?"

1983

Chronology

<u>January.</u> W. A. Criswell, pastor of FBC Dallas, claims SBC erosion due to infidels in colleges and seminaries and decline in evangelism.

<u>March 21.</u> Thirty-three women meet in Louisville KY to initiate the formation of SBC Women in Ministry.

<u>April.</u> First issue of moderate newspaper *SBC Today.*

<u>May.</u> Moderates, dissatisfied with the recently announced Committee on Boards nominees, announce they will not challenge Draper for the SBC presidency. This is the only time from 1981 to 1989 that an incumbent president was not challenged.

<u>June.</u> Formation of Women in Ministry, SBC (later Southern Baptist Women in Ministry). See documents 21 and 24.

<u>June 14–16.</u> SBC, Pittsburgh, 13,740 messengers, Jimmy Draper presiding.

—Jimmy Draper is unopposed for reelection as president.

—Moderates hold "reception," the forerunner to the SBC Forum, counter-organization to the SBC Pastors' Conference.

—Fundamentalist Charles Stanley, the next president of the SBC, became visible at the SBC as the new president of the SBC Pastors' Conference and chair of the Committee on Boards. Previous efforts by moderates to challenge nominations from this committee had been successful but failed in Pittsburgh.

—Resolution on women adopted that was not as harsh as the 1984 resolution would be. Joyce Rogers sought to amend 1983 resolution so it would read that "this resolution should not be interpreted as endorsing the ordination of women" but the messengers defeated the amendment.

—Resolution "On Freedom and Responsibility in Southern Baptist Seminaries" adopted. While milder than previous statements and rhetoric, the resolution's emphasis fell clearly on the side of "responsibility" rather than "freedom."

—Resolution "On Religious Liberty" adopted that fundamentalists sought in vain to amend. This resolution softened the 1982 resolution "On Prayer in Schools," but religious liberty issues and the role of the BJC become extremely controversial this year. See related stories in documents 22 and 23.

June 27. Samuel T. Currin, newly appointed chair of the SBC Public Affairs
    Committee, speaks without authorization for the committee opposing BJCPA
    position on public school prayer amendment. See documents 22 and 23.
November. Fundamentalist SBC President James Draper proposes "some mini-
    mum things" Southern Baptists must believe, but his creedalistic proposal
    goes nowhere. Other fundamentalist leaders prefer their creedalistic interpre-
    tation of the BFM, while moderates wanted no creed of any kind.

Document 21
Nancy Sehested's Sermon at Women in Ministry Meeting

"We Have This Treasure"
by Nancy Hastings Sehested

Greetings to you, sisters and brothers, in the name of our Lord Jesus Christ, who did not count equality with God a thing to be grasped; in the name of our Lord, who no longer calls us servants, but friends; in the name of our Lord, who welcomed Mary to his teaching, saying that she had "chosen the good portion"—the one thing that was needed (Luke 10:42).

Wherever the Spirit of Christ rules, there is freedom! Wherever the Holy Spirit blows, the neat corners and taut strings on the package created to box God in are torn and unraveled. Our ancestors in the faith lived in tents which could easily be broken down and carried on the journey to a new land and a new home. The temple itself was portable—God would not be enclosed with bricks and mortar, stone and wood.

God's spoken self-identity as the great "I AM WHO I AM" can also be translated as the great "I WILL BE WHO I WILL BE."

Our spiritual pilgrimage as women is also like the lives of our spiritual ancestors in another way. As the Hebrews passed out of bondage and slavery in Egypt, there was great anticipation, great excitement, a vision of new lives and new possibilities. A new land. A new place.

Ah, but then there was the desert. The expectation and vision of a new place, a new way of living, came crashing into the experience of the desert. Maybe Egypt wasn't so bad after all. At least we could eat good.

. . . .

Think with me for a minute. In what ways have your expectations—your hopes and dreams and callings and visions—in what ways have they been preyed upon and victimized by your experience of attempting to live them out in flesh and blood?

The scripture passage you've heard read from 2 Corinthians this morning is a good one for us to dwell on. In fact, Paul's famous image—"We have this treasure in earthen vessels"—is worth considering as a mirror to reflect on our common spiritual pilgrimage. I'd like to suggest something of a novel way of entering into the text: starting at midpoint, moving backwards to the beginning and then confronting the end.

Before anything else, there is the treasure. Before anything else, the undifferentiated Good News. Gospel news. News of God's grace. And not just news, as in information, but news as in experience. And not just a word, but *the* Word, in living color, flesh and blood, a walking portrait of divine mercy and forgiveness and promise.

But there's more still. Not just Good News generally, but Good News—treasure—for us, for me. Not just timeless, cosmic, nameless Good News, but Good News for me, with my name of it, in my life. The Good News gets specific. It calls my name and bids me to follow.

And I say, "WHO, ME? You gotta be kidding. I'm a woman! I've got a high voice and no hair on my chest. I'm emotional, I cry, and I can't think straight. I prefer cooking and diapers and diets and cleaning up after Wednesday night church suppers. At least I'm supposed to. Don't I?"

Maybe yes, maybe no. What does it matter? Martha wasn't distracted with serving, but with *much serving*; anxious and troubled about many things, but not the one thing needed. Blocked, by unseen forces, from choosing the "good portion." Old Pharaoh would have liked her. Every busy pastor would love to have a stable of Marthas.

But stables are for horses. Not women. Not men.

But back to Paul and treasure—our treasure—not as a thing to be grasped, but a call to a new order of service, as different from the old as night is from day, as east is from west.

We have this treasure.

But there's trouble in paradise. We have this treasure in earthen vessels. We share this "earthen vessel" quality—this not-yet-perfected, this not-yet-mature, this not-yet-fully-refined quality—along with all others whose name has been called, whose heart has been gripped, whose devotion has been commanded.

And our fellow earthen vessels look at us much the way St. James and the other leaders of the first church at Jerusalem must have looked at Paul when he first suggested he go over and preach to the Gentiles.

Gentiles in the fellowship? Women in the ministry?

You're gonna baptize a what? You're gonna ordain a what?

The uncircumcised at our table? Skirts in our pulpit?

Putting treasures in earthen vessels is something like putting an ice cream cone in two-year-old's hands. Things can get messy.

How are we to live, how are we to carry on, how are we to keep hope alive when visionary expectation intersects with the concrete details of this time and this place and our lives?

Were we foolish to come here? If not foolish, maybe just misguided? If we speak loudly enough, to be heard doors away and blocks away, we would certainly be met with a chorus of "yeses." Old master Pharaoh will take us back if we're good girls and learn to behave ourselves.

But most of us just feel trapped. We feel afflicted, perplexed, persecuted and struck down—sometimes even on the edge of being crushed, driven to despair, forsaken, and destroyed. We simply can't go back. Our eyes have been opened and our ears have popped. The way back is blocked by a force far greater than Pharaoh's army ever was. But so far the future only chokes us with dust and blinds us with sand. These desert storms give us a bad case of spiritual dyslexia, spiritual disorientation, not knowing which way is forward and which is backward.

With these experiences fresh in our minds—sometimes even branded upon our hearts—we come to Paul's affirmation of hope, his vital sense of expectation, with a certain measure of puzzlement. And with a discreet tone of voice, we ask, Run that by me again?

Afflicted, but *not* crushed; perplexed, but *not* despairing; persecuted, but *not* forsaken; struck down, but *not* destroyed; we can get into the part about being given up to death for Jesus' sake. But Paul continues: "So we do not lose heart."

The first thing that comes to mind as a response is: Says who?

Sisters and brothers, here is my testimony. May God bless and use these words as is needed and fitting.

We live in the great in-between time. We are ready, but still waiting. We are called, but not confirmed. We are trained, but not employed. We are willing, but not able.

Pastors tell us their congregations are not yet ready and able to accept us. Congregations tell us their pastors are not yet ready and able to accept us. We are to our Convention like Paul's early Gentile converts.

We live in the great in-between time. Our calling is clear and our gifts are manifest. But the desert is a severe, unforgiving place. Many have already parted company, taking on other careers in other fields, or taking positions with other denominations. Are there many among us who have not entertained such options? For those who have moved on, we bid Godspeed. Some of us feel that if we had any sense, we would do the same. But we remain. It is no special virtue, no special righteousness. Stiff upper lips won't do.

We can't fully understand why we stay, although all of us would have some partial reasons. The deepest reason is not fully fathomable. The best we can say is that this is where we're called to be. And that's enough.

We live in the great in-between time. We hope for brighter futures, assured of nothing but God's continued fidelity to undergird our spirits and nurture our souls. We see glimmers of light here and there shining in the darkness, and we celebrate and cultivate it. But we know that light shines from a great distance. It will be a while yet before the whole room is lit up.

We live in the time of great in between. I propose that we make a covenant with each other.

That we covenant to care for each other, to listen to each other, to be open to each other's encouragement and counsel.

That we stay in touch with each other, allow each other the freedom to make different choices, that we burn our bitterness as a sacrifice to the Lord.

That we confess to each other, treat each other with gentleness.

That we open our communion to new brothers as well as sisters. That we pray for each other, challenge each other, rejoice with each other, weep with each other.

That we covenant to meet again with each other, for mutual support and correction, for study of the Scriptures with each other, for singing spiritual songs and hymns together.

Why? Because we have this treasure.

We have this treasure in earthen vessels.

Vessels that need filling and refilling again and again.

Vessels filled to spill over with healing waters to a hurting world.

The treasure is not buried.

It is here among us and in us.

For what we preach is not ourselves, but Jesus Christ as Lord.

We are afflicted in every way, but not crushed.

Perplexed, but not driven to despair.

Persecuted, but not forsaken.

Struck down, but not destroyed.

Let the light shine in our hearts.

Let the light shine on out of darkness.

For we have this treasure.

Document 22
News Story: Currin vs. BJCPA on Prayer in Schools
Baptist Press, 28 June 1983, 1-2

"New Trustee Opposes BJCPA On School Prayer Amendment"
by Larry Chesser

WASHINGTON (BP)—In opposition to testimony presented by the Baptist Joint Committee on Public Affairs, a newly elected Southern Baptist Convention representative to that agency has urged a Senate panel to pass President Reagan's proposed school prayer amendment.

In a letter to Senate Judiciary Committee chairman Strom Thurmond, R-S.C., North Carolina attorney Samuel T. Currin cited a 1982 SBC resolution supporting the Reagan prayer amendment as clear evidence "that Baptists favor a restoration of voluntary prayer to the public schools."

Thurmond's committee is considering two proposed constitutional amendments approved early in June by the Subcommittee on the Constitution. The Reagan proposal, S.J. Res 73, would allow state-written oral prayer in public schools. A substitute supported by Sen. Orrin G. Hatch, R-Utah, and other members of the subcommittee would permit "individual or group silent prayer and meditation" and provide "equal access to the use of public schools by all voluntary student groups."

Thurmond entered the Currin letter and a copy of the 1982 SBC resolution into the record after hearing testimony from BJCPA General Counsel John W. Baker urging the panel to reject both proposals.

Currin's letter quoted the 1982 resolution's erroneous declaration that the Reagan amendment "does not constitute a call for government-written or government-mandated prayer." A printed White House explanation of the amendment's impact said the proposal would empower state and local officials to compose prayers to be used in public schools.

"If groups of people are to be permitted to pray, someone must have the power to determine the content of such prayers," the White House document stated.

In his testimony, Baker referred to the recent 1983 SBC resolution adopted in Pittsburgh which urged Baptists to "express their confidence in the United States Constitution, and particularly in the First Amendment, as adequate and sufficient guarantees to protect these freedoms (free exercise and no establishment of religion)."

Told by Baker the 1983 resolution rejected the previous year's position, Thurmond said, "I wonder just why they sent this letter then."

"Because that's an old resolution which agreed with Mr. Currin's position," Baker responded. "It's not the position which the Southern Baptist Convention took just two weeks ago."

Baker further reminded Thurmond, himself a Southern Baptist, "each Southern Baptist Convention meeting speaks for itself and (the 1982 resolution) was the expression of opinion of those people there at the time."

Earlier Baker told the committee the BJCPA opposes "any attempt to amend the First Amendment" and warned "amending the Constitution should be the last resort rather than a first resort."

"Neither the judicial nor the legislative processes have run their full course on the issues of a period of silence or equal access," Baker said.

"If the judicial processes as well as the ordinary legislative processes are allowed to run their course, the need which some Senators see for a constitutional amendment may well be removed," he added.

Baker's assessment of the Hatch substitute was underscored by an administration witness who urged the panel to stay with the Reagan amendment.

Deputy Attorney General Edward Schmults said the silent prayer and equal access issues of the Hatch amendment have not yet been finally decided by the Supreme Court and a constitutional amendment to deal with them "seems to be premature."

Schmults suggested legislation might accomplish the same goal as the Hatch substitute, a view also pushed by Sen. Mark O. Hatfield, R-Ore., who asked the committee to consider his equal access legislation rather than either of the constitutional amendments.

Hatfield, also a Southern Baptist, has introduced legislation (S. 815) to provide equal access for high school students to meet voluntarily for religious purposes.

Further action on the proposals is yet to be scheduled but a committee spokesman said it will "most probably" occur after the July 4 recess.

Document 23
News Story: SBC Public Affairs vs. Currin
Baptist Press, 1 July 1983, 1-2

"Public Affairs Committee Disclaims Chairman's Letter"
by Dan Martin

FORT WORTH TX (BP)—Twelve of the 15 members of the Southern Baptist Convention's Public Affairs Committee have publicly disclaimed a letter from the newly elected chairman of the group, Samuel T. Currin of Raleigh, N.C., which supports President Reagan's proposed school prayer amendment.

On June 27, Currin wrote a letter to U.S. Sen. Strom Thurmond, R-S.C., chairman of the Senate Judiciary Committee, in which the former aide to U.S. Sen. Jesse Helms, R-NC, identified himself as chairman of the committee, the SBC's standing committee which relates to the Baptist Joint Committee on Public Affairs.

Currin, currently U.S. District Attorney for the Eastern District of North Carolina, cited a 1982 resolution supporting the Reagan prayer amendment as clear evidence "that Baptists favor a restoration of voluntary prayer to the public schools."

His letter noted that "as chairman of the Southern Baptist Convention's Public Affairs Committee, I am pleased to submit for the record a copy of a resolution supporting President Reagan's proposed constitutional amendment. . . . "

Currin was elected to the committee June 13, during the 1983 annual meeting of the SBC in Pittsburgh. He was recommended to be chairman of the committee, even though he has not served on the body previously, nor has he held any national denominational post.

Four days after Currin's letter was made public, 12 members of the committee wrote a letter to Thurmond which disclaimed the Currin letter. The letter was drafted by Russell H. Dilday Jr., president of Southwestern Baptist Theological Seminary in Fort Worth, and immediate past chairman of the Public Affairs Committee.

The letter pointed out Currin "was recently elected" and says: "He does not speak for the committee."

Grady C. Cothen, president of the Baptist Sunday School Board in Nashville, and a member of the committee by virtue of his position, said: "In my opinion, no Baptist can speak for another Baptist and no committee chairman can speak for a committee without proper authorization. The committee itself needs to meet and authorize any statement that purports to speak for the committee."

In addition to disclaiming that Currin was speaking for the committee, the 12 members of the Public Affairs Committee signing the letter went on record supporting the Baptist Joint Committee on Public Affairs position opposing both the Reagan prayer proposal and a substitute offered by U.S. Sen. Orrin G. Hatch, R-Utah.

The position was detailed in testimony before Thurmond's Senate committee by John W. Baker, general counsel of the BJCPA, who referred to a resolution adopted during the 1983 annual meeting of the SBC, which urged Baptists to "express their confidence in the United States Constitution, and particularly in the First Amendment, as adequate and sufficient guarantees to protect these freedoms."

SBC Bylaw 18 specifies the Public Affairs Committee shall have 15 members including the president of the convention and the executive secretary-treasurer of the Executive Committee. Other mandated members include "executive officers or staff representatives" of the Foreign Mission Board, Home Mission Board, Christian Life Commission, Sunday School Board, Brotherhood Commission and Woman's Missionary Union.

Also included are the "president or executive officers" of two other agencies, and five at-large members.

Those signing the letter include Dilday, Harold C. Bennett, Executive Committee; and agency executives R. Keith Parks, FMB; William G. Tanner, HMB; Foy Valentine, CLC; Cothen, BSSB: Carolyn Weatherford, WMU: Jimmy R. Allen, Radio and Television Commission, and James H. Smith, Brotherhood.

At-large members signing the document are R. G. Puckett, editor of the *Biblical Recorder*, news journal of the Baptist State Convention of North Carolina, and chairman of the Baptist Joint Committee on Public Affairs; Donald R. Brewer, an attorney from Chicago, Ill., and Donald P. Aiesi, a professor at Furman University, Greenville, S.C.

SBC President James T. Draper Jr., pastor of First Baptist Church of Euless, Texas, declined to sign the letter. Albert Lee Smith, a layman and former one-term congressman from Birmingham, Ala., who was elected during the 1983 meeting as an at-large member, was unavailable when members of the committee attempted to contact him.

Draper told Baptist Press he declined to sign the letter "because I don't have enough information. I am not trying to avoid anything, I just don't have enough information." He added he has not seen a copy of the Currin letter, nor a copy of the Dilday draft.

He added he is "against state composed prayer," and noted the White House paper prepared as background information on Reagan's proposed amendment "indicated someone would have the authority to compose the prayers. I cannot agree to that. However, the amendment does not say that, just the White House explanation."

He noted the Supreme Court decision "has been interpreted as outlawing prayer" and said he wishes "the court had the courage to clarify their ruling."

He added he believes the Baptist Joint Committee and its executive director, James M. Dunn, have been "cast in the role of being against prayer. They are not against voluntary prayer, but against state mandated and written prayer. I am not for state composed prayer, either, but I want voluntary prayer in schools."

Draper added he believes Currin "an outstanding young man, who is just not familiar with the ins and outs of Southern Baptist life. I am quite sure Sen. Thurmond or the White House contacted him about making some statement about prayer in the public schools. I don't think he was being malicious; I just don't think he realized he needed to check with the committee before writing the letter."

Document 24
Formation of Women in Ministry Organization
The Christian Index, 23 June 1983, 7

"Women In Ministry Move To Form Group"

SBC—Taking steps to create an official organization for mutual support and encouragement, about 75 Southern Baptist women in church-related vocations adopted a purpose statement and unanimously agreed to hold a third annual meeting preceding 1984 Southern Baptist Convention in Kansas City.

The need for women in ministry within the denomination to be servant-leaders and to challenge cultural barriers were themes sounded by several speakers in the two-day meeting.

Debra Griffis Woodberry, associate minister at Ridge Road church in Raleigh, N.C., said, "Cultural mores, attitudes and expectations about who women are constitute the greatest obstacle to enabling women to actualize their calls to vocational ministry."

Other speakers included Christine Gregory, president of Baptist General Association of Virginia; Anne Neil, visiting professor of missions at Southeastern seminary; and Nancy Hastings Sehested, associate minister of Oakhurst church in Decatur.

The purpose statement says an organization for women in ministry should: "provide support for the woman whose call from God defines her vocation as that of minister, or as that of a woman in ministry within the Southern Baptist Convention, and to encourage and affirm her call to be a servant of God."

Anne Davis, convener of the meeting and assistant professor of social work at Southern seminary, said the eight-member task force which planned the meeting envisions an organization "on the model of the pastors conference or religious education conference. This ought to be an independent group to speak to its own needs and not be tied to an agency of the Southern Baptist Convention."

An ad hoc group of women from Louisville unveiled the first issue of a newsletter, *Folio*, for Southern Baptist women in ministry.

Reba Cobb, minister of younger youth at Crescent Hill church in Louisville, said the group will publish four issues of *Folio* during the next year at their own expense and hopes the SBC organization will be in place to take it over in 1984.

Part II
1984–1987

Introduction to Part II

The four-year period 1984–1987 marks a decisive momentum swing toward the fundamentalists. Some signs of this swing existed at the 1983 SBC meeting in Pittsburgh, though it was one of the calmest conventions during the entire controversy. Amidst the apparent Pittsburgh tranquility, James Draper, the third successive fundamentalist to be elected SBC president, went unopposed by the moderates for a second-year term. Deciding not to challenge Draper, moderates then unsuccessfully challenged nominations of the fundamentalist-stacked Committee on Boards. This was moderates's first failure at modifying the nominations of this powerful board.

Also amidst the Pittsburgh calm, fundamentalists displayed Charles Stanley for one of his first major appearances at a meeting of the Southern Baptist Convention. Elected president of the SBC Pastors' Conference prior to the Pittsburgh convention, Stanley, the popular television preacher and pastor of First Baptist Church, Atlanta, Georgia, also gained platform time as chair of the powerful Committee on Boards. Elected president of the SBC the next year, Stanley was crucial for the fundamentalist machine during the years of the fiercest struggle of the controversy.

Some interpreters have seen the 1985 SBC in Dallas as the single most important turning point in the conflict. Others thought it came a year later in Atlanta in 1986. Both Dallas and Atlanta loomed huge in the outcome of the controversy. The momentum swing, however, that pushed the fundamentalists to eventual victory came a year earlier in 1984 in Kansas City.

What happened in Kansas City that was so telling for the future? Two elections. In that year Southern Baptists spoke volumes about the change they were undergoing when they elected as their president a person who had been, until the previous year, on the very margin of Southern Baptist life. Messengers to the 1984 SBC elected Charles Stanley on the first ballot over John Sullivan, a nonaligned Shreveport pastor and Grady Cothen, a man of impeccable denominational service. Cothen had served Southern Baptists faithfully for decades as a popular preacher, a local church pastor, a state convention executive, the president of a Baptist college, the president of a Baptist seminary, and most recently as president of the Baptist Sunday School Board. For messengers to reject Grady Cothen, a staunch biblical conservative and devoted denominationalist, for Charles Stanley, a biblical fundamentalist and marginal Southern Baptist, meant that fundamentalists had been enormously successful in heralding the fundamentalist program as the new badge of denominational identity.

The messengers went further, however. They elected Paul Pressler, one of the two architects of the fundamentalist takeover of the convention, to a crucial position on the Executive Committee of the SBC. Pressler had been viewed by many elements of the conflict as one of the genuine extremists among fundamentalists. While moderates challenged his election, Pressler's accession to the most powerful committee in Southern Baptist life marked the legitimation of a theological and political extremism within the denomination unprecedented in Southern Baptist history. If absolutely nothing else had happened in Kansas City, the elections of Stanley as president and Pressler to the SBC Executive Committee suggested that "school was almost out" for the moderates and the SBC as it had been known.

The Kansas City Convention was also a defining moment for women in the future SBC. By a vote of 58% to 42% messengers adopted a hotly debated resolution entitled "On Ordination and the Role of Women in Ministry." Accenting their hierarchical understanding of the world and a clearly submissive role of women to men, fundamentalists announced that, "While Paul commends women and men alike in other roles of ministry and service (Titus 2:1-10), he excludes women from pastoral leadership (1 Tim 2:12) to preserve a submission God requires because the man was first in creation and the woman was first in the Edenic fall (1 Tim 2:13ff.)."

Moderates saw the resolution as antithetical to the spirit of Jesus, abusive of women, and an example of biblical and theological interpretation used to reinforce unbridled male egos and sinful self-centeredness. No issue in the controversy more starkly contrasts the fundamentalist and moderate approach to Scripture than does the role of women in the church. Using Galatians 3:27-28 where Paul says, "There is no longer Jew or Greek, there is no longer slave or free, there is no longer male and female; for all of you are one in Christ Jesus," moderates countered the fundamentalist prooftexting with some of their own. In a 1991 public document designed to distinguish moderate from fundamentalist Southern Baptists, moderates declared:

We take Galatians as a clue to the way the church should be ordered. We interpret the reference to women the same way we interpret the reference to slaves. If we have submissive roles for women, we must also have a place for the slaves in the church.

In Galatians Paul follows the spirit of Jesus who courageously challenged the conventional wisdom of his day. It was a wisdom with rigid boundaries between men and women in religion and in public life. Jesus deliberately broke those barriers. He called women to follow him; he treated women as equally capable of dealing with sacred issues. Our model for the role of women in matters of faith is the Lord Jesus.[1]

Southwestern Seminary president Russell Dilday issued a stinging rebuke of the attitudes and efforts of the fundamentalists in his 1984 convention sermon entitled "On Higher Ground." Fundamentalists never forgave Dilday for this sermon and his public opposition to their efforts: in March 1994, in gestapo-like fashion, fundamentalists fired him from his presidency at the seminary. Among other things, Dilday, in one of the most powerful SBC sermons of the controversy, lamented the death of denominational diversity:

Incredible as it sounds, there is emerging in this denomination built on the principle of rugged individualism, an incipient Orwellian mentality. It threatens to drag us down from the high ground to the low lands of suspicion, rumor, criticism, innuendoes, guilt by association and the rest of that demonic family of forced uniformity.[2]

Dilday continued, excoriating fundamentalists for playing footsy with political powers and ignoring historic Baptist principles:

Go ahead. Engage the government as your ally. Since you're a major political force today, and hold the power to influence Congress, breech the wall of separation and bend the guarantees of religious liberty a little bit so that your faith enjoys the support of the state. If the sword of Federal support is offered, grasp it and use it. But remember, our Lord said, "They that live by the sword shall die by the sword."[3]

Repudiating what he saw as a grab for power by fundamentalist leaders such as Patterson and Pressler, Dilday said, "When proud brokers of

---

[1]See document 50, p. 268.
[2]See document 27, p. 114.
[3]Ibid., 116.

power manipulate the democratic processes of this convention in order to promote themselves, they've slipped from the high ground to the misty swamps of selfish ambition and conceit."[4]

Despite Dilday's powerful public rebuke of their attitudes and efforts, fundamentalists won every major vote in 1984. Moderates managed to derail their adversaries' effort to defund the Baptist Joint Committee on Public Affairs, but that was the best they could do. It was their lone victory in Kansas City. Moderate defeat at the 1984 SBC, however, never meant acquiescence.

Following Kansas City, denominational agency heads, especially seminary presidents Russell Dilday of Southwestern, Randall Lolley of Southeastern, and Roy Honeycutt of Southern, entered the fray in a public way, flailing away. They and others worked indescribably hard, but it was too little, too late. Even though the 1985 and 1986 SBCs in Dallas and Atlanta hosted the largest crowds in SBC history, and even though moderates showcased their most electable presidential candidate in Winfred Moore for both years, they could not muster the necessary votes to win the presidency.

The turning point was at Kansas City, not Dallas or Atlanta. Referring to the so-called "Shootout in Dallas" in 1985, Paige Patterson said, "Our hearts had been in our mouth every year up until Dallas but coming off the victory in Kansas City we had more confidence than ever before. By then we knew how to communicate effectively."[5] He understated. At Kansas City his group had learned more than how to communicate effectively; they had learned to win impressively with some of their most extreme people.

If fundamentalists delivered a decisive blow in Kansas City in 1984, knockdowns of moderates came in rapid succession at annual meetings of the SBC.

—Dallas, 1985: Stanley reelected president over Winfred Moore by a margin of 55.3% to 44.7%, and the appointment of a "Peace Committee," which would be adroitly used to further SBC fundamentalism.

—Atlanta, 1986: Adrian Rogers elected president over Winfred Moore by a margin of 54.22% to 45.78%, and a bylaw amendment adopted that guaranteed the appointive powers of the president and fundamentalist control.

---

[4]Ibid., 119.
[5]As quoted in Winston, 21.

—St. Louis, 1987: Adrian Rogers reelected president over Richard Jackson by a vote of 59.97% to 40.03%, and acceptance of the Peace Committee Report, a major triumph for the right wing of the SBC.

With the election of the fundamentalist presidential candidates at these three conventions, the Pressler-Patterson coalition tightened their grip on the SBC political machine and increasingly attracted the previously fence-sitting pastors to the side of power and triumph.

Not only were fundamentalists winning, some denominational leaders began capitulating to the steamroller. In many ways the single most demoralizing event for the moderate cause came on 22 October 1986, in Glorieta, New Mexico. On that day the seminary presidents presented to the SBC Peace Committee what came to be known as "The Glorieta Statement." While some seminary presidents, especially Lolley, Dilday, and Honeycutt, were among the staunchest opponents to the takeover, "The Glorieta Statement" constituted little less than a theological surrender to fundamentalism, especially to its language about the Bible.

"The sixty-six books of the Bible," said the seminary presidents, "are not errant in any area of reality." Nothing could have pleased Adrian Rogers more. Moderates and fundamentalists both saw this as nails in the moderate coffin. Later some of the presidents would seek to "clarify" and "explain" and even back away from that statement, but the damage was done. Cecil Sherman, the most militant moderate voice on the Peace Committee, resigned in protest and despair. Later he wrote that

> The Glorieta Statement was shameful. It was not the truth, and the people who wrote the statement knew it. The presidents said what they thought they had to say to "save" their schools, but in so doing, they gutted serious theological education among Southern Baptists for at least a generation. Well-placed people will deny my assessment of the effects of the Glorieta Statement, but the exodus of good teachers from our seminaries, the rape of Southeastern Seminary, the exodus of top-notch faculty members . . . from Southern Seminary and the resulting transformation of that historic school, and the climate of fear and intimidation that now exists at places that once were free makes my point.[6]

Unfortunately, subsequent events at Southeastern where both President Lolley and Dean Ashcraft resigned, at Southwestern with the

---

[6]Cecil E. Sherman, "An Overview of the Moderate Movement," in Shurden, ed., *The Struggle for the Soul of the SBC*, 41. For a copy of "The Glorieta Statement" see document 37, p. 195.

precipitous firing of Russell Dilday as president in March 1994, and the horrendously tyrannical actions at Southern Seminary by fundamentalist president Al Mohler in 1994 and 1995 proved Cecil Sherman right. Mohler forced out Molly Marshall, a tenured female theologian, fired Diana Garland as dean of the School of Social Work, and effectively gagged his faculty and gutted their freedom. At Glorieta the seminary presidents made the mistake which many Southern Baptists made during the fight: they thought one might be able to negotiate with nonnegotiating fundamentalists. Not so.

A pivotal turn in the controversy came in St. Louis in 1987 with the adoption of the ironically named "Peace Committee Report." Appointed in Dallas in 1985, the fundamentalist-dominated committee gave an interim report to the SBC in 1986. More of a report of exhaustion than anything approximating an authentic peace consensus, the 1987 document was completed after an all night committee session. Symbolic of the SBC itself, the committee, stalemated to the very end,[7] failed to produce the report in time for the messengers to the Convention to read it critically or seriously before voting on it.

No one can question that the Peace Committee Report ended as a total triumph for fundamentalists. A paradoxical document, the report is, in fact, a fundamentalist document. Fundamentalists would creedalize it in the future and use it to rigidify Southern Baptist theology. While affirming theological diversity in the SBC on the one hand, the report calls for theological uniformity in the hiring practices of SBC agencies and institutions on the other. Those agencies and institutions are to "only employ" those who agree with the fundamentalist interpretation of scripture.

Moreover, the committee report blew both cold and hot air at the same time about the character of the Baptist Faith and Message. While affirming the noncreedal nature of the Baptist Faith and Message in one sentence, the committee recommended in the next sentence that Southern Baptists "Reaffirm the 1963 Baptist Faith and Message statement as *the guideline* by which all of the agencies of the Southern Baptist Convention *are to conduct* their work [italics added]." This is in striking contrast to the motion presented in 1962 at the SBC in San Francisco calling for the

---

[7]Cothen, *What Happened to the Southern Baptist Convention?*, 219. Peace Committee Chairman Charles Fuller described the situation in the committee as "an impasse."

committee to draft the Baptist Faith and Message "which shall serve as information to the churches, and which *may serve as guidelines* [italics added] to the various agencies of the Southern Baptist Convention."[8] The Peace Committee Report, and especially its later use by fundamentalist leaders, violated the original preamble to the Baptist Faith and Message. That preamble said:

> Throughout their history Baptist bodies, both large and small, have issued statements of faith which comprise a consensus of their beliefs. Such statements have never been regarded as complete, infallible statements of faith, *nor as official creeds carrying mandatory authority* [italics added].[9]

The careful and judicious church historian Claude L. Howe, Jr., gave the following appraisal of the Peace Committee Report:

> The Peace Committee brought not peace but a sword. When a confessional statement becomes creedal then it must be interpreted uniformly and applied universally, which often means it is elaborated upon frequently. Now Southern Baptists must adhere not only to the Baptist Faith and Message, but to the Glorieta Statement and the Peace Committee report.[10]

In his book on the changes in Southern Baptist thought resulting from the controversy, theologian Fisher Humphreys points to the Peace Committee Report as evidence of the growing creedalism in Southern Baptist life. He contended that the report is tantamount to a formal and official biblical interpretation for Southern Baptists. "The question, then," says Humphreys, "is whether the existence of formal, official interpretations of the Bible constitutes an interference with the traditional Baptist principle of having no creed but the Bible. The answer, simply, is that it does."[11] Humphreys continues by saying that "what was done in the report of the peace committee was unprecedented in Baptist life."[12]

By the end of the convention in 1987 fundamentalists were riding high on a mighty wave of momentum. Strong enough in 1984 to elect Charles Stanley, heretofore a marginal player in Southern Baptist life, as SBC president, the fundamentalists also legitimized their entire movement the same year by engineering Paul Pressler's election to the Executive

---

[8]See the preamble to the *Baptist Faith and Message*.
[9]Ibid.
[10]Howe, 112.
[11]Humphreys, 155.
[12]Ibid., 156.

Committee of the SBC. Strong enough to reelect Stanley in 1985 against a formidable opponent in Winfred Moore, fundamentalist leaders negotiated the appointment of a Peace Committee favorable to their point of view at the Dallas Convention. Moreover, while fundamentalist Adrian Rogers won the SBC presidency in 1986 and 1987, he also became the dominant voice on the Peace Committee, shaping its report to his theological and denominational whims. As early as March 1984 Pressler had predicted that "the direction of the convention is irrevocably set. I do not think there will be any reversing of the direction that is now set."[13] Not all fundamentalists were as confident as Pressler. But by the time of the St. Louis convention in 1987, no one had any question about the radical changes that were occurring in the SBC. The fight, however, becoming increasingly bloody and nasty, was not quite finished.

---

[13]See document 25, p. 103.

1984

Chronology

<u>March.</u> Paige Patterson and Paul Pressler indicate their pleasure at the progress of their movement to transform the SBC. See document 25.

<u>May.</u> James Dunn, under fire for the work of the BJC which he heads, describes in an interview the work of the BJC and its relationship to the SBC. See document 26. The interview comes a few weeks after the U.S. Senate defeats President Reagan's proposed constitutional amendment regarding prayer in public schools, a proposal Dunn and the BJC strongly opposed.

<u>June 12–14.</u> SBC, Kansas City MO, 17,101 messengers, Jimmy Draper presiding.

—Fundamentalist Charles Stanley elected president with 52.18% of the vote over moderate Grady Cothen with 26.28% and independent John Sullivan with 21.53%.

—Resolution "On Ordination and the Role of Women in Ministry" adopted 58.03% to 41.97%, advocates woman's submission to man, her exclusion from pastoral leadership in the church, and her priority in the Edenic Fall. The resolution implies that this specific interpretation of the role of women had priority over the views of a local Baptist church. See document 28.

—Motion to eliminate funding for Baptist Joint Committee fails but prophesied what is to come for BJC.

—First meeting of the SBC Forum. Among the speakers were Ken Chafin, Kirby Godsey, Duke McCall, Cecil Sherman, and others.

—Paul Pressler elected to serve on the executive committee of the Southern Baptist Convention.

<u>June and following.</u> Denominational executives, especially seminary presidents Russell Dilday of Southwestern, Roy L. Honeycutt, Jr. of Southern, and Randall Lolley of Southeastern, launch all-out attack on fundamentalists. Dilday preached a fiery sermon at the SBC in Kansas City deploring the political machinations of Pressler and Patterson (see document 27); Honeycutt used the "Holy War"

metaphor from the Old Testament in a convocation address at Southern Seminary (see document 29); Randall Lolley defended in a spirited manner the role of women in ministry. All these efforts pointed toward the next SBC (Dallas) and unseating incumbent president Stanley.

November 1984. Former SBC president Franklin Paschall proposes "Peace Committee."

Document 25
**News Story: Pressler\Patterson Statement
on Progress of Their Movement**
Baptist Press, 15 March 1984, 2-4

"Progress Pleases Inerrantists; Say SBC Course Irrevocably Set"
by Dan Martin

WAKE FOREST NC (BP)—Three leaders of the inerrancy movement in the Southern Baptist Convention say they are "encouraged" by progress they have made in the past five years in getting "equity" for their views in the nation's largest protestant denomination.

Paul Pressler, an appeals court judge from Houston, and Paige Patterson, president of Criswell Center for Biblical Studies in Dallas, emerged into the spotlight in 1979 with their claims the denomination was becoming increasingly liberal and a concerted campaign to wrest political control of the 20 national agencies—particularly the six seminaries—from the "enormous bureaucracy" running them.

The focus of their campaign has been the boards of trustees. The strategy has been to elect "solid conservative presidents" who will make key appointments insuring placement of inerrantists on the boards.

The structure of the effort has been a network of "those who had a conservative disposition" in every state. The method is to "inform" interested Southern Baptists of what is being written and promulgated by denominational employees and to encourage active involvement.

Pressler and Patterson have been the point men. Several years ago, they were joined by Russell Kaemmerling, Patterson's brother-in-law, who established and edits the independent inerrantist publication, *Southern Baptist Advocate*.

During a recent symposium on the campus of Southeastern Baptist Theological Seminary, the three say they want their view that Scripture is without error taught at the six Southern Baptist seminaries and reflected by the other 14 agencies.

Kaemmerling said the effort "is not a matter of imposing interpretation," but is a "matter of being represented." He cited a Gallup Poll which claims 96 percent of Southern Baptists are inerrantists, and said: "Assuming that he (Gallup) is only half right, where is the 50 percent of faculty members who hold to an inerrant Bible? My money is being expended, but my views are not being represented."

Patterson said: "We have seen no substantive effort on the part of any institutions or agencies to date to rectify the injustice that presently exists in representation," he said. He answered with an unequivocal "No!" when asked if any agency is approaching "equity."

Patterson did, however, say he "must put in an asterisk because I think in the case of the Home Mission Board . . . Dr. Bill Tanner is very much sensitive to what conservative Southern Baptists feel and are saying . . . I think if it were as simple as his just declaring it is going to be fair, it would be tomorrow, but things don't happen that easily."

He added, however, that in the case of the Home Mission Board, "things are moving in that direction (toward 'equity')."

Pressler mentioned Golden Gate Baptist Theological Seminary in Mill Valley, Calif., and said: "Frank Pollard (the new president) is a very conservative, Bible-believing man. He has two openings on his faculty, and what he does with them will probably affect their future."

Progress, Patterson said, is being made on the trustee level. "We do feel we have seen some progress in establishing more nearly an equitable situation in terms of the people who serve on the boards of directors. There has been some progress made there."

Patterson said it is a "logical deduction that provided we continue to be able to rectify the inequity on the boards it would have to follow that at some point or another the inequities that actually exist . . . would also begin to straighten themselves out."

He said: "We knew we wouldn't get to the break-even point on the trustees in five years unless we started the process of knocking people off. I think the people who have been serving on the committee on boards have wisely chosen not to take that action. We are not up to the elimination of people. What we want is to gain adequate representation and that means that we have to spread it out over a longer period of time."

Pressler said the group has "no timetable," for when political control will shift. "When rank and file Southern Baptists are involved, the problems are going to work themselves out."

Previously, "nobody understood how the system worked; nobody was sufficiently involved. The convention (machinery) was overwhelming," he charged. "There was an enormous self-perpetuating bureaucracy that was not sensitive to lots of issues."

Now, however, Pressler claimed the inerrancy movement has had an impact and "the direction of the convention is irrevocably set. I do not think there will be any reversing of the direction that is now set."

Patterson said inerrancy "is a life and death matter" to him because he "believes heaven is real and hell is real and that lost people go to hell. The only difference is the vicarious substitutionary death of Jesus Christ. I believe that is only maintained by an absolute allegiance to the word of God as infallible and inerrant in every statement that it makes."

"It is unconscionable for me to be forced to pay to support the propagation of another view," he said, comparing it to asking him to "send money to Russia to propagate communism."

He added he believes the denomination was "rapidly moving toward a day of disintegration" when the inerrancy effort began and warned that "if something isn't done to rectify the inequity it (the Southern Baptist Convention) is going to disintegrate."

During the symposium, sponsored by the Conservative/Evangelical Fellowship, a group of 25 students at the 1,200-student school, Patterson was asked: "If you have it your way would all seminary faculty be inerrantists or would you allow those who don't feel that way to teach?"

Patterson said "we are 40 million light years away from that," but responded: "If I were personally selecting the faculty . . . yes, the whole faculty would be inerrantists."

"If I were in the position of the presidency of one of the seminaries—which I think is exceedingly hypothetical—my first move would be to replace existing faculty members . . . with folks who have no questions about the full validity of the scriptures," he said.

His second move would be to make chapel programs "vibrant affairs with people coming in to represent primarily that viewpoint." The third would be that no faculty member or staff member "would fail to be a personal soul winner. Dismissal for that would come more quickly than for any other reason. This is the first work as far as I am concerned, and the emphasis on personal witnessing, evangelism and missions would do much to solve difficulties," he added.

He said if he still had people on the faculty "after a period of time who were advocating that the Bible was not entirely accurate, I would try very hard to spend special time with them, to listen to them, but also to persuade them of my view."

Patterson admitted he did not know what would happen "if all that doesn't work. I haven't faced that yet; I don't have that problem at Criswell Center."

Patterson also explained that students at Criswell Center are taught the other major "strands of theology," but added: "Very honestly, we provide an evangelical answer to those."

During the symposium, Pressler was asked what his goal in the movement is. He replied that "in some of our institutions there are individuals who undermine the faith of our young people in the complete authority of the scripture."

"My goal," he said, for the Southern Baptist Convention "is that any student who goes to any one of our Baptist institutions comes out with his faith built up, his faith encouraged and as a stronger believer and a stronger witness than when he entered."

Document 26
News Release: James Dunn's Description of BJC
Baptist Press, 31 May 1984, 1-4

"Dunn Answers Questions about Joint Committee"

WASHINGTON (BP)—Southern Baptists, like the rest of the nation, have struggled with religious liberty issues in recent years. Caught in the crossfire of that struggle has been the Baptist Joint Committee on Public Affairs and its executive director, James M. Dunn. In an interview, Dunn responded to many of the questions raised by those who object to the role played by the Baptist Joint Committee during the religious liberty debates.

The interview was conducted by Bobby S. Terry, editor of Word and Way, newsjournal of the Missouri Baptist Convention.

It is presented in question and answer format in order to present Dunn's comments as clearly as possible.

TERRY: What is the Baptist Joint Committee on Public Affairs?

DUNN: The Baptist Joint Committee on Public Affairs (BJCPA) is a Washington-based arm of nine major Baptist conventions and conferences in North America which focuses attention on its common commitment to religious liberty and its corollary of church-state separation. The BJCPA functions as a service agency in the nation's capital.

TERRY: Why has the Baptist Joint Committee become the center of controversy among Southern Baptists in recent years?

DUNN: For two principal reasons. First, religious liberty and church-state separation have never received more national attention than in the last three years. That is just documentable—school prayer; tuition tax credit; the constitutional convention; court stripping, which is the removal of the jurisdiction of federal courts from certain religious and civil liberty issues; an ambassador to the Roman Catholic Church. Emotional and controversial court cases such as the issue of tax exemption for church-related schools were brought to a focus in the Bob Jones case. A great deal of attention has been given to a wide range of government intrusion questions related to the Internal Revenue Service, local zoning ordinances, historical commissions, city councils and lots of others.

The other thing is the apparent erosion, or the illusion of erosion, within Southern Baptist life of their historic commitment to a very dedicated stance on church-state separation. These two major, easily documentable trends have converged.

TERRY: Your membership in People for the American Way has been a source of controversy. You have been linked to Norman Lear, the organization's most visible member. Why did you associate yourself with People for the American Way?

DUNN: In October 1980 before I came to this agency, the BJCPA board passed an official policy statement on the dangers of civil religion. The statement expressed the fear that "the current activities of the religious right may pose a more dangerous threat to the American principle of church-state separation than any previous similar movement." It called on all Baptists, together with other concerned citizens, to work for political cause and, at the same time, cautioned against judging candidates as Christian or non-Christian, moral or immoral on the basis of essentially political rankings by the religious right. Those are precisely the same goals of People for the American Way.

The board was made up of church corporate leaders; a broad-based group of all major religious types, including Father Hesburg, president of Notre Dame University; Barbara Jordan, a black Baptist congresswoman from Texas; Ruth Carter Stapleton; Claude Hugh Broach; John Buchanan, a former congressman from Alabama who is now chairman of the board of People for the American Way; David Matthews, the former president of the University of Alabama and a Republican secretary of the old Department of Health, Education and Welfare, and a long list of others. The board brought together church leaders and corporate leaders who care about religious liberty and sat them down together on the same board. That had not been true anywhere else. The board decided deliberately from the outset to use television to counter those threatening the First Amendment. Obviously, that is why Mr. Lear was so visible.

I am not convinced that everything I do is always right. I would not say absolutely and irrevocably the judgment call to be a member of the board was correct. I am convinced that it was proper for me to know what they were doing and to participate in the activities of People for the American Way, as a citizen concerned about First Amendment issues, relating to them in the same coalition way that we relate to all the other major actors on religious liberty issues on the Washington scene.

That may sound like a bland generalization but it is not one at all. Recently, we signed a letter to the Congress, put out the letter, did the physical work in our office against an ambassador to the Roman Catholic Church, and the American Civil Liberties Union, the National Council of

Churches, the Seventh Day Adventists and the National Association of Evangelicals joined us in that.

It is virtually impossible to communicate effectively or work well in a political climate without being aware of, participating in and aggressively engaging in single issues or cluster issue coalitions on those things where there is a high degree of commonalty with other groups.

TERRY: One critic of the American Way described it as "pornographic smut peddlers, homosexual activists and baby-killing abortionists." How accurate is that description?

DUNN: Totally inaccurate. There has never been a position taken, a paper written or a posture assumed by People for the American Way on those issues—pornography, homosexuality or abortion. The strong Roman Catholic leadership on the board is evidence that we have not been involved in those myths of overheated rhetoric that have been injected into the criticism of People for the American Way. It simply is not true. It is not the agenda, purpose or intent and never has been.

TERRY: Are you a member of People for the American Way or do you support the organization financially?

DUNN: No to both.

TERRY: Some of your critics say that if you had not been so vocal in opposition to earlier proposals by President Reagan, you would have been more successful in opposing the appointment of the ambassador to the Vatican. How do you respond to such critics?

DUNN: It reflects a misunderstanding of how the political process works in Washington. It shows a lack of awareness of the degree to which this office led the fight in opposition to the ambassador to the Vatican and a misperception of how that process was accomplished and announced. I think it is a far-fetched criticism.

TERRY: Why has the Baptist Joint Committee been silent about abortion and other public policy issues of concern to Southern Baptists when it has been extremely vocal about religious liberty?

DUNN: Well, a simple rereading of our charter and program assignment would make it clear that our primary focus is in the religious freedom, church-state separation realm. Secondly, there are program assignments for other denominational agencies which have those other areas of abortion, peace, hunger. For Southern Baptists, it is the Christian Life Commission. It would be poor stewardship for us to do their job or them to do ours. Thirdly, the overwhelming workload I referred to earlier makes it very difficult to do justice to even the religious liberty issues.

TERRY: It has been suggested that Southern Baptists need their own lobbying group in Washington, one that would combine religious liberty concerns with issues assigned to the Christian Life Commission such as abortion, world hunger, etc. What is your reaction to that?

DUNN: Twice in the last 20 years this issue has come to the attention of the SBC Executive Committee, the full convention and then back to the Executive Committee. In both instances, Southern Baptists have overwhelmingly affirmed the present arrangement with the Joint Committee majoring on religious liberty and the Christian Life Commission majoring on the broader sweep of social issues. The last times were 1979 and 1980.

There is a substantive response as well. We are already in a very close working relationship with the Christian Life Commission. To identify the religious liberty and church-state issues, we have to read the federal register every day all the way through and the Congressional record. Since we do that, it would be silly to have that duplicated. We alert the Christian Life Commission to any and all issues that relate to their agenda. We cover, at their request, as a news service, all of those issues and feed them through Baptist Press. We make the formal request for them to testify when it is appropriate or when they request any other "shoe leather" services.

TERRY: If Southern Baptists decide that part of the funds now designated for the Baptist Joint Committee should be used to finance a separate Southern Baptist agency in Washington, what to you think would happen to the Baptist Joint Committee?

DUNN: It is difficult to know, it is so hypothetical. I can only affirm that there are a great many individuals with a passionate commitment to remain with this office. A good many churches have expressed a strong desire to see to it that we maintain the integrity and reputation for consistency and continuity on religious liberty issues and the visibility that we have in Washington. The 40 years of hard work by those who have gone before are very meaningful to a good many churches and individuals across the SBC.

TERRY: What impact would such a development have on the cause of religious liberty?

DUNN: I don't know. I could see a wide range of possibilities. Some would be very bleak. Others are very optimistic. I just can't be more specific than that because I am not a fortune teller.

TERRY: How Southern Baptist is the Baptist Joint Committee?

DUNN: In terms of staff, eight of the 10 present staff members are Southern Baptists in history, roots and involvement. It is Southern Baptist in the great volume of its work. When you take the time which is devoted to serving, writing materials for, speaking to and doing stuff for Southern Baptists, 90 percent or more of our work is done for Southern Baptists.

TERRY: Some people complain that Southern Baptists pay most of the bills for the Baptist Joint Committee but the Baptist Joint Committee doesn't reflect Southern Baptist positions. The 1982 resolution on the school prayer amendment is a case in point. How do you respond to this?

DUNN: I think the 1982 resolution on the school prayer amendment is an excellent argument for us that we do respond to Southern Baptist positions and reflect them. The 1982 resolution caused one to look at what other resolutions on that subject have been passed during the last few years. When you do that you see that nine resolutions have been passed since 1964, including the 1983 resolution that spoke against any constitutional amendment and supported the 1962 and 1963 Supreme Court decisions. The 1982 resolution was an aberration.

In 1983, we said once again the First Amendment offered adequate and sufficient guarantees for religious liberty. If that were not true, we had 10 state conventions in the fall of 1982 that explicitly or implicitly repudiated the 1982 SBC resolution.

We took the position on the amendment that Southern Baptists have repeatedly said they wanted us to take. Southern Baptists, through their state conventions at the grassroots, have reaffirmed that they wanted us to take that position also.

TERRY: In light of the overwhelming financial support coming to the Joint Committee from the Southern Baptist Convention, do you feel there are enough Southern Baptists on the trustees?

DUNN: Probably not. I inherited an awkward governing structure. One of the pluses of a serious reevaluation is that we may, in fact, by scrubbing the present representation system and starting over, get a more balanced representation that more accurately reflects the fiscal support for the agency.

A very prominent South Carolina Baptist leader said the importance of a Baptist witness in the nation's capital is significant enough that if we had to pay other groups to let us use their names, we probably should do so. He is convinced, as I think a good many are, that the "jointness" of the Joint Committee is a very important value in itself. Being biggest carries with it some responsibilities, bigness of spirit, not just bigness of budget.

TERRY: Are Southern Baptists getting their money's worth from the Baptist Joint Committee?

DUNN: I am convinced they are getting one of the biggest bargains that they get anywhere in the country for what they put into the Baptist Joint Committee. If you simply want to look at it dollar-wise, the revision of the pension reform act, the ERISA legislation, saved the Annuity Board annually, more than our budget every year. That says nothing of the ultimate savings to the retirees who benefit from the Annuity Board's savings.

The overseas-earned income is a problem related to the Foreign Mission Board where we had foreign missionaries literally having to pay double taxation—once in each country. (R.) Keith Parks (FMB president) estimated a savings for the Foreign Mission Board of a million dollars a year. The second phase of that legislation almost slipped through Congress without public attention and, unless we had been here monitoring it and caught it, it would have.

So, yes, I think if you look at issue advocacy, services to the denomination on matters that affect us in our pocketbook or news reporting, they get their money's worth out of the Joint Committee.

Document 27
Russell Dilday's SBC Convention Sermon
"On Higher Ground"
by Russell H. Dilday, Jr., 13 June 1984

Introduction

The title of the message is taken from a well-known hymn:

Lord, lift me up and let me stand,
By faith on heaven's tableland,
A higher plane than I have found,
Lord, plant my feet on higher ground.

The biblical text for the message is Philippians 3:14, "I press toward the goal for the prize of the *upward* call of God in Christ Jesus," and Colossians 3:1-2, "If then you were raised with Christ, seek those things which are *above* where Christ is, sitting at the right hand of God. Set your mind on things *above*, not on things on the earth."

The Bible repeatedly calls us upward to higher ground, to turn our backs on the petty, the trivial, and the unworthy, and to take instead the high road of uncompromising integrity. We are to stand on higher ground with the One who himself is High and Lifted Up.

To every man there openeth A Way, and Ways, and a Way,
The High Soul climbs the High Way,
The Low Soul gropes the Low,
And in between, on the misty flats,
The rest drift to and fro,
And every man decideth, The Way his soul shall go.

—John Oxenham

The challenge of the message to this Convention is that we obey the Word of God that calls us to a more excellent way, and redeploy our messengers, our institutions, and our churches to God's tableland where they belong.

Our hearts have no desire to stay,
Where doubts arise and fears dismay,
Though some may dwell where these abound,
Our prayer, our aim is Higher Ground.

I. Let's Turn from Forced Uniformity
to the Higher Ground of Autonomous Individualism

Baptists have stood tall in their courageous defense of individual autonomy. We call it "the priesthood of the believer," "the axiom of soul competency." It's that cherished truth that no one can stand between a person and God except the one mediator, Jesus Christ. No church, no priest, no ordinance, no creed, nothing but Jesus. Our heroes have been those rugged individuals who died for the right to answer to God for themselves and to worship him as they pleased.

We take that concept of individualism from the Bible. Psalms 49:7 says, "None of them can by any means redeem his brother nor give to God a ransom for him." God created us individually, and each of us is both responsible and free to live his own life. That's why Jesus asked the disciples in Matthew 16:13, not only "Whom do you say that I am?" but "Whom do YOU say that I am?" And one of the clearest verses about individual autonomy is John 18:34, where Jesus confronted Pilate with the question, "Are you speaking for yourself, or did others tell you this?"

But unfortunately, in contradiction to the Bible, there are some among us who, fearful of standing alone, and determined to get ahead in denominational life, surrender that sacred privilege of individualism. They go along with the crowd, accepting the canned thinking of the majority. Swayed by public opinion, and glibly mouthing the popular cliches of the party in power, they are quick to espouse those causes that are in vogue. They cater to the powerful, play to the gallery, and flow with the tide.

Isn't it a shame to be caught in the grip of a mentality like that? Even if only one person among us believes that "to get recommended to a better church you have to signal your loyalty to the party in power by using certain flag words. If you disagree, you'll be labeled. Be careful who you sit with in the sessions or talk to in the halls. Watch out how they see you vote. You may have a deep conviction about the issue being decided, but you'd better raise your hand with the majority." Even if only one believes that, he is one too many. And over the dying ashes of autonomous individualism we will hear the probing question of Jesus, "Are you speaking for yourself, or did others tell you this?"

But lost individualism is a two-sided coin. One side is the fear of standing alone, but the other side is the refusal to let another person stand alone. In his famous novel, George Orwell painted a grim picture of society in 1984, a society of forced uniformity. Everyone was obliged to mouth the party line or else. Spies listened and reported any diverse unorthodoxy to the Ministry of Truth. Individual disagreement was punished as heresy.

Incredible as it sounds, there is emerging in this denomination built on the principle of rugged individualism, an incipient Orwellian mentality. It threatens to drag us down from the high ground to the low lands of suspicion, rumor, criticism, innuendoes, guilt by association, and the rest of that demonic family of forced uniformity. I shudder when I see a coterie of the orthodox watching to catch a brother in a statement that sounds heretical, carelessly categorizing churches as liberal or fundamentalist, unconcerned about the adverse effect that criticism may have on God's work. But surely this would never happen in our convention, would it?

Three experiences I've had recently led me to say it might happen here. Last year, a pastor publicly critiqued the book I wrote on biblical authority. It was a broadside criticism in which he disagreed vehemently with my position. That's O.K., except for the fact that he obviously misunderstood my position. Much of the criticism was so unjustified that it was obvious: he couldn't have read the book. I called him, he acknowledged that he wrote the criticism without having read the book for himself. I sent him a copy, and we eventually established an open relationship of discussion. But as I reflected on that experience, I couldn't help but remember the question of Jesus, "Are you speaking for yourself or did others tell you this?"

Illustration number two. We had on campus recently a preacher who during our recent controversies, has been very vocal in his defense of the denomination. He preached a powerful evangelistic sermon in chapel that moved our student body and visiting guests. There were rousing "Amens" and spontaneous ovations. After the service, one of our guests said to me, "I was really going to let you have it, Mr. President, for inviting that liberal to preach today, but I was wrong. That was a great message, but do you think he really believes what he preached today?" It was obvious the guest had let other people shape his opinion of our preacher, and I remembered the scripture, "Are you speaking for yourself or did others tell you this?"

Number three. A few years ago I attended one of those Bible conferences where criticism was so often leveled at our seminaries. The rhetoric was especially hostile that day. Later, upon discovering I was present, some of those who spoke so strongly, came by to say, "I didn't have you in mind. I'm not really with this crowd; I'm for you." Well, the disclaimers may have been sincere, but I couldn't help but remember the biblical admonition in Colossians 3:22, "Serve the Lord with singleness of heart, not with eyeservice as men-pleasers," and the passage "Are you speaking for yourself or did others tell you this?"

How much better to be a godly individualist who with open mind listens to all sides of an issue, prayerfully measures those issues by the Word of God, and then humbly takes a position and stands courageously by it no matter what others think. How much better, like Luther, facing abuse if necessary, to say, "Here I stand. I cannot do otherwise, God helping me." And how much better to allow that same freedom to others without pressing for lockstep uniformity. That's the rugged individualism to which the Bible calls us. And that's the higher ground where we Baptists have stood and where we need to stand today.

II. Let's Turn from Political Coercion
to the Higher Ground of Spiritual Persuasion

Jesus made it unmistakably clear by his commands and example that the power we are to employ in our work for him is not political or conscriptive power, but spiritual power. Consistently, Jesus refused to use even subtle coercion in his mission. He rejected the low ground of political force and chose instead the higher ground of spiritual persuasion.

Our Saviour wept over Jerusalem, but he never besieged it, never rallied its legislature or courts to favor his cause, never formed a political coalition to advance his kingdom. He preached, and prayed, and served, and loved, and to the end he steadfastly rejected worldly force. Jesus chose the higher ground of spiritual persuasion.

Heaven's entire angelic army was at his command. With the snap of a finger, he could have brought Herod and Pilate to their knees in surrender and enthroned himself as king in Jerusalem. But he didn't. John 6:15 says, "Perceiving then that they were about to come and take him by force to make him king, Jesus withdrew again to the mountain by himself." He came not to be an autocrat, but a servant leader.

John 9:54 says that even though James and John thought it was a great idea, Jesus would not call down fire from heaven on those who disagreed with him. Respecting that fragile treasure of free will, Jesus refused to manipulate, coerce, or commandeer the people. He chose persuasion, reason, and love as his weapons. He who could wither a fig tree with a spoken rebuke, and with one word defang a howling windstorm into a whimpering breeze, would not force his will on others. Jesus could have pulled the trigger of his power and with one divine laser blast vaporized the ones who nailed him to the cross, but instead he prayed, "Father forgive them, for they know not what they do."

In Matthew 26:52 Simon Peter drew his weapon in the garden, and Jesus rebuked him, "Put your sword back into its place, for all who take up the sword will perish by the sword." We can learn from that verse, for it may seem appropriate at times for us to enlist the civil powers of the state in our witness for Christ. But beware, that's the low road to the misty swamps, not the way to God's higher ground.

Go ahead. Engage the government as your ally. Since you're a major political force today, and hold the power to influence Congress, breech the wall of separation and bend the guarantees of religious liberty a little bit so that your faith enjoys the support of the state. If the sword of Federal support is offered, grasp it and use it. But remember, our Lord said, "They that live by the sword shall die by the sword."

Call on Big Brother in Washington to help you witness and worship, and Big Brother will trivialize your Lord, sanctioning his sacred birth as nothing more than a folk festival, giving Bethlehem's manger no more significance than Rudolph's red nose. Ask the Supreme Court to endorse your Christian faith, and they will relegate the virgin-born Jesus, the only begotten of the Father, the King of Kings and Lord of Lords, they will relegate him to the company of Santa Claus, Frosty the Snowman, and Alvin the Caroling Chipmunk.

Better to have enemies who know who Christ is and detest him, than political friends in high places who classify the eternal incarnation with fairy-tale symbols of godless folklore.

No wonder Jesus said to Simon, the would-be swordsman, "Stop! No more of this! I need no political allies. Do you think that I cannot appeal to my father and he will at once put at my disposal more than twelve legions of angels? But I will not stoop to coercive arm twisting. Put away your sword; for all who take up the sword shall perish by the sword."

Some day in the future, as so often in the past, other political forces, hostile to religious liberty, will hold the advantage. They will have the political clout you have today, and they may breech that crack you so casually made in the wall of separation, and circumvent the guarantees you brazenly bent a little bit, and they may steal away the liberty you carelessly abused. And future generations of Americans will look back on our twentieth century and wonder what happened to that country which a Baptist musician described as "sweet land of liberty."

Have you ever studied the sad experience of Baptists in Germany during Hitler's rise to power? We who've never lived under a repressive regime like the Third Reich should be slow to condemn, but the lessons of their failure are so timely. Church historian Stephen Brachlow has a disturbing study you ought to read.

German Baptists, rightly concerned about immorality in their country in the 1930s rallied behind Hitler's drive to rid society of pornography, prostitution, homosexuality, and other social sins. Deceived by the Orwellian doublespeak of Nazi propaganda, and impressed with Hitler's righteous campaign against degenerates, and his pious commitment to what he called "positive Christianity," German Baptists temporarily lost sight of their traditional antipathy toward establishment religion. They developed alliances with the government and received unprecedented privileges while other religious groups were being persecuted. As one Baptist leader put it, "the German Finance Ministry favored Baptist churches in tax matters and the Secret Police were uninterruptedly friendly." For the first time in 100 years German Baptists enjoyed the paternal care of their government. In contrast to their forebears who had struggled as a persecuted minority, they were now the privileged ones.

They dismissed the government restrictions placed on Lutheran and Evangelical congregations as divine judgment for the years they had harassed Baptist churches. So long as they remained unmolested by the authorities, these Baptists shrank from endangering their own privileged freedom by challenging the state. And they discovered too late that they were duped.

The lesson is clear. Individual Baptists should be involved as Christian citizens at every level of our democratic processes of government, but only to insure that personal freedom and justice are maintained, never to secure privileged support from the state nor encourage its entanglement in religious affairs. We must never give up our historic concern for religious liberty. Even when we find ourselves in positions of prominence and in league with the powerful, we must not fail to protect the freedom of the minorities who differ from us.

Oh twentieth-century Baptists, where is your distinctive biblical message: "Render unto Caesar the things that are Caesar's and unto God the things that are God's"? Where is your voice so consistently raised in past days for religious liberty? Where is your ancient conviction that it is "not by might nor by power, but by God's spirit" that we conquer? We should put away the sword of government alliance and political clout, and reclaim instead our historical Baptist legacy of separation of church and state. We must choose, as Jesus did, to employ only spiritual weapons. For Baptists stand tallest when we look not to a benevolent uncle in Washington, but to an omnipotent father in heaven. Let's turn from political coercion to the higher ground of Spiritual Persuasion.

III. Let's Turn from Egotistic Self-Interest to the Higher Ground of Christ-Like Humility

Who can forget that embarrassing incident in Mark 10:37 when James and John asked their special favor of Jesus. He had just predicted in graphic detail how he would soon be crucified, how they would mock him, scourge him, spit on him, and kill him. And do you remember how James and John responded to that solemn prediction? They said to Jesus, "Grant us that we may sit, one on your right hand and the other on your left in your glory." Incredible! In fact, it seems Jesus was always catching the disciples at each other's throats about who was the greatest. No wonder the Holy Spirit inspired Paul to write in Philippians 2:3-7:

> Let nothing be done through selfish ambition or conceit, but in lowliness of mind let each esteem another better than himself. Let each of you look out not only for his own interest, but also for the interests of others. Let this mind be in you which was also in Christ Jesus, who being in the form of God, did not consider equality with God something to be grasped, but emptied himself by taking the form of a servant. . . .

The moment we imitate James and John in looking for personal advancement, or the moment we imitate the Pharisees in seeking the chief seats, in that moment we are bogged down in the muddy flats of egotistic self-interest. But the moment we imitate Jesus, and let his lowliness of mind be our example, in that moment we climb to the higher ground of Christ-like humility.

Weren't you shocked to read that the U.S. government, following the military rescue mission in Granada, awarded 8,614 decorations for bravery in action? We were shocked because only 7,000 troops were involved in the fighting. Many of the medals for bravery under fire went to bureaucrats in the Pentagon or Fort Bragg who sat behind desks and were never in danger. We really know how to congratulate ourselves, don't we? Somebody said God created us with our arms out in front to make it almost impossible to pat ourselves on the back, but we learned to do it anyway. We're experts at giving ourselves medals, promoting our own careers, and looking out for number one.

I had lunch a while back with a famous television evangelist who is often introduced as "The Next Billy Graham." His secretary called to ask if I would please arrange for a private room. She said the evangelist was so well known that he could never eat in a public restaurant. His fans would mob him and interrupt his meal. Well, it sounded a little presumptuous, but I followed her suggestions for privacy.

However, I couldn't help but remember my moment of glory a few years ago in Atlanta when I entertained the *real* Billy Graham. The crusade committee asked me to arrange a golf game and a luncheon one Monday. I was really excited. The best clubs were closed on Mondays, so I pulled strings and enlisted the famous golf pro at the Atlanta Country Club to open his course just for Dr. Graham and our foursome. Then I set up an elegant luncheon in one of Atlanta's best restaurants.

But when I called Dr. Graham to tell him my plans, do you know what *he* asked me to arrange? After hearing my suggestions, he thanked me, but humbly asked if we might make some changes. He would rather play at a public golf course and eat at a cafeteria near the hotel. I couldn't believe it.

When I picked him up, Dr. Graham had on an old golf cap and dark sunglasses, we played on the sorriest golf course in Atlanta, right under the flight path of the Airport. Then, believe it or not, we pushed our trays through the line at Morrison's Cafeteria for lunch. There I was fighting an irresistible urge to point to this man in golf cap and sunglasses to say to everybody, "Do you know who this is? Do you know who I'm with?" No one recognized him until halfway through the meal, and he greeted that one nervous intruder graciously and kindly. The contrast between the two men was startling. One walked in the misty flats of self interest, the other walked on higher ground.

What do you think Jesus, who rebuked James and John for their petty self-promotion, would say about our blatant scramble for denominational chief seats today? It sounds so much like the egotistic self-interest of the Sons of Thunder, doesn't it? "We've been left out, it's our turn to be elected, put us on the boards and committees, give us the positions." When proud brokers of power manipulate the democratic processes of this convention in order to promote themselves, they've slipped from the high ground to the misty swamps of selfish ambition and conceit. And the Bible says, "Let nothing be done through selfish ambition or conceit, but in lowliness of mind let each esteem another better than himself."

Whatever happened to the biblical concept of servant leadership? Lloyd Elder is right when he says we must examine our denominational reward system. We have so glamorized some standards of success that the other standards so essential to winning our world to Christ have been overlooked. Dr. Elder said:

Right now the reward system is based not on faithfulness, but largeness and notoriety. You have to make it to the headlines in order to be recognized among the brethren as being faithful in ministry. Super churches are important, but we must begin to recognize the super work being done by untold thousands in smaller congregations.

We don't need "king of the mountain" competition today, we need compassionate cooperation. God didn't put us here to see through each other. He put us here to see each other through. First Peter 5:5-6 says, "All of you be submissive to one another, and be clothed with humility, for God resisteth the proud, but gives grace to the humble. Therefore humble yourselves under the mighty hand of God, that he may exalt you in due time."

The first chapter of John's Gospel describes the first man to carry the name Baptist. He was the forerunner of Jesus. Jesus called him the greatest man who ever lived. But look again at that first chapter. Every reference to John the Baptist is one of personal depreciation. Verse 8 says, "he was *not* that light, but was sent to bear witness of that light." In verse 15 John the Baptist says of himself, "He who comes after me was before me. He has a higher rank than I have." He claims in verse 27, "He who comes after me is preferred before me. His sandal straps I am not worthy to unlatch."

John's enemies thought it would make him jealous when they told him in chapter 10 that Jesus was baptizing more people than he was. (What would some of our preachers say if they were told that a neighboring pastor reported more baptisms than they did?) John's response was, "I must decrease; He must increase." In John 1:20 a delegation from Jerusalem asked him, "Who are you?" His reply: "I am *not* the Christ. I'm not the Prophet, I'm not even Elijah. I am a voice"—literally a *phono*, that's all, a voice.

Ask a compass, "Are you north?" No answer; it just swings its faithful arrow toward the magnetic pole and points. Ask John, "Are you the light?" No answer, he just points to Jesus and says, "Behold the Lamb of God." John made humility a sacred art form. He never filed an IRS tax return, but if he had, his "personal depreciation schedule" would have been a classic!

But isn't it a shame today when a person becomes the focus of his own ministry? When self-promotion, autocratic leadership styles and success goals become our highest priorities? Or worse, isn't it tragic when a church begins to worship its pastor instead of the Lord who called him, focusing on the herald instead of the King. No matter how great your pastor is, he's not the light, he's just a *phone*, just a voice pointing to the true light, announcing the King whose sandals none of us is worthy to unlatch.

Let's reclaim that vanishing quality of humility that was personified by Jesus and lived out so convincingly by John, the first Baptist. Let's turn from egotistic self-interest to the higher ground of Christ-like humility.

Conclusion

When Nehemiah, the cupbearer to King Artaxerxes, was busy obeying God's command to rebuild the walls around Jerusalem, he was tempted to turn from his lofty work to take up lesser pursuits. His response to that temptation is the one I pray Southern Baptists will give. It's in Nehemiah 6:3, "I am doing a great work and I cannot come down. Why should the work stop while I leave it and come down to you?"

Stay on the heights, Southern Baptists. You're doing a great work. Stay close to the Lord and to the task he has called you to perform. Be faithful to your historic heritage. Don't dabble in controversies or exhaust your energies arm wrestling for denominational control. This convention is too valuable to let it become a volleyball bounced back and forth across the political net by shrewd game players. Stay on higher ground of spiritual persuasion, autonomous individualism, the Christ-like humility where you belong.

Shakespeare was right, "They that stand high have many blasts to shake them." But when we stand high with Christ those blasts will not be jealous potshots we lob at each other; they will be Satan's blasts hurled against a united family of faith. And we won't be afraid, because we'll be with the one who promised to make us more than conquerors. We'll be on higher ground.

So, Southern Baptists, our prayer should be:

Lord, lift us up and let us stand,
By faith, on heaven's table land,
A higher plain than we have found,
Lord, plant our feet on higher ground.

Document 28
SBC Resolution on Ordination and Role of Women
SBC Annual 1984, 65

"Resolution No 3—
On Ordination and the Role of Women in Ministry"

WHEREAS, We, the messengers to the Southern Baptist Convention meeting in Kansas City, June 12-14, 1984, recognize the authority of Scripture in all matters of faith and practice including the autonomy of the local church; and

WHEREAS, The New Testament enjoins all Christians to proclaim the gospel; and

WHEREAS, The New Testament churches as a community of faith recognized God's ordination and anointing of some believers for special ministries (e.g., 1 Timothy 2:7; Titus 1:15) and in consequence of their demonstrated loyalty to the gospel, conferred public blessing and engaged in public dedicatory prayer setting them apart for service; and

WHEREAS, The New Testament does not mandate that all who are divinely called to ministry be ordained; and

WHEREAS, In the New Testament, ordination symbolizes spiritual succession to the world task of proclaiming and extending the gospel of Christ, and not a sacramental transfer of unique divine grace that perpetuates apostolic authority; and

WHEREAS, The New Testament emphasizes the equal dignity of men and women (Gal. 3:28) and that the Holy Spirit was at Pentecost divinely outpoured on men and women alike (Acts 2:17); and

WHEREAS, Women as well as men prayed and prophesied in public worship services (1 Cor. 11:2-16), and Priscilla joined her husband in teaching Apollos (Acts 18:26), and women fulfilled special church service-ministries as exemplified by Phoebe whose work Paul tributes as that of a servant of the church (Rom. 16:1); and

WHEREAS, The Scriptures attest to God's delegated order of authority (God the head of Christ, Christ the head of man, man the head of woman, man and woman dependent one upon the other to the glory of God) distinguishing the roles of men and women in public prayer and prophecy (1 Cor. 11:2-5); and

WHEREAS, The Scriptures teach that women are not in public worship to assume a role of authority over men lest confusion reign in the local church (1 Cor. 14:33-36); and

WHEREAS, While Paul commends women and men alike in other roles of ministry and service (Titus 2:1-10), he excludes women from pastoral leadership (1 Tim. 2:12) to preserve a submission God requires because the man was first in creation and the woman was first in the Edenic fall (1 Tim. 2:13ff.); and

WHEREAS, These Scriptures are not intended to stifle the creative contribution of men and women as coworkers in many roles of church service, both on distant mission fields and in domestic ministries, but imply that women and men are nonetheless divinely gifted for distinctive areas of evangelical engagement; and

WHEREAS, Women are held in high honor for their unique and significant contribution to the advancement of Christ's kingdom, and the building of godly homes should be esteemed for its vital contribution to developing personal Christian character and Christlike concern for others.

Therefore, be it *Resolved,* That we not decide concerns of Christian doctrine and practice by modern cultural, sociological, and ecclesiastical trends or by emotional factors; that we remind ourselves of the dearly brought Baptist principle of the final authority of Scripture in matters of faith and conduct; and that we encourage the service of women in all aspects of church life and work other than pastoral functions and leadership roles entailing ordination.

Document 29
Roy Honeycutt's "Holy War" Convocation Address
at Southern Seminary

"To Your Tents O Israel!"
Roy L. Honeycutt, Jr., August 1984

For two centuries Israel's war cry rang through Canaan's rugged mountains and fertile plains. Waging holy war, Israel believed her wars were the Wars of Yahweh. So strong was this conviction that her national epic was sung in a book called the "Book of the Wars of Yahweh."

Gathering for the fall convocation of 1984, the context of Israel's holy war is more appropriate for Southern Seminary and the Southern Baptist Convention than we might imagine. Even the word "convocation" derives from the Latin *convocatio* which Cicero used to describe a calling together of Roman citizens to defend the republic.

We who constitute this fall convocation—this *convocatio* of God's people—are heirs to both the holy traditions of Israel and the calling of the New Testament church. Consistent with that heritage, this convocation is a calling together of the seminary community with a focus on duty, unity, and honor.

Convocation Is a Call to Duty

Unlike ancient Israel, Southern Seminary has never developed a war cry. But like Israel, for 125 years this seminary has lived with heroic qualities of integrity, fulfilled its duty with honor, and matched its convictions with courage. Our heritage demands that we hear again that ancient call to battle—calling us to duty, unity, and honor.

The focus of our challenge is neither the bureaucracy of a denomination nor the continuity of an institution. The crucial issue of this year and of this era in the life of Southern Baptists probes the inner core not only of what it means to be a Baptist, but what it means to be a Christian redeemed by Jesus Christ.

For many of you, it may appear to be extremism of the highest order for me to use the Old Testament commitment to holy war as an image for the nature of our denominational struggle. Yet, such imagery can be used legitimately in a Christian context. Because, in God's providence, Old Testament concepts of holy war and the kingdom of God have been purged of nationalism, stripped of militarism, refined by the ethical imperative of Jesus, and transformed by the power of the resurrected Lord.

That I should be either so bold or so presumptuous as to suggest "holy war" as an analogy for our current struggle grows out of my conviction that "unholy forces" are now at work—which, if left unchecked, will destroy essential qualities of both our convention and this seminary.

Among those crucial ingredients of our heritage now being eviscerated by the myopic and uninformed action of independent fundamentalists and the sincere but naive individuals recruited to support their political party are:

The priesthood of the believer, the primacy and authority of scripture, competence of the individual, soul freedom of conscience, pluralism in worship and in witness, liberation through Christ as the Lord of life, leadership of the Holy Spirit in our convention decision making, separation of church and state, a worldview of the gospel through cooperative missions, and excellence marked by integrity in all aspects of our election to be on mission with God in his world.

The inerrantist political party now seeking to hijack the Southern Baptist Convention is *damaging* local churches, *risking* the destruction of our denominational heritage, and *compromising* our Christian witness to the world! If you doubt this, consider, please:

What is happening to that crucial Baptist heritage, the *priesthood of the believer*. The Bible insists that we are our own priests, with no mediator between God and humanity than Christ our Lord (1 Tim. 2:5). We also are priests for one another, with a priestly mission to the world; and that may well be both the most significant and the most neglected aspect of our belief in the priesthood of the believer.

How long can this treasured Baptist principle survive the assault of those who believe that someone other than God now defines priestly relationships; that priestly calling and functions are determined by convention resolutions; that priestly roles are defined by gender rather than by theology; and that someone else in the "divine chain of command" must provide definitive answers to the soul's deepest longings, for which believers, both male and female, previously sought answers in the sanctity of their priesthood with God?

Such views are not only an aberration of our heritage, they are an absolute danger to our cooperative mission commitment.

What is happening to our *historic emphasis on the primacy of scripture, its authority, and its infallibility when rightly interpreted*? For a century and a quarter, Southern Seminary faculty and staff have affirmed with other Baptists the primacy and authority of scripture.

During C. H. Toy's inaugural address in 1869, he spoke on "The Claims of Biblical Interpretation on Baptists." This first alumnus to teach at Southern Seminary made biblical authority a primary element in his hermeneutic of biblical interpretation: "A fundamental principle of our hermeneutics must be that the Bible, its real assertions being known, is in every iota of its substance absolutely and infallibly true."

Yet how long can this fundamental commitment withstand the subversive action of inerrantists who substitute a theory about the Bible for the reality of biblical revelation? For in the most contradictory action, adherents of the inerrantists political party have succumbed to a radical form of scientific rationalism. Holy scripture, according to their insistence, now must give account of itself before the bar of human reason. Consequently, inerrantists propose fidelity to their particular and restrictive theory about biblical origins as a test of both faith and fellowship.

Where also is the future of the soul competence of the individual, freedom of conscience, and pluralism in worship and witness—if we succumb to the demands of independent fundamentalists?

What is the future of our historic affirmation of the New Testament gospel of freedom through Christ as Lord of Life? Hostile critics are misinterpreting both freedom and lordship by propounding a Bill Gothard-like "chain of command" which places males second only to God; while relegating women and children to the same essential role as families of the Old Testament patriarchs.

I ask you, do we believe in a limited atonement by which Christ achieved degrees of redemption, forgiveness, and freedom according to an individual's race, gender, social rank, political views, or ecclesiastical position? Or do we believe He died for all and set humanity free from the bondage of sin and evil, principalities and powers, cultural and religious traditions?

I ask you, did Christ set only some persons free; or only some parts of our personalities free; or only some of our institutional relationships free? No, he set the whole person free.

To every twentieth-century Judaizer now seeking to realign our convention and to purge our institutions, I say without apology, restraint, or hesitation: We shall not submit again to slavery's yoke.

If Christ has made us free, then we are free indeed. We are free before God. We are free in the family. We are free in society. We are free in the church. There is no dimension of God's Kingdom in which we are not free—for Christ who is the pioneer and perfecter of our faith, for the joy that was set before Him endured the cross and despised the shame (Heb. 12:2) that He might make us free. Because Christ is freedom's continuing creator, we shall never go back to the bondage from which he set us free!

Those in the Southern Baptist Convention who are seeking to legalize life by eviscerating freedom from the gospel have more in common with Judaizers of ancient Galatia than with the apostle set free on the Damascus Road.

So, if you meet one of the Southern Baptist Judaizers, give him this message: those of us who are free by the grace of God in Jesus Christ, are free forever. For us there's no turning back to a limited legalism untouched by the grace of God—no turning back, no turning back!

As Israel raised the war cry to rebel against the oppressive rule of Rehoboam, so every person who is responsive to duty and who is committed to the integrity of the biblical covenant as the norm of life should raise a denominational battle cry against injustice and oppression, whatever the source of its leadership.

For this denominational war cry constitutes a clarion challenge undimmed by the passage of time. It is a call to arms and a call to duty, one to which we pray history shall judge us faithful!

"And when all Israel saw that the king did not hearken to them, the people answered the king, 'what portion have we in David? We have no inheritance in the son of Jesse. To your tents, O Israel! Look now to your own house, David.' So Israel departed to their tents" (1 Kgs. 12:16).

Convocation Is a Call to Unity

Convocation as a call to duty is no less a call to unity. The name for our assembly today, "convocation" (*convocatio*), presupposes that we are called (*vocare*) together (*com* or *cum*, with together).

So also of ancient Israel, whose unity came from their response to charismatic leadership or the gravity of national crises. Whatever the circumstances, as a holy people they were totally committed to the Lord's will. Whether in worship or in war their devotion to Yahweh created a magnetic force which overcame their fragmentation.

To debate whether unity is prerequisite or consequence of community is like arguing about which side of your hand goes into your pocket or purse first. The sides are inseparable and they go together. Yet, there are some who act as though unity is optional for community. By definition and usage, unity is not a discretionary choice. Authentic community cannot exist with isolated internal fragmentation.

On this special day which opens the academic year, we cannot celebrate authentic "convocation" as a divided people. Hence, my forthright and candid appeal to you is for a unique quality of unity consistent with the Old Testament concept of *shalom*, or solidarity, more commonly translated "peace."

The continuing challenge for this seminary as a community of faith and learning, as well as the Southern Baptist Convention as a community of believers on mission, is to discover a focus of unity that transcends our differences. It is this quest that both haunts our journey and hallows our shared life. On such a pilgrimage, we reach out in faith for authentic community with God and with one another in the human family; so broken by discord, distrust and strife.

Honesty compels us to confess that unity cannot be coerced. Yet, there are times when we so long for authentic community as to seek it by force. Or in more subtle ways we manipulate freedom's birth into the fragmented family of God. But in the process we forget that authentic community cannot be coerced, manipulated, or massaged into the plastic form of our own image. Unity is authentic only as it is created in the image of God.

Artificial unity conceived by coercive action soon withers or evaporates. Despite this caution, some seek spurious manifestations of unity and generate artificial responses to duty by following strategies which include both indirect and direct forms of pressure. Such coercive efforts to generate unity remind one of Saul, that tragic Old Testament figure who was the last judge and the first king of Israel. His earliest national leadership emerged when he rallied Israelite tribes against the Ammonite siege of Jabesh-Gilead.

When the spirit of God came upon Saul (1 Samuel 11:6), he cut into pieces the yoke of oxen with which he was ploughing, and sent a piece to each of the tribes. With those bloody parts of the oxen, went this message: "Whoever does not come out after Saul and Samuel, so shall it be done to his oxen." Needless to say, Saul received instant and unanimous cooperation!

Persons in our generation seeking unity by autocratic and dictatorial control, should remember that individuals cannot be coerced into community. History is replete with horror stories of political bosses and demagogic tyrants. Then, as now, that style of leadership always exists in the context of dishonesty, manipulation, and depersonalization.

As in *Cat On a Hot Tin Roof*, "Big Daddy" is always ready to dominate and control those who are willing to submit. But the price of that kind of unity is often too high and millions have struggled to overthrow those who would impose it on unwilling subjects. Yet, some people in every age demand a king, saying "Big Daddy" rather than "Our Father"!

Not all that some identify as unity is the real thing. For some forms of unity are no more than syrupy sentimentality substituted for the hard realities that inevitably attend the biblical concept of unity. Authentic unity neither sublimates differences artificially nor dismisses disagreements inappropriately. Distinctions are maintained and differences of opinion and conviction are not only tolerated but affirmed. Christian community has no disposition to substitute an insipid, bland sameness for the stringent substance of diversity.

Unity does not mean uniformity, because you can't limit God. He established the boundaries of Christian community with such breadth as to embrace our diversity within the larger unity created by the cosmic Christ. Thus, Christian unity does not drive diversity into exile, nor force it to live in the bondage of an ecclesiastical ghetto. Biblical unity absorbs our differences within a larger purpose discovered in Jesus Christ who is the Lord of history.

As already implied, an authentic community of faith does more than merely tolerate differences—it celebrates their creative presence. Communities such as this seminary and the Southern Baptist Convention should affirm, not stifle or otherwise restrict, pluralism.

Such diversity is a necessary precondition for the maturation of faith and for continuing our participation in cooperative missions. Therefore, at Southern Seminary we affirm the diversity of individuals and the idiosyncratic nature of human personality. We affirm freedom of conscience in the interpretation of scripture and the affirmation of theological conclusions. We affirm the priority of God's call for Christian ministry and concurrently reject artificial disqualifiers which society may erect, whether those barriers are social, racial, political, ecclesiastical, or gender. We affirm the variety of cultural patterns and provincial traditions that characterize a people so diverse as Southern Baptists and a Seminary so international in scope as to include students from more than 700 colleges and universities, forty-eight of the fifty states, and twenty-three foreign countries.

For Christians who believe in God's inclusion of all creation within his redemptive purposes, diversity is not a discretionary option but a divine imperative.

Consequently, when some are tempted to substitute isolationism for mission commitment, myopic self-interest for a worldview of the Gospel, and first century legalism for the Gospel of God's grace, we should hear the Lord chastening Simon Peter's ghetto religion: "What God has cleansed, you must not call common" (Acts 10:15).

If the pluralism of the Gospel means that God hears the prayer of a non-Christian Roman centurion named Cornelius of the Italian cohort who was a "Godfearer" "who prayed constantly to God" (Acts 10:1ff.)—but a member of neither a synagogue nor a church—then we need to rediscover authentic, New Testament pluralism as an essential quality of the church on mission with God.

Assuming the validity of pluralism as a necessary quality of community, then we Southern Baptists in 1984 should reconsider our commitment to a pluralistic convention. Without question, events of the five most recent years inscribe this question indelibly on the agenda of every loyal Southern Baptist: will authentic pluralism survive among Southern Baptists?

Historically, there has been a place in the denomination for every Southern Baptist church and individual identified with the Convention through cooperative mission commitment. The fundamental issue currently facing Southern Baptists is not now nor has it ever been whether a church is large or small, rural or urban; whether ministers are graduates of one particular seminary or of no seminary; whether one ministers in one part of the nation or overseas in missionary service.

Nor is the issue theological. We cooperated in missions, evangelism, and education for eighty-one years before we ever got around to adopting a statement of faith. As for liberalism in educational institutions, one would be at a loss to discover a classical liberal among Southern Baptists, whether in pulpit or classroom, college or seminary.

Nor does the issue focus on who serves as president of the Southern Baptist Convention, as convention officers, or as members of the executive committee, or as trustees of agencies and institutions of the Convention—so long as those individuals are authentic, "convention" Southern Baptists committed to the priority of cooperative missions, evangelism, and education and to an open process for the election of convention officers and members of boards.

No, none of those issues constitutes our problem. Our problem is that *independent-fundamentalist revisionists* are rewriting Southern Baptist history to suit their agenda. They would reshape our Convention by excluding from both our history and our current polity the Southern Baptist commitment to authentic pluralism.

Unity within diversity has characterized our denomination during its entire history, and pluralism continues to be a necessary ingredient for our cooperative mission commitment.

As Southern Baptists respond to that call, God weaves from the threads of our varied lives a masterful tapestry which displays the richness of his grace and the all-encompassing power of his love. God calls us to exclude no one, but to include everyone committed with sincerity to Christ's Great Commission and to cooperative missions as a means to its fulfillment.

What future is there for pluralism among Southern Baptists? Can we recover that historic emphasis on pluralism already so seriously eroded by the independent political party in our convention? Or shall we harden convention lines of relationship into an iconoclastic exclusiveness that affirms only the clones who duplicate a single style of ministry and a monolithic biblical and theological system? That is the fundamental issue, and this is the determinative question: Where now, Southern Baptists?

Convocation Is a Call to Honor

Honor is no stranger to the household of faith, no matter how alien it may have become for street life in our society. Authentic community not only clamors for the moral implementation of justice, honor, and integrity. Those fundamental qualities of covenant life also motivate our response to duty and our demonstration of unity.

Virtuous words like honor, justice, and integrity echo in our generation with the hollow ring of forgotten ideals like chivalry and civility.

Yet, how different it was for ancient Israel, demonstrating the demands of covenant faith. Prophetic leaders never forgot the singular demand for duty, honor, justice, and integrity. As Micah summarized God's demands for covenant living (Micah 6:8): "and what does the Lord require of you but to do justice, and to love kindness, and to walk humbly with your God?"

Or, look at Job—responding to unbearable, undeserved, unexplained catastrophes. Yet, again and again reaffirming his integrity. Even his wife complains about his absurd fidelity to God: "Do you still hold fast your integrity?" she asked, "Curse God, and die" (Job 2:9). With inspired fidelity, Job endured her scolding as he did his suffering and God's silence. Through successive catastrophes he manifested the same resplendent faithfulness—steadfastly insisting, despite all adversities, "I will not put away my integrity from me" (Job 27:5).

Such commitment stands in marked contrast to the prevailing attitudes of religious zealots who believe that the end justifies the means—and who give little spiritual evaluation to the morality of ends or means!

For example, it is amazing to observe the unscrupulous use of power and manipulation that characterizes the current political party created in the Southern Baptist Convention by Judge Pressler of Houston and Paige Patterson of Dallas.

Or, consider the practice of enlisting a few disgruntled seminary students to provide tapes of lectures by seminary professors, or chapel sermons and lectures, as well as addresses such as this convocation address, for the Dallas war room with its reported information banks.

I was not unduly surprised by recent reports of unscrupulous and unethical acts by politicians heading the Independent Fundamentalist Party in the convention. Their actions only confirm that in every generation there are individuals committed to religious causes who walk on the dark side of ethical conduct.

For example, one of the Texas leaders of the inerrantist political party recently invaded the privacy of the president's office, to say nothing of my personal life. He was in Louisville and called a student acquaintance of former years who also is a friend of the president and who frequently drives the president's car to the airport. The politician asked whether the president may have said anything to the student during those trips to the airport which might "be of help," to the caller and other political leaders of the Independent Fundamentalist's Party. To my student friend's credit, he talked to me the next day—rather than to report our conversations to the politician who sought to corrupt the student's conscience, and his friendship with the president.

Or, consider that a professor reported to me only last week his conversation with a student concerning a breakfast meeting in Kansas City during the Southern Baptist Convention which involved several Southern Seminary students and a Dallas leader of the Independent Fundamentalist Political Party who sought to enlist them as campus subversives, "moles," or "quislings," to tape faculty lectures at Southern Seminary.

Such espionage is needless. And we would gladly provide appropriate taped materials; so long as the recipients were worthy in motivation and committed to study such materials within their appropriate context. This seminary has nothing to hide, whether at the classroom lectern or the chapel pulpit. At Southern Seminary, we seek to teach and to live without reproach. We invite all the world to hear and see our actions and our words that they may know to whom we belong.

After five years of harassment, Professor Bruce Corley of Southwestern Baptist Theological Seminary summarized the issue for many faculty persons in his chapel message on July 3, 1984:

> For five years the light has been blazing on me . . . why all the subterfuge, misinformation, secrecy games and clandestine activity. Do you assume that I will lie unless spied upon? Why should anyone ever come to this seminary [SWBTS] in order to spy and report to a watchdog? My classes, my books, my sermons, my meetings, and my heart are open; ask what I believe, and I will tell you. I still regard personal integrity a Christian virtue.
>
> . . . I have drawn a line of truth in the sands of my life; it runs deeply, as deep as the truth of the Gospel. I have asked, Is this a time that silence can pass as a virtue?
>
> I have measured my convictions on the Word of God, made them clear, and here I stand. I call others of courage to stand with me.

Truth needs to engage neither a defense lawyer nor a prosecuting attorney. For truth is both its own surest defender and its most stalwart advocate. Those who stand in the light need not fear the darkness; nor do they need to fear those who stand in the darkness to abuse the light!

Should we as faculty, staff, or student—or external critic of the seminary—disagree with a friend, another student, a professor or a staff person; if we misunderstand what another person says; or if we object to an individual's views for whatever the reason—why not demonstrate the integrity and courage of your deeply held conviction by first talking with the other person? If you have problems the two of you cannot resolve, then talk with other appropriate persons in your school or division.

By so doing we would be faithful to Jesus' imperative counsel: "If your brother sins against you, go and tell him his fault, between you and him alone" (Matt. 18:15). By manifesting such honor and respect toward one another we would fulfill our duty, maintain the unity of this community, and magnify our personal honor.

So, my friends and colleagues, whether student, faculty, staff, or visiting friend—hear my plea this morning. There are few if any qualities or relationships which we have in life that are more crucial than the honor with which we live and the integrity by which we are remembered. Let us, therefore, make this Joban confession our own:

As God lives, who has taken away my right, and the Almighty, who has made my soul bitter; as long as my breath is in me, and the Spirit of God is in my nostrils; my lips will not speak falsehood, and my tongue will not utter deceit . . . till I die I will not put away my integrity from me. I hold fast my righteousness, and will not let it go. (Job 27:2-6)

When your children and loyal Southern Baptists in the next generation ask what you and I did during the struggle to preserve the integrity of the Southern Baptist Convention and our historic commitment to cooperative missions; may it be said of us that within the limits of divine opportunity and human possibility we fulfilled God's calling.

For this reason, Convocation 1984, is a time to hear the call of duty, unity, and honor. When the story of the conflict is written, may it never be said of us that their call to battle fell on deaf ears, unresponsive hearts, or unwilling lives.

1985

Chronology

<u>February.</u> SBC Executive Committee approves statement regarding Baptist Press and charges of Paul Pressler against BP. Fundamentalists accuse the Baptist Press, the denominational news agency, of bias and BP becomes target of increasing attack. See document 30.

<u>March.</u> Former SBC president James Draper warns of Cooperative Program collapse if Charles Stanley is not reelected at the SBC in Dallas in June.

<u>April 19.</u> Keith Parks, president of the Foreign Mission Board, declares that he will not vote for Charles Stanley for president of the SBC. Parks sees threat to SBC cooperative missionary enterprise.

<u>April 29.</u> Adrian Rogers and Paul Pressler lead a "Confronting the Issues" Rally in Knoxville TN, rallying support for Charles Stanley's reelection in Dallas and criticizing Roy Honeycutt, president of Southern Seminary, and others for theological liberalism. Honeycutt responds by saying the attacks represented a distortion and misrepresentation of his biblical beliefs.

<u>May.</u> *The Theological Educator* publishes special issue entitled "The Controversy in the Southern Baptist Convention." Patterson and Pressler lay out their concerns. See documents 31, 32.

<u>June 2.</u> The Sunday edition of the *Atlanta Journal-Constitution* contains names of 2,000 people opposed to Charles Stanley's reelection as SBC president.

<u>June 9-19.</u> Largest SBC Pastors' Conference in history completely dominated by fundamentalist preachers. W. A. Criswell depicts decline of denominations due to biblical criticism; Presbyterian D. James Kennedy receives standing ovation with sharp criticism of Baptists' traditional position on separation of church and state; Morris Chapman elected president of the conference.

<u>June 11-13.</u> SBC, Dallas, 45,519 messengers (largest in SBC history), Charles Stanley presiding.

—Charles Stanley reelected president with 55.3% of the vote over moderate Winfred Moore with 44.7%. Billy Graham allegedly endorses Stanley, and that report circulates on Monday among the messengers to the SBC. SBC elects Moore first vice president, supposedly placing him in good position to be elected president the next year in Atlanta.

—Appointment of the "Peace Committee," with Charles Fuller as chair, "to determine the sources of the controversies in our Convention, and make findings and recommendations regarding these controversies." See document 33.

—Charles Stanley overrules the SBC regarding the Slatton motion. James H. Slatton's motion would have amended the Committee on Committees' report by substituting state convention presidents and state WMU presidents as a more inclusive and representative group to serve Southern Baptists as the Committee on Boards. See document 34.

June. Three-time Southern Baptist Convention parliamentarian William J. Cumbie criticizes SBC president Charles F. Stanley's "flagrant misuse" of parliamentary procedure regarding the Slatton motion at the denomination's annual meeting in Dallas, June 10-12.

December 5. Robert and Julia Crowder of Birmingham and Henry C. Cooper of Windsor MO, file a lawsuit against the denomination and its executive committee because of Charles Stanley's ruling on the Slatton motion.

December. Homer Lindsay, Jr., announces at meeting in Jacksonville FL that Adrian Rogers would be the fundamentalist nominee for SBC president in June 1986 in Atlanta.

Document 30
News Story: SBC Executive Committee Statement
on Pressler-Baptist Press Debate
Baptist Press, 20 February 1985, 3-5

"SBC Executive Committee Approved Statement On BP"
by Jim Newton

NASHVILLE TN (BP)—After almost three hours of testimony and discussion, the Southern Baptist Convention Executive Committee concluded two Baptist Press news stories last September "when taken together" gave a balanced presentation of the news.

The final vote was taken with almost no discussion, although the stories had stirred heated debate in two preliminary meetings.

The stories were released Sept. 17 and 18, 1984. The first article reported that a seminary student, J. Stafford Durham, had filed a "formal complaint" with the Federal Communications Commission alleging Houston judge Paul Pressler had secretly tape recorded a telephone conversation "in violation of his civil rights." The second story gave Pressler's response to the charges.

The Executive Committee said it was "untimely" and "unfortunate" the first story appeared separately without an appropriate rebuttal from Pressler.

The committee also expressed support for the Baptist Press staff for "their strong recommitment to timely, accurate, and well-balanced news reporting;" reaffirmed "its longstanding policy of openness in its deliberations and actions," and "its support for a responsible and free press as an essential element for an informed Southern Baptist constituency."

The committee also was told a "Baptist Press operating policy" is being formulated by the Executive Committee staff.

While the recommendations were adopted by the 69-member committee virtually without comment, two preliminary meetings featured heated debate. Both meetings took place under "background rules" which prevent direct quotations from individuals during debate.

The chairman of the public relations workgroup, Jimmy Jackson of Huntsville AL, ruled during the workgroup's meeting on Feb. 18 that discussion on the matter would be limited only to the procedure in handling the two stories, not whether anyone was right or wrong; and that only members of the workgroup would be allowed to discuss the matter.

Pressler, who brought into the room a suitcase full of printed materials, objected strongly to the ruling which prevented him from presenting four hours of testimony he said he had prepared.

In interviews after the meeting, Pressler complained the ruling was grossly unfair. "I don't know why these people are suppressing the truth. I had 35 grievances against Baptist Press I wanted to present, but they wouldn't let me speak."

Instead of hearing testimony by Pressler and Baptist Press Director Wilmer C. Fields, the public relations workgroup discussed wording of the recommendation which finally was adopted by the full Executive Committee.

On the second day of the meeting, the administrative and conventions arrangements subcommittee voted 15 to 6 to allow a full and complete discussion of the issue, including testimony by any who wanted to speak. Pressler, a leader in the movement some claim is trying to gain control of the SBC, is a member of the subcommittee.

Frank Ingraham, a Nashville attorney and chairman of the subcommittee, ruled the committee would allow Pressler and Fields 45 minutes each to present their arguments.

Pressler passed out a seven-point, 65-page stack of documents detailing his complaints against Baptist Press.

In his written presentation, Pressler admitted tape recording the telephone conversation with Durham on Sept. 1, but denied he had done anything unethical or illegal. "I took the precaution of taping the conversation for several reasons," he said. He claimed "certain individuals on the liberal side in the convention have completely and totally misrepresented conversations I had with them."

He added he recorded the conversation "for self-protection . . . to have a record of the telephone conversation."

Pressler listed 35 objections to the story, including a charge Durham, in his complaint, had given "a bogus citation to the FCC code which has no relevance to the matters involved." He suggested someone must have advised and manipulated Durham to contact the FCC.

Pressler also charged Baptist Press gives "liberals" in the convention "full and ample opportunity to respond" to accusations, but "conservatives are not always afforded that privilege." He further complained about use of writers "with fixed prejudices."

"The question is whether the present employees of the Baptist Press are so firmly directed in their mind set that they are unwilling or unable to look at what is occurring in the SBC from an alternate viewpoint from their own, or whether they are incapable of separating their personal prejudices from their reporting of the events that are occurring within the convention," Pressler concluded.

He asked the committee to examine the two stories and determine if "libel" was committed, and argued he was defamed by the articles which show "an intent to harm or malice."

In response to Pressler's charges, Fields made a brief statement and passed out copies of the related Baptist Press articles. He said Baptist Press carried 1,118 stories last year, and only 22 of those stories (1.9 percent) could be considered "negative stories" about controversial issues to which someone might object. Of the 1,118 stories carried, Baptist Press received complaints on only about three articles, including the Pressler complaint, according to Fields.

Fields said he regretted very much that time and space limitations caused the mailing of the second story to be delayed one day. He said that if the incident could be done over again, the two stories would have been mailed the same day.

Much of Baptist Press' response to Pressler's charges was devoted to a presentation by Southern Baptist Association President Bobby S. Terry, editor of Word and Way, newsjournal of the Missouri Baptist Convention, who summarized a six-page "Report of Special Inquiry" commissioned and paid for by the press association.

The six-page report was prepared by journalism professors John Merrill of Louisiana State University, Clifford Christians of the University of Illinois and John DeMott of Memphis State University. All three are members of the ethics subcommittee of the Association for Education in Journalism's committee on professional freedom and responsibility.

The journalism professors said they found no "evidence of ill will toward Pressler," and no evidence the BP staff was "motivated by unprofessional intentions to damage the reputations of the principals involved."

"Release of the report of Sept. 17, without the response of Pressler, was not unfair under the peculiar circumstances existing, and therefore did not constitute poor journalism," the professors said. They described BP's dilemma this way: "Should a reporter report the news immediately, even though the response to some accusation contained in it cannot be included in the first report . . . , or should he suppress the news temporarily while getting the response?"

"It is difficult to fault BP for the decision it made, and few news editors would do so," the professors said. "The decision made by BP is one made every day by many news organizations practicing the highest standards in our profession.

The professors said the BP stories in question "show exemplary restraint and discretion in what is admittedly a potentially sensational event. They are both news accounts which refrain from editorializing. They do not speculate regarding motives, editorialize about the ethics involved, or entertain reflections from unattributed sources."

"The news releases," they continued, "appear to us to show the commendable vigor of effective journalism combined with the restraint that is demonstrated among the most responsible in the news profession today."

Pressler was not satisfied with their study, however, saying in an interview afterwards it was done by "hired guns" who were "paid" to say what they did.

After the hearing, Pressler said he was pleased the committee had heard his complaint, and that his side of the story had been told.

Fields observed the Executive Committee members and staff had talked themselves together on the proper role of Baptist Press. "It is highly significant that the committee voted to reaffirm its support for a responsible and free press as an essential element for an informed Southern Baptist constituency," he said.

Document 31
Paige Patterson's Article in *The Theological Educator*
The Theological Educator, Special Issue, 1985

"Stalemate," by Paige Patterson, 3-10

Initially, I wish to express to Dr. Fisher Humphreys, the *Theological Educator*, and the New Orleans Baptist Theological Seminary my deepest appreciation for their kindness and fairness in allowing me to express in unedited form that perspective which, though it is my own, is shared by many other conservatives. Whether or not one believes the words to follow, at least the forum has been provided for an open presentation of both sides without repression or distortion. The present apparent impasse might never have developed if this had been the case throughout this controversy.

Controversy has been an ever-present accompaniment of Christianity from its inception. The tone of Galatians and the vivid and poignant language of the Acts 15 recital of the events of the Jerusalem Conference demonstrate the existence of conflict in the early church. The intense Christological battles of the Reformation are linchpins of the history of Christianity. In our own denomination the Landmark and missionary conflicts are only representative of many others. Though some bad resulted from all of these, infinitely more good proceeded from the same events. Greater understanding, sharper definition, increased evangelistic fervor and, most of all, fervent and humble supplication to God for His intervention in the affairs of men are among those favorable consequences.

The present controversy in the Southern Baptist Convention may result in the demise of the Convention as we know it, but more likely, it will yield to an epoch of unprecedented growth and to a renewal of Baptist doctrinal commitment. Nevertheless, it may prove helpful to examine the nature, causes, and extent of the present crisis and propose a potential solution from the viewpoint of one conservative.

Why the Controversy?
The present controversy would have occurred sooner or later. Had there been no Martin Luther, there would still have been a Reformation. The only point of this analogy is simply that the conditions existing in sixteenth-century Europe made the Reformation inevitable. Similarly, conditions in the Southern Baptist Convention in the last quarter of the

twentieth century dictated the inevitability of such a confrontation. Too many contemporary Southern Baptists sat through classes in Baptist colleges or seminaries in which alternatives to the faith of their homes and churches were presented as certainties. In my own experience some of the doctrinal truths I had been taught to hold precious were not only debunked but also ridiculed. On occasion my precious pastor Dr. Criswell was held in derision. The fires of evangelism and fervency of heart were often doused with the condescending remark of a lofty academe.

During those years I often wondered why no one looked into this. I found incongruous the apparent anomaly of professors who accepted their wages from churches whose positions they proceeded to undermine. But most painful of all, for one who believes in the realities of heaven and hell and in the substitutionary atonement of Jesus as the only way men can be saved from eternal condemnation, was the spectacle of formerly aggressive evangelistic young ministers no longer interested in the plight of the lost. This loss of zeal is the apparent result of "delving more deeply into study"—study dominated by the use of the historical-critical method and its accompanying loss of confidence in the accuracy of the Bible.

Actually, the threats to evangelism and missions posed by both classical liberalism and neoorthodoxy are well known. For many conservatives, the controversy in Southern Baptist life is a battle for the souls of men. Denominations, churches, schools, and other institutions which have begun to shed aspects of their conservative theology appear to forfeit their zeal for the conversion of the lost also. Denials of such allegations are unconvincing. Invoking slogans such as Bold Missions [sic] Thrust is also a futile enterprise. When neoorthodox churches and schools demonstrate extensive personal involvement in direct evangelism resulting in church growth and the calling out of missionaries and pastors, conservative Southern Baptists will be less concerned about the effects of New Theology on worldwide evangelization.

The irrepressible conviction that Southern Baptist people were unaware of much of what was transpiring in the schools led to the examination of other serious questions. How did a theological direction established by Boyce, Robertson, Mullins, Carroll, and Scarborough reverse itself so quickly? How could one justify all the talk about Baptists as being people of local church autonomy and emphasis when in fact the denominational control and focus seemed to increase year by year?

Once in the full-time pastorate, denominational pressures began to be experienced in new ways. Sometimes threatened, sometimes ostracized by the "establishment," I soon learned the coercive potentials of a burgeoning bureaucratic denomination. The perils of bucking the tide were reinforced whenever an apparently threatening but sincere question was ventured. This whole process seemed inscrutable to one who had so often defended the integrity of the denomination in which he was reared and to one whose father was for thirteen years the executive secretary of Texas Baptists. The existence of these things in the denomination which has been my very life was unthinkable!

Eventually disillusionment gave way to resolution to work through the existing structures in an attempt to do my part in a return to the former moorings of our Southern Baptist Zion. A number of other Southern Baptists who shared similar concerns met for fellowship and prayer. From the outset it was our desire to address issues, not persons. We were aware that the two were often packaged inseparably. To the best of our ability, however, we set our sights on issues and prayed that God would guard our lips from haste or from any uncharitable remark. Sometimes this has been difficult amid the acrimonious assaults against our persons and motives and the distorted portrayals of our positions. There have been times of failure when conservatives spoke unwisely. Hopefully these have been rare, but where they have occurred, I seek the forgiveness of God and of my brethren. The actions of others never provide license for us to respond in other than a Christ-honoring way.

The Theological Issue

The reasons which drove many of us to action may be summarized as *theological, historical,* and *ecclesiastical.* The theological reasons that produced the conservative resurgence can perhaps be most easily presented in the thought of two Kentuckians who have noted the invasion of many of our schools by the historical-critical method. C. R. Daley, then editor of the *Western Recorder,* said on May 1, 1984,

> Reactions to doctrinal directions in the Convention and especially in the seminaries is not a new thing. The growing use of the historical-critical approach to the study of the Bible in Southern Baptist seminaries and acceptance of some conclusions from some such studies had brought earlier reactions from more conservative Southern Baptists. (C. R. Daley, "Southern Baptists are becoming a new and different denomination," *The Western Recorder,* 1 May 1984.)

The same theme is again voiced by E. Glenn Hinson in the initial chapter of *Science, Faith, and Revelation*, a *Festschrift* volume devoted to Eric Rust. Dr. Hinson says of Dr. Rust's approach,

> The time was not right for wholesaling his approach. Consequently, he has constructed a bridge which some, especially of the present generation, are ready to cross. He has equipped others to lead the next generation across. We must remember that historical-critical interpretation had barely gotten started even in Southern Baptist seminaries when Eric Rust first began teaching at Southern in 1953. (Robert E. Patterson, editor, *Science, Faith, and Revelation: An Approach To Christian Philosophy*, Nashville: Broadman Press, 1979, p. 24.)

These two references to the historical-critical method focus on the fact that by the admission of these neoorthodox writers themselves, the historical-critical method in theology has been making its inroads into Southern Baptist life. These advances belong to the modern period, and conclusions associated with this method do not reflect the historic Baptist position. The advances of the historical-critical method and neoorthodox theology of the European continent are causes for alarm among conservative Southern Baptists. The results of such thinking are reflected, for example, in the current situation at Southern Baptist Theological Seminary in Louisville, Kentucky.

On the one hand the faculty unanimously adopted a resolution of gratitude and commitment to Southern Baptists on October 4, 1984. That resolution reaffirms that "We believe without reservation in the inspiration and authority of the Bible and all that the Bible affirms about itself." It also reaffirms the Baptist Faith and Message statement concerning the Bible, which in part says that the Bible has "truth, without any mixture of error, for its matter." On the other hand, Dr. Roy Lee Honeycutt in his comments in *The Broadman Bible Commentary* repeatedly raises serious questions about the historicity of events which purportedly took place according to the author of 2 Kings. On page 238, vol. 3, speaking of the reported restoration of the life of the dead child in 2 Kings 4:32-37, Dr. Honeycutt says:

> One should hear the stories as they were intended, as a person living two and a half millennia ago, prior to the modern, scientific era. Whether one interprets the stories literally or as wonder stories in the category of saga and legend, the narrative suggests that Elisha did in fact restore the life of the child. That this is most likely a wonder story in the category of saga and

legend is most probable; even so, that the story should be weakened by rationalistic explanations is to miss the point of the redactor's purpose. (Roy Lee Honeycutt, Old Testament consulting editor, *The Broadman Bible Commentary*, vol. 3, Nashville: Broadman Press, 1970, p. 238.)

Elsewhere, Dr. Honeycutt finds ways to question the historicity of other miracles presented in the book of 2 Kings. He finds "helpful" the suggestions of John Gray that in 2 Kings 6:1-7, Elisha secured the ax head with a long pole. Therefore, the "iron" did not really float to the surface as the story indicates. It is "an example of the manner in which historical events were elaborated across successive generations until the narrative becomes a combination of saga and legend, inextricable woven together" (ibid., 242).

The reason for the apparent discrepancy between the reaffirmation of faith adopted by Dr. Honeycutt's faculty and his own hesitancy to affirm the historicity of many biblical narratives is found in the philosophical distinction as to the nature of truth. Like most neoorthodox writers, Dr. Honeycutt apparently adheres to what is sometimes called the "intentionalist" view of truth, rather than the "correspondence" view of truth. The "correspondence" view of truth insists that in order to be true a statement must conform to reality. If, for example, I invite a man to leap from a building into a safety net that he cannot see, promising him the presence of that net, I have told him the truth only if the net is actually there. However, according to the "intentionalist" view of truth, if I know that the man will perish in the building which is being consumed by flames, and I encourage him to leap into a net that is not there, knowing of other provisions to break his fall and, hopefully, prevent his demise, the only thing that is important is that the man should jump and thus be saved. It may be true that the facts as I have reported them to the man do not strictly correspond to the reality below. Nevertheless, if my intention is to save his life and I succeed, then actually I have told him the truth.

Dr. Honeycutt suggests that what the redactors and biblical writers had in mind was to present spiritual truth, which might not actually always correspond to the historical circumstances which they reported. Such cavalier handling of the biblical materials, based on minimal evidence, is intolerable at best for most Southern Baptists. The problem is not the right of someone to believe those things which Dr. Honeycutt has expressed. As a Baptist profoundly convinced of the absolute necessity of religious freedom, I must defend Dr. Honeycutt's right to believe, write about, or proclaim his own understanding of the Scriptures.

On the other hand, this kind of exegesis not only calls into question the individual passages, but also raises the more serious epistemological question as to exactly what methods are to be used to distinguish in Scripture that which is historically reliable from that which is not. For example, if Elisha did not actually cause the "iron to swim" as reported by the biblical writer in 2 Kings 6, then how are we to know that the writers who reported the resurrection may be counted reliable? When serious questions about biblical accuracy are engendered by those who are supposed to be preparing ministers for the pulpits of churches, those of us who find such views unconscionable cannot justify providing Cooperative Program "missions money" to sustain such instruction. Furthermore, we find it incomprehensible that Broadman Press owned by the Sunday School Board of the Southern Baptist Convention would publish such material when what is so greatly needed is an affirmative presentation of the veracity and authority of the Scriptures.

Dr. Honeycutt claims that the entire faculty at Southern Seminary is committed to the Bible as "truth without mixture of error." Clearly when Dr. Honeycutt speaks of error, he has something different in mind from what "error" normally implies. One of the most subtle dangers in neo-orthodox theology is the use of conventional evangelical and biblical vocabulary with new meanings attached. Only the initiates realize fully what is being said. The solipsistic nature of neoorthodoxy may generate widely disparate conclusions, but the theological method remains essentially unchanged. What is at stake here is not an argument over whether or not "inerrancy" is a good word to describe the Bible. Rather, Dr. Honeycutt is interpreting the Bible in an unprecedented way as far as Baptist history is concerned. He says that he believes it, but then he proceeds to provide examples of "legend" in which what is recorded by the author of Scripture is not actually what transpired at all.

Is Dr. Honeycutt aware of this distinction? I cannot judge his heart. But it is alarming that in a recent interview in the *Indiana Baptist*, Dr. Honeycutt noted that both he and a friend recognized that there was danger in making known his own view.

> I remember when writing the commentary on Exodus—since I was one of the consulting editors, I couldn't serve as editor on that particular book—they sent it to a friend in another school. He suggested, "I think it would be much safer if you didn't identify your own view." (David Simpson, "Personal Interview with Dr. Roy L. Honeycutt, President, Southern Seminary," *Indiana Baptist*, 20 November 1984.)

Concerning the recent reaffirmation of the Southern Seminary faculty, Dr. Honeycutt says that

> Anyone dissatisfied with their commitment cannot be satisfied; and it is likely that other agenda are operative for such critics than honest concern for the authority of the Bible at Southern Seminary. (Roy Lee Honeycutt, "President's Journal," *The Tie*, November/December 1984.)

Overlooking for the moment another instance of the judging of motives, a province reserved for God alone, the affirmation itself *is* satisfactory. But it is just this point that intensifies division. Dr. Honeycutt's own contributions to *The Broadman Bible Commentary* in both Exodus and 2 Kings call into question the historicity or at the very least the accuracy of reporting of numerous passages from the burning bush of Moses to the swimming iron of Elisha. How can this incredibly strange way of handling the Scriptures be reconciled with the affirmation recently tendered?

Conservative Southern Baptists do not intend blanket inclusion of all in concerns expressed. They recognize that not all Baptist colleges, universities, and seminaries are dangerously adrift from New Testament roots. Not all denominational leaders have been insensitive to the concerns of the churches. To the contrary, there is much that conservative Southern Baptists applaud and support. The concern is with the general drift. After all, as Paul wrote the Corinthians, "a little leaven leaveneth the whole lump." Unqualified blanket endorsement of all convention agencies and programs is no less reprehensible than blanket questioning. Neither can valued doctrines be misconstrued any longer. In this controversy, appeal to the doctrine of "the priesthood of the believer" has become a popular tactic for justifying whatever belief one might cherish. But this is far removed from the intent of the New Testament and Baptist doctrine of the priesthood of the believer. If this doctrine is a umbrella to shelter every belief, then we must admit Moslems and Hindus to church membership and we could schedule the Ayatollah Khomeini to teach the next miniterm in one of our seminaries. No one advocates such absurdities. All draw line of fellowship and doctrine somewhere. The doctrine of the priesthood of the believer proclaims access to God for every penitent soul. It further stresses the saints' responsibility to take Christ to a lost world. Maring and Hudson stated it well:

> Unfortunately, this doctrine has often been misunderstood, for its conventional interpretation is that it means no more than the right of every man to

approach God directly. It is true that Christ is our High Priest, and that his priestly work is unique and unrepeatable. We may indeed come to God in prayer and in humble confession of our sins without the intercession of a human advocate, but for that matter people under the Old Covenant could also do that! This interpretation is not what the doctrine of the priesthood of believers was originally intended to stress; it emphasized responsibilities more than rights. The idea of priesthood indicates something done on behalf of another; one cannot be a priest to himself. (Norman H. Maring and Winthrop S. Hudson, *A Baptist Manual of Polity and Practice*, Valley Forge: Judson Press, 1963, p. 91.)

The Historical Issue

The history of denominations tends to resemble a bell curve. Slow and often maligned beginnings give way to rapid growth, followed by slow and painful decadence and ineffectiveness. English Baptists, Canadian Baptists, and American Baptists are all examples. Often this process witnessed the loss of invaluable educational institutions such as the University of Chicago or Brown University. Within the Southern Baptist family, states which were influenced by more liberal theology frequently reported diminishing baptisms. Universities such as Wake Forest and the University of Richmond were lost to Baptist state convention control. Lip service was paid to "Bold Missions," but many institutions notably were not aggressively evangelistic. Baptist Student Union programs, once openly acknowledged as the most aggressive and successful evangelistic forces on the college campus, have forfeited their reputation. Campus Crusade, Fellowship of Christian Athletes, and the Navigators are now the recognized leaders in campus evangelization. The number of students in Baptist colleges preparing for the pastoral ministry has experienced an alarming decline over the past ten years. Many conservatives fear that our own denomination is repeating the deadly errors of our brethren before us.

The Ecclesiological Issue

The ecclesiological difficulty may be observed in various ways. The gradual change in nomenclature for those in denominational positions is one such case in point. In many associations the man who was once an "associational missionary" has now become an "executive director" of the association. Those formerly spoken of as "denominational servants" are increasingly distant from the constituencies they serve, surrounded by burgeoning bureaucracies, which continue to demonstrate lack of sensitivity to many of those who actually provide funding. Associations pressure new churches and missions to place deed restrictions on the property of the church stating that should members cease to cooperate with Southern Baptists or the association or both, the property would revert to the association. This is at best a threat to the local church's autonomy—at worst the continuing development of a "connectional church."

Examples of changes in the direction of denominational centralization abound. For example, at the time of the establishment of the Sunday School Board, J. B. Gambrell was opposed to the establishment of such a board. The reason for his concern was stated in a paragraph which he himself wrote, Gambrell said:

> In conclusion, your committee, in its long and earnest consideration of this whole matter in all its environments, has been compelled to take account of the well-known fact, that there are widely divergent views held among us by brethren equally earnest, consecrated, and devoted to the best interest of the Master's Kingdom. It is therefore recommended that the fullest freedom of choice be accorded to everyone as to what literature he will use or support, and that no brother be disparaged in the slightest degree on account of what he may do in the exercise of his right as Christ's freeman. But we would earnestly urge all brethren to give to this Board a fair consideration, and in no case to obstruct it in the great work assigned to it by this Convention. (Joe Burton, *The Story of the Sunday School Board*, Nashville: Convention Press, 1966, pp. 44-45.)

As I have commented elsewhere, the phrases "fullest freedom of choice" and "no brother be disparaged in the slightest degree" sometimes seem to be lost to the modern, supercorporate convention structure. Disparagement is often present, usually in one of the following ways:

(a) Damaging suggestions that a pastor or a church is "really not Southern Baptist" and would "probably like to become Independent."

(b) Allegations of failure to have a "cooperative spirit."

(c) Efforts to isolate pastors and churches from the participation in denominational activities.

> Major denominational leaders are seldom guilty of such harassment. But many who would never personally venture into such activities condone and encourage them by their silence. The fact is that *while Baptist churches are technically free to choose their literature*, if they do not choose the literature of the Sunday School Board, *these churches face the probability of pressure and even harassment*. Where are our Baptist liberties? Are we free only from physical constraint and reprisal? (Paige Patterson, "Strange Fire in the

Holy of Holies," *The Shophar Papers*, Dallas: Criswell Center for Biblical Studies, p. 17.)

In fact, the fear of the growing centralization of the Southern Baptist Convention is not a novelty. Fifty years ago in 1934, William Wright Barnes, professor of Church History at Southwestern Baptist Theological Seminary, published a book entitled *The Southern Baptist Convention: A Study in the Development of Ecclesiology*. In that small monograph, Barnes cited the alarming evidences, which had come to exist even in 1934, of a movement toward the development of what constituted in effect a Baptist hierarchy. Barnes wrote:

> In the following pages the effort has been to show that there has been an ecclesiological development in Southern Baptist life comparable to the development that took place in the first centuries of Christian history. A development that laid the foundation of the medieval Catholic church, out of which came the Roman Catholic church of modern times. (W. W. Barnes, *The Southern Baptist Convention: A Study in yhe Development of Ecclesiology*, Seminary Hill, Texas: By the Author, September, 1934, p.1.)

Barnes continues:

> Southern Baptists in the meeting of 1925 declared that they did not believe in evolution, but they have been practicing it through the years. They have crossed two distinct species—association and convention bases of representation—and have evolved, or are in the process of evolving, an entirely new species—the ecclesiastical. (Ibid., p.34.)

He points to the state ownership of religious papers as a cause for concern:

> Another result of centralization and at the same time a cause of further centralization is the denominational ownership of religious papers. There is objection to private ownership, but the objections to denominational ownership are greater. When an individual owned and controlled the paper the responsibility for the policies was his. Under present public ownership the responsibility is denominational. So long as the denomination retains an editor the denomination is responsible. If the policies are objectionable the editor may be dismissed. But it is not so easy to dismiss the editor of a Baptist paper as it is a French prime minister or a Cuban president. The most objectionable feature of denominational ownership is that it is but another link in the chain of centralization. (Ibid., p. 60.)

Dr. Barnes concludes:

By the fourth century, the developed Catholic church had become sacrosanct, visible and invisible, to rend which was the deepest sin. It mattered not about anything else if one were in communion with this church. Unification is the cry of the hour today. (Ibid., p. 78.)

That tragic development, which our great Baptist historian W. W. Barnes saw developing, has become increasingly the case in our own day. The criticism to which the so-called "super churches" have been subject is just another case in point. Ostensibly our denomination is concerned to maintain the autonomy of the local church and a determination to reach the world for Christ. Yet, when churches begin to succeed in reaching their cities for Christ in a remarkable way and in some sense or another become models for other churches to imitate, these same churches become the objects of criticism, particularly in some state Baptist papers.

In conclusion, it may be fairly stated that the three concerns which activated the present conservative resurgence were:

(1) The criticism to which the Scriptures have been subject, as serious questions have been raised about the veracity of that document which Baptists have always held to be a sure and certain word from the Lord.
(2) Observation of the tendency of denominations historically to move to the left and decline in efficiency and effectiveness.
(3) The gradual development of a powerful ecclesiastical bureaucracy, which, if not in theory at least in practice, increasingly threatens the autonomy of the local churches.

The Extent of the Present Crisis

Apparently there is agreement among most Southern Baptists about one thing: our Convention faces at the present moment the most serious crisis which it has faced since its inception. There is probably little to be gained by elucidating the extent of the crisis to readers who are already painfully aware of it. Perhaps the matter may be set in perspective in the following way.

Conservative Southern Baptists have a deep desire to be loyal to the Convention, to support its institutions and agencies, and to be a part of the entire program. Knowing, however, that there comes a day of reckoning where they must give account to God for every word and work, conservatives cannot continue in good conscience to support that which they feel to be contrary to the teaching of the Word of God and to our historic Baptist principles. On the other hand, those who fear the conservative resurgence seem convinced that what is on the drawing board is a "conservative takeover," which will result in mass terminations of employment and the establishment of an Independent Fundamentalism that will in effect cause the demise of the Southern Baptist Convention. Those holding views on all sides of the issue have met together on several occasions, but as yet no consensus has been achieved. At the moment, the June 1985 meeting of the Southern Baptist Convention in Dallas, Texas, looms before us as the great confrontation, with apparently no solution in sight.

All of this has been greatly exacerbated as far as conservatives are concerned by the plethora of allegations concerning conservative behavior, all largely unsupported by facts. Through sermons preached, news releases provided, and editorials written, conservatives have been accused of having at the Southern Baptist Convention floor managers dressed in black suits, white shirts, and red ties; of busing in enormous numbers of messengers; of maintaining in Dallas a "War Room" with "heresy files"; of maintaining large computer banks with sophisticated mailing lists capable apparently of reaching almost every Southern Baptist; and of prospering through large financial endowment, making it possible for conservatives to launch almost any kind of campaign they wish to launch. Worse still, unfounded, unproved, and unprovable accusations have been made about the motives of conservatives. Although conservatives have repeatedly denied such allegations, readers of state newspapers have been assured that the conservative resurgence is a massive power play designed by a conservative oligarchy to take control of the convention for its own purposes. Readers have been assured that these conservatives are not true Southern Baptists but are actually "Independent Fundamentalists" whose agenda is actually the establishment of dispensational premillennialism and the financing of their own "independent" schools. Space does not permit the elucidation of all of the charges that have been made concerning the motives of conservatives. Suffice it to note that the judgement of men's motives belongs to God who alone can adjudicate in matters of the heart. Probably no single factor other than the discrediting of the Bible itself has so polarized and astonished conservative Southern Baptists as this willingness on the part of the "moderates," the neoorthodox, and sometimes even denominational leaders such as Dr. Honeycutt and Dr. Dilday, to judge the motives of others. These assailants are entitled to disagree with methods and positions. But are they omniscient? How can they read the hearts of others?

Is There a Solution?

Recently Dr. Franklin Paschall, past president of the Southern Baptist Convention, has proposed that the Southern Baptist Convention officially appoint a committee consisting of at least some of the agency and institutional leaders together with concerned conservatives. The committee would be charged with the necessity of reporting back to the Southern Baptist Convention the following year on a proposal to end the controversy and get on with the work. Dr. Paschall's proposal has the advantage over former efforts of envisioning an official committee faced with the necessity of an official report to the convention. I applaud Dr. Paschall's proposal and confess to the hope that such a proposal may become reality.

However, the potential that such a proposal carries with it may be one year too late, unless some major changes can be made. What would those major changes be? First, there must be on the part of state Baptist newspapers, Baptist Press, and denominational leaders, as well as pastors who consider themselves in the moderate camp, a cessation of those allegations which would construe concerned conservatives as anything other than loyal and committed Southern Baptists. False and unsupported charges concerning the exact nature of political activities of conservative Southern Baptists not only must be dropped but also should be repudiated by those who have formerly made those accusations. This does not mean that such persons must agree with conservative conclusions or even methods. It simply means that the inaccuracies about those methods must be corrected.

In the second place, there must be a disposition on the part of Convention leadership to face openly and honestly the issues that lie before us. I do not know of any conservative who expects every issue to be resolved to his own satisfaction. All seems cognizant that discussions of many issues will produce conclusions not altogether as one might prefer. One thing *there must be* is an agreement not to question the truthfulness, the historicity, or the authority of the Scriptures.

An open challenge by denominational employees to the election of Charles Stanley as president of the Southern Baptist Convention for a second year, while totally within the bounds of the procedures provided in the constitution and bylaws of the convention, would certainly be construed by concerned conservatives as a further sign of the determination of many in denominational leadership to remain insensitive to conservative concerns. The only accusation being lodged against Charles Stanley as a reputable president of the convention is that his church has not given an appropriate percentage of its gifts to the Cooperative Program. The church has given all that is required and much more besides to the Cooperative Program in order to send its messengers to the Southern Baptist Convention; therefore, any of its members may serve in any of the offices of the convention. Many of those who seem most concerned about the threat of a doctrinal creed inconsistently espouse "monetary credalism" and avow that a church must give a certain percentage before one of its members is qualified to serve the Convention as an officer. Such continual emphasis upon monetary matters alone is becoming labored even to those of us who have always been the most ardent proponents of the Cooperative Program.

People frequently raise the question, "What is going to become of the Southern Baptist Convention?" It seems to me that there are three possibilities. There is always the possibility of a formal split. Although I am now prepared for the first time to acknowledge that possibility (due to the challenge to Dr. Stanley's reelection and the declaration of "holy war" being made by the presidents of two of the denominations' seminaries), I still do not feel that there is much likelihood of such a split. For this I remain thankful. We have not yet arrived at the fateful crossroads confronted by Spurgeon and the English Baptists at the middle of the last century. Conservative Southern Baptists have spoken now in order to avoid that tragic but necessary checkmate described by Spurgeon on September 14, 1856:

> We live in very singular times just now. The professing church has been flattering itself that, notwithstanding all our divisions with regard to doctrine, we were all right in the main. A false and spurious liberality has been growing up, which has covered us all, so that we have dreamed that all who bore the name of ministers were indeed God's servants—that all who occupied pulpits, of whatever denomination they might be, were entitled to our respect, as being stewards of the mystery of Christ. But, lately, the weeds upon the surface of the stagnant pool have been a little stirred, and we have been enabled to look down into the depths. This is a day of strife—a day of division—a time of war and fighting between professing Christians. God be thanked for that! Far better that it should be so than that the false calm should any longer exert its fatal spell over us. The day is come when we must know who are for the Lord and for His truth, and who are on the side of error. The time is now come when some men, once distinguished among us for the attractiveness of their preaching, must be ranked amongst those who are opponents of the truth. We did once imagine, in the blindness of our charity that we all preached one gospel; but now the enmity

of the carnal mind hath appeared. Carnal churches have chosen to themselves carnal teachers, who have begun to teach strange doctrines, which
they mystify by their words, garnish with their eloquence, and try to support
by specious logic, apart from simple Scripture.

The time is coming when it shall be openly proved who is on the Lord's
side; at this very hour, separations are everywhere taking place. We weep
for the cause—we do not weep for the effect. We weep that there should
have been such heresies growing up in the midst of the church; but we do
not weep when we see those heresies brought out to the day, and slaugh-
tered, with what some think remorseless cruelty, but what we believe
unflinching justice. We desire that God may spare to us the men who are
still faithful, and who will never cease, at the risk of being called bigots, to
drag out to the light those who lie against God's gospel—to bring them
publicly before the world as opponents of the faith which is in Christ Jesus,
whereby we hope to be saved. May God give us courage to stand up for the
right. (C. H. Spurgeon, "The Church Of God And The Truth Of God,"
Metropolitan Tabernacle Pulpit, vol. 54, Pasadena, Texas, Pilgrim Publications, 1978, p. 241.)

The second possibility I would describe as a functional division. If
the continued erosion of confidence in the leadership of many of the denomination's agencies and institutions occurs, the day will certainly
arrive when congregations far more numerous than most people realize
will devote most of their monetary support to associational mission
projects both at home and abroad. These projects would be those
missionary and educational efforts in which those doctrines of the faith
held most dear will be the guidelines. Such a state would clearly be
preferable to the formal split, but one wonders just exactly what the
eventual ramifications of such a functional division might be.

The other possibility is that of a sweeping revival within the denomination. It is my conviction that such a revival would be welcomed by
"moderates" as well as conservatives. The stupendous importance of
prayer for the intervention of God not only in the coming convention, but
also in all of Convention life assumes an importance of inestimable mag-
nitude. Perhaps our problems can only be solved by direct intervention
of God. Such a thought, however, is hardly objectionable. In fact, this
would be the best of all developments. Is such a thing impossible? Other
periods of controversy have certainly lent themselves to such results. The
confrontation between the hyper-Calvinists of England and the missionary
impulses of William Carey were surely painful for those representing
both positions. The end result was the birth of the modern missions

movement. At this time, we must all devote increasing amounts of our time and energy to seeking just such intervention of God and just such rebirth of missions and evangelism.

Conservative Southern Baptists are willing to forgive the unkind and uncharitable accusations which have been lodged against them. Even judgment of motive will be quickly forgiven. Conservatives do no seek "control" of the Southern Baptist Convention, only the reducing of the bureaucratic structure and the return of the Convention to the people. Conservatives do not insist that every decision and policy conform to their own thinking. They do not insist that everyone use the word "inerrant" to describe his view of the Bible. They do seek genuine parity in the faculties and administrations of the schools and insist that employees of the convention never, under any circumstances, call into question any statement of the Bible or say anything that might be construed as disbelief in the veracity of the Scriptures. Conservatives will accept and support current denominational leadership. However, the monotonous response, "just trust us," is no longer sufficient. "Trust" must be earned, and in any case never functions without accountability. As J. B. Gambrell liked to state the matter, "Baptists never ride a horse without a bridle."

Document 32
Fisher Humphreys's Interview with Paul Pressler
The Theological Educator, Special Issue, 1985

"An Interview with Judge Paul Pressler," 15-24

Educator. I would like to begin with some background questions, Judge Pressler. Am I correct that both your family and your wife's family have been Baptists for several generations?

Judge Pressler. No, my family have been Baptists for about seven generations on the Towns and Garrett side. On the Maddox side I know of only about five generations that would have been Baptists; on the Pressler side only three generations down to me; my children make four. My wife is descended from Julian Cave who led the traveling church from Culpepper, Virginia, and was the first Baptist pastor in Kentucky, but some of her relatives went off and were Presbyterians prior to the time we were married. Her mother's family were French Reformed and then Methodists. Her father's family were Presbyterians, and she was Presbyterian when we were married and was baptized a few weeks after we were married.

Educator. Did you yourself attend a Baptist College or seminary?

Judge Pressler. No. I have never had any seminary education. I went to prep school at Phillips Exeter, in Exeter, New Hampshire, and then attended Princeton University and graduated from Princeton University. Then I got my Doctor of Jurisprudence degree from the University of Texas law school.

Educator. Have you been in Baptist churches all of your life?

Judge Pressler. Yes.

Educator. And am I correct that you now teach a Sunday School class at First Baptist here in Houston?

Judge Pressler. That is correct.

Educator. Is that an Adult class?

Judge Pressler. I have taught in three different departments there at First Baptist. I am now teaching twenty-five-year-old single men in Sunday School.

Educator. When did you first become concerned about theological trends among Southern Baptists?

Judge Pressler. I was saved in South Main Baptist Church in Houston where my grandfather was chairman of the deacons and taught a major

Bible class. I did not realize that there were any theological issues existent until I went away to Phillips Exeter Academy. It was a school founded by a man to train young men in the Word of God, and when I went there it was completely secular with no Christian influence whatsoever. My Baptist pastor in Exeter, a seminary graduate, told me that he did not know what it was for a person to be saved. He said, "I don't know what you people from the South mean when you say somebody has been saved." So I had the privilege of explaining the way of salvation to my pastor, a seminary graduate. I saw a church there in Exeter that was on its last legs because theological liberalism had killed it. I came on down to Princeton University and saw a university that, again, had been founded by believers to train people in the Word of God, which was then completely secular and humanistic and was undermining the basic truths of the gospel. I saw the same thing in the chapel there at Princeton. I knew some of the children of the professors at Union Theological Seminary [in New York] and I had the opportunity of visiting with a faculty member in some situations there at Union Seminary.

So I found what liberalism was in the East. I found out the extremely negative impact that it had had on culture and society and presentation of the gospel. I did not think that this was existent very much among Southern Baptists until I came back here. I have a letter I wrote in 1953 to the editor of the *Baptist Standard* complaining of some liberalism that I had come across. But I didn't realize that it was here until I came back to law school and went to the University of Texas. The first Sunday I went down to the University Baptist Church where my great-grandfather, Judge John C. Towns, had led the organization of the Baptist Bible chair; in Austin is the John C. Towns' Bible Chair, named after my great-grandfather. Blake Smith was pastor of University Baptist in Austin at that time, and I found the same type of liberalism there that I had known in the East, and that was the first awakening to me that we had problems in the Southern Baptist Convention. I then went down to First Baptist Church where part of my family had been since the 1850s and where my grandmother had taught Sunday School for fifty years; and Carlyle Marney was there and I found some very disquieting things going down at First Baptist. So that was the beginning of my acquaintanceship with liberalism in the Southern Baptist Convention.

Educator. What steps did you try to take to influence the theological direction of Southern Baptists when you encountered these problems? I mean steps before 1979.

Judge Pressler. The first step I took was to leave the two family churches—not to join the two family churches—in Austin. I went to Hyde Park Baptist Church, and I joined there soon after I got to Austin. I taught Sunday School while I was in law school there. I tried to minister to students, just as I organized a Baptist Student group on the campus at Princeton, which I taught. So up through that, it was just positively asserting the gospel.

When Ralph Elliot wrote the book, *The Message of Genesis*, in which he said that perhaps a man named Abraham never lived, and that Melchizedek was a priest of Baal—although both in Genesis and Hebrews he is called a priest of the most high God—I became very concerned about the failure of Southern Baptists to deal quickly and decisively with the matter.

I had been elected deacon at Second Baptist Church and ordained there at Second Baptist Church. A committee of deacons was set up to study our seminary situation. I served on that committee. As a result of serving on that committee, I wrote a little pamphlet called *A Message to Southern Baptists* which was published in the early sixties, which grew out of my concern about where we were headed, based upon the Elliot controversy and other things which I had observed up until that time. Shortly thereafter, after reading my pamphlet Dr. Eddleman, who was president of New Orleans Seminary at that time, asked his local representative, his development man, to stop by and see me, and we discussed raising some development funds for the New Orleans Seminary. I informed him at that time that I was not interested in helping endowment of the school because I had seen too many schools take the endowment funds given by God's people and use it to undermine the very basic principles that motivated their founding of the school. So I got together with some of the best legal talent in Houston, and we decided to set up a foundation to support New Orleans Seminary so long, but only so long as, in the opinion of the self-perpetuating board of trustees, the school adhered to the doctrinal statement set forth in the Articles of Incorporation of that foundation that we had created. So up until that time, my concern had manifested only in seeking to teach the Word affirmatively and raise money in such a way that the money would never be used to undermine the principles that motivate its donation.

Educator. I wasn't aware of the committee at Second Baptist. Was this a committee elected by the church at large or appointed by the Pastor?

Judge Pressler. No. It was appointed by the chairman of the board of deacons. It was voted on by the deacons. It was a committee of the deacons and was appointed by the chairman of the board of deacons.

Educator. What was the name of the Foundation?

Judge Pressler. The Evangelical Christian Education Foundation.

Educator. Is it still a functioning foundation?

Judge Pressler. We used a good deal of money for scholarships. We helped a number of people go to New Orleans Seminary. We used money for various purposes related to Seminary, and at the present time there is $4,000.00 deposited with the Seminary, that if we made a determination the Seminary was not adhering to the doctrinal position that motivated the setting up of the Foundation, we have the right by the agreement signed by the Seminary to withdraw that money.

Educator. But it is not as active as it was before?

Judge Pressler. We are not soliciting funds, and we are not awarding scholarships. We are just letting the money stay at the $4,000.00—which we did not use for the other purposes—stay at the Seminary at the present time.

Educator. Up until 1979, the Southern Baptist Convention was almost certainly the most effective large missionary and evangelistic organization in the world. I know that you share the commitment to missions and evangelism of the Convention. In light of God's blessing on our missions and evangelism, did you not feel some hesitation about setting out to redirect the Southern Baptist theological enterprise?

Judge Pressler. Your question is such that it is rather difficult to answer. I think that we have to go back in the history a little bit further than you have gone. Southern Baptists were not always the greatest missionary agency in the country. The Methodists and the Presbyterians had the largest mission force, were really the most evangelical, and the Methodists greatly outnumbered Southern Baptists. This was back a number of years ago. In my lifetime I saw Southern Baptists overtake Methodists and Presbyterians in their missionary efforts and in their evangelistic zeal. And I saw those denominations peak and start to go down. When you trace what happened to them, you'll see the same thing that happened to the Congregationalists and the same thing that happened to various other denominations. Once their schools became liberal, then they lost their evangelistic imperative, they lost their mission zeal, and their mission forces dwindled to almost complete insignificance. You'll find that situation existent in Presbyterian and Methodist circles in the United States today, in the parent organizations. The liberalism of the Presbyterian denomination has fermented a division with the conservatives pulling out and creating the Presbyterian Church of America. The Presbyterian church is in extreme difficulty today because of the liberal takeover of its institutions. You'll find the same problem in the Methodist denominations.

Now Southern Baptists had resisted, up until much more recently than the Methodists and Presbyterians, the inroad of liberal theology. Anybody who studies history will notice that liberal theology kills, and although a group still might be keeping its evangelistic force and its missions in numbers, if that denomination has lost its theological institutions, the handwriting is on the wall for that institution unless that is reversed. Therefore I think that anybody who is a fair judge of history—who studied the Downgrade Controversy with Spurgeon in England, studied the history of the Methodist Church in the United States, studied the Presbyterian Church—would realize that when Southern Baptists lost their institutions to theological liberalism, they also would be destroyed.

Now the question was, Do we wait for the complete deterioration to set in, or do we act to avert the disaster which happened to the Presbyterians and Methodists while there is still time? So what we did was try to turn the situation around while there was still hope. I praise God that there was hope, that we have seen victory, and we are turning to where we can maintain our evangelistic pace, our evangelistic zeal, our missionary imperative, and our desire to reach the world for a saving knowledge of Jesus Christ. If we do not believe that Jesus Christ died on the cross to pay the price of our sins with his blood shed on the cross; if we do not believe that the only payment of the price for man's sins is the blood of Christ; if we do not believe that there is no salvation in any other; then we do not have the missionary and evangelistic imperative. And once we start losing that—which we were—the handwriting was on the wall, "Ichabod" was beginning to be written on the doorposts of our Southern Baptist institutions. And therefore we would have taken the same demise as taken by the Presbyterians and the Methodists.

No, there was no hesitation whatsoever, because I believe in being a student of history, and anybody who studied history would necessarily have come to the same conclusion as to what was happening in Southern Baptist ranks, if they had any understanding as to what was occurring.

Educator. Would you describe the way in which you and your friends work as you attempt to influence the direction of Baptist theology. I'm thinking in particular about publications, meetings, talking to students, talking to pastors, collecting evidence of the problem, and so forth.

Judge Pressler. You have a multifarious question which is rather difficult to answer. At law that would not be allowed. So I am going to try to remember to break your question down. If it is not broken down sufficiently, would you please re-ask those portions which you do not think are adequately addressed.

First of all, the acuteness of the problem came to me when some students who had trusted in the Lord through a Bible study which I had here in Houston had gone to Baylor University, called me and told me that they were being very much confused, and asked that I come to Waco and meet with them, and study the Word with them and see their textbooks and listen to what had been going on in class, so that they would have an opportunity to try to understand all these things that were being thrown at them. So I went up there. Coming back from Waco that night after reading *People of the Covenant,* seeing where it talks about the errors in Daniel, where it talks about the historical inaccuracies, and the other things that were in the book that was written by the one who would soon become chairman of the Baylor Religion Department, and who was teaching the same thing along with the rest of the faculty members in the class; according to these students, I felt that I was not going to sit around any further, any longer, and help finance the destruction of the faith of my young people, that something had to be done.

So I started asking other people if they shared my concern. Back when the effort to assist New Orleans Seminary in the early sixties, I had some people that contributed to it that were concerned about the same things we were concerned, and we began talking. Paige Patterson had been a friend of mine since the mid-sixties and I talked to him. We just began communicating. Then, as a lawyer does, I began to study the structure of the Convention because I felt that the conservatives had been fighting battles without knowing what the war was. The liberals had analyzed the Convention structure and manipulated it for their own purposes. And the conservatives had been out winning people to Christ and not attending the conventions, and not paying any attention to the Convention institutions. So, first of all we began to pray and think and communicate, just informally, to see whether there was something that could be done. We studied the constitution, studied the bylaws, and, not wanting to be dissident, we decided that we would work within the system to effectuate the changes that needed to be made, and obviously needed to be made, by working within the system.

We just communicated with people. The first thing we had to communicate was how the system worked. There were people that had been president of the Convention that didn't even know how the system worked. We talked to some of them and got insights. It was a very informal thing, always has been, just because we needed to see whether people were interested in the things we were. When we found out they were, then we started praying about, let's all come to Houston to the convention. And they showed up. God convicted Adrian Rogers at 2:00 o'clock in the morning the day of the election that God had put his hand on him to run. Adrian ran, and he was elected. That's the story.

Educator. I will repeat a little bit of the question. Could you comment on the use of things like: do you have meetings, do you have publications, do you regularly talk to students, pastors, and so on. And do you keep records of theological misconduct in any formal sort of way?

Judge Pressler. I regularly communicate with everybody I can communicate with. I've spoken to pastor's conferences across the country. I've preached in churches across the country. I've responded to invitations to speak to two or three people, or to two or three hundred people, or two or three thousand people, constantly, for the last seven years. And I felt that communication is the name of the game. That is, we have to communicate. The Baptist Press has constantly misrepresented our intentions, misrepresented our motivations, misrepresented what we have been doing and so we have a method of getting behind the Baptist press in order to let people know what is actually going on, other than that which they read in the propaganda agencies which the liberals control.

Educator. If all of your ideals for the Southern Baptist Convention were reached, Judge Pressler, how would the Convention differ from what it is today?

Judge Pressler. Every young person that went to one of our institutions would be built up in their faith and would come out with a deeper and more wonderful appreciation for the fact that God wrote his book, and would not have his faith undermined in the institutions. That does not mean that the liberal position would not be made known to the students. It would mean that it would not be advocated and that we would not have ones in our institutions which sought to belittle the faith of our students.

Educator. This is more of a speculative question than the others: In order to reach this ideal that you have just described, what must be done? People are very interested to know what you think needs to be done. Do we need to close schools, start new schools, replace administrators, replace faculty? Do we need to set up a committee to watch these things? Do we need a creed or confession in addition to what we have?

Judge Pressler. It is a multifarious question again, but I'll try to answer. If you'll ask specifically about the things that you want me to cover then I'll be glad to do it, but it is kind of hard for me to answer.

All right, how should it be proceeded? Now I've been open in the entirety of this situation, as to what I think should be done. The trustees are ones that are entrusted with power by the Southern Baptist Convention. The trustees and the trustees alone are responsible to the Convention for the manner in which they have these institutions run. Obviously, the administrations, the faculty, the others in the institutions, are also responsible, but they are responsible secondarily where the trustees are responsible primarily. My position always has been, I have clearly enunciated it, and there should be no reason why anybody misunderstands what my position is; my position is that the trustees should run the institutions responsive to the wishes of their constituency. And they should run their institutions in such a way that individuals within the Convention do not have ground and basis for suspicion and concern about what the institutions are doing. When we have confidence in our institutions, we'll have no problems with contributions, we'll have no problems with conflicts. The problem is that the institutions have enclosed, self-perpetuating cliques that have become in some ways unresponsive to Southern Baptists.

So all I want is the trustees to be people who believe what Baptists have always believed; and I am not talking about peripheral issues, I'm talking about what the Bible is. The liberals have made every effort in the world to change the issue, to peripheral issues from what the real issue is. The real issue is, What is Scripture? Is it absolutely true? Is it completely reliable? Is it God's book or is it man's machinations? Now if we have trustees that believe that it is completely God's book, that it doesn't make mistakes because it is God-given, then we are going to have institutions—if they take their charge and commitments from Southern Baptists seriously—we are going to have institutions that are responsive to their constituency, and then the problems will be gone.

Let me negate some of the things you asked me about.

No, I am not for the creating of new institutions. No, I am not for creating a watchdog committee because the trustees are already such. No, I am not for creating a creed, because most of the institutions already have their statements of faith, and a statement of faith or creed is no better than the integrity of the person who signs it. We do not need more creeds, we need more integrity. If there is anything in the question that I have left out, please remind me.

Educator. No, that is fine, thanks. Is your ideal for the seminaries, and other schools as well, parity on the faculties, or is your ideal that only theologically acceptable people remain on the faculties?

Judge Pressler. My ideal is that everybody who is in one of our institutions, paid with Southern Baptist money, will be responsive to his constituency. Now we have a diverse constituency in a number of ways. I think a responsiveness to the constituency is not having somebody out militantly to undermine the faith of any of our young people.

I do not feel that our institutions should be institutions where only one viewpoint is espoused. We should have a great breadth of interpretation of Scripture, and there is all the difference in the world between an interpretation of Scripture and an understanding of what Scripture is. If we do not believe that the Scripture is completely authoritative in all that it says, then we make ourselves the judge of Scripture and we can leave out those portions that do not suit our sensitivities. Now I would like everyone in our institutions to adhere to a position that we are going to take the Bible as it is, believe it as it is, and try to understand what it says.

Now when you talk about parity, I don't know what you are talking about parity in. Are you asking me if we should have people who deny that the Bible is true in our institutions as a means of promoting parity, or are you talking about, should we have a parity, a divergence of opinion in interpreting the Scripture?

Educator. Let me come at this question in a different way. I know that you yourself are committed to the inerrancy of the Bible. In your view, what action should the Convention instruct institutional trustees to take toward faculty members or other employees who love Jesus Christ, believe the gospel, accept the Bible as the uniquely inspired Word of God and the ultimate authority on earth for Christian faith and practice, but who reject biblical inerrancy?

Judge Pressler. Well, it depends on what you mean by rejecting biblical inerrancy. First of all, you explain to me how much of the Bible you can reject and still believe in the authority of the Scripture. You explain that to me, and then I'll answer your question.

Educator. Let's suppose we have a faculty member in a seminary who says, "The Bible is the Word of God; there is no other book that is the Word of God. The Bible is uniquely inspired, not like Shakespeare, but it is uniquely inspired by God. It is God's Word to us. That Word has come to us through human beings. And I believe in the message of the Bible, the great truths that there is a transcendent, personal, creator God who is Father, Son, and Holy Spirit; the Son of God became incarnate as Jesus of Nazareth; he died upon the cross for our sins, and was raised on the third day."

Judge Pressler. When you say raised on the third day, are you talking about a bodily resurrection?

Educator. Let's say a bodily resurrection.

Judge Pressler. So you're putting in a doctrinal requirement for belief in the bodily resurrection?

Educator. I'd be glad to include that. It doesn't matter.

Judge Pressler. It does matter. How much can you disbelieve and still believe, is what I am asking.

Educator. Let me go ahead—who believes in the bodily resurrection, who believes in salvation by grace through faith, who believes that the church is the people of God, who believes in baptism, and in evangelism, and in missions. . . .

Judge Pressler. The trouble is, Dr. Humphreys, I am not asking what you believe, but what can you disbelieve about Scripture and still believe in the authority of Scripture? I am asking you to put it negatively. What can you disbelieve?

Educator. I was coming to that. Let me go through the positive side again.

Judge Pressler. The problem that I have is—there is a lot of theological gymnastics that are exercised, a lot of mental gymnastics are exercised in the theological world, where words do not mean to the theologian what they mean to the person in the pew. Therefore I would like to have a negative of what you cannot believe in the Christian gospel, and what you cannot believe in the Scripture, what part of Scripture you can believe is wrong and still teach our young people.

Educator. All right. Let's suppose we have a professor in the Seminary. This person says, "I love Jesus Christ. I trust him. I believe in the message of the Bible. I believe in one God the creator, who is a personal God. . . ."

Judge Pressler. Again, you are putting it affirmatively and not telling me what you are negating.

Educator. " . . . and this loving God became incarnate as Jesus of Nazareth, he died upon the cross (and I'm using these words just as they are used by ordinary Baptists) for our sins, he was raised bodily from the dead on the third day by the Father; he gave his Spirit to the church; the church is the people of God; salvation is through Jesus Christ by grace through faith in him who died and was raised again from the dead; and then there is the hope in the hearts of all these people for the coming of Christ and for heaven." But you have such a person who nevertheless says, "I will not describe the Bible as inerrant."

Judge Pressler. Nobody wants him to describe it in any terms that anybody has. I want to know what he doesn't believe about Scripture and what you would say that he can disbelieve that is contained is Scripture and still use Scripture as authoritative.

Educator. Let's say the person says, "I will not use the word 'inerrancy'."

Judge Pressler. Nobody has ever asked anybody to use the word "inerrancy." What can you disbelieve in Scripture, and still feel that you ought to be paid with Southern Baptist money to teach in one of our institutions?

Educator. First of all, I am not sure the question that I would want to deal with is the question of what you disbelieve.

Judge Pressler. You asked me whether a person couldn't believe in inerrancy and teach in Seminary. I'm asking you to define your question and what he doesn't believe about Scripture. And I think we'll go a long way towards understanding if you all will define what you can deny about Scripture and still be in our Southern Baptist frame of communion.

Educator. You want an illustration?

Judge Pressler. Yes.

Educator. From the Bible?

Judge Pressler. I want an illustration of what a person can disbelieve about what the Scripture teaches.

Educator. This is something I very much regret being asked to do. I've taught at. . . .

Judge Pressler. You are the one who brought the thing up.

Educator. But you haven't answered my question.

Judge Pressler. I can't answer it because you haven't defined your terms.

Educator. The man says, "Some people would say that the Bible is inerrant. I say it is the inspired, unique, authoritative, Word of God for faith and practice. I do not say that it is inerrant."

Judge Pressler. Nobody is asking. I'm talking about what you mean behind the phraseology. What can you disbelieve in Scripture? What can you disbelieve about the Bible? Because if you don't feel that it is inerrant that means that you feel it has errors.

Educator. I don't know. . . .

Judge Pressler. Well, that is what I am trying to get to. So if you don't believe that there are any errors in Scripture, regardless of how you phrase it, we have no trouble. If you are saying, outside of the fact that Jack Flanders and two others wrote a book where it talks about the errors in Daniel; I could cite the fact that Temp Sparkman talks about ascribing terrible things to God by the writers of the Old Testament in his book, that says that the writers of the Old Testament ascribe terrible things to God, in his book *Being a Disciple.* Now I don't believe I want anybody teaching in an institution that I pay for, that says the Old Testament ascribes terrible things to God. Would you want somebody like that teaching in an institution that you supported?

Educator. I'm not familiar at all with all that he said. I'd rather not comment on what Temp Sparkman has said.

Judge Pressler. Well, tell me what a person can disbelieve about Scripture. If you want me to answer that prior question, you tell me what a person can disbelieve about Scripture and you still want him to teach in an institution.

Educator. My question has to do, not with what I advocate; my question has to do with what you advocate.

Judge Pressler. If you will explain to me what it is that he doesn't believe when he says that he doesn't believe in inerrancy, then I'll be glad to answer your question. Nobody in the conservative movement is ever trying to get anyone else to use our terminology. We want to know what they are talking about, though. And until now, "inerrancy" has been a concrete word, subject only to one interpretation. I don't care what word we use, as long as we know what is being said. So if you are asking me if I would have only people who have used the word "inerrancy" teaching in our institutions, I would say no, because the issue is not over words. If you are asking your question as to how much of the Bible you have to believe to teach in Scripture, then I would ask you, How much are you defining as disbelief so I can tell whether that person ought to teach in an institution or not, according to my thinking. Of course, the trustees of the individual institutions are the ones who are going to decide it, and I am not going to have anything to do with it. But if you would define to me what a person can disbelieve about Scripture and you think he still ought to teach in our institution, then I'll be very happy to answer your question.

Educator. I hear you saying that it isn't the word "inerrancy" that you would require.

Judge Pressler. That is what I have always said.

Educator. All right. Let me ask you then, if a person believes in the full religious message but does not believe in scientific accuracy of the Bible, would that amount to disbelief?

Judge Pressler. Who is going to define what is religious and what is scientific? Is the resurrection of Jesus Christ religious or scientific? Which is it?

Educator. Let's stipulate that the person denied the resurrection shouldn't teach in our seminary.

Judge Pressler. You are setting us a doctrinal creed. What I am asking is, How much can you disbelieve? You are telling me that a person ought to believe in the bodily resurrection to teach in one of our schools. Are you?

Educator. Judge, I really intended for me to interview you, not for you. . . .

Judge Pressler. But you're asking me questions you want me to answer.

Educator. What I want to know, is, Do you think that a person must believe not only in the message of the Bible about God and Jesus and faith and the church and salvation, but also that any allusions in the Bible that have to be scientifically accurate?

Judge Pressler. What is an allusion to science? The bodily resurrection is science, because it describes something that is not in accordance with regular scientific events, a supernatural event. Now that deals with science. I believe that where the Bible touches on science, it is scientifically accurate. Now what is it that you can disbelieve and say that the Bible is wrong about?

And what you've done if you say that you believe that the Bible can make mistakes, then you define the areas where the Bible makes mistakes, and you define the term "scientific," and so you have made yourself the judge of Scripture rather than Scripture being your judge, when you set up categories where the Scripture can be wrong. And with the resurrection, I am trying to show you that it depends on your definition of "scientific" as to whether a person can be a Bible-believer and deny the bodily resurrection of Christ, in the terminology that you are seeking to make me use.

Educator. So you had really rather not say outright that a person who denies the scientific accuracy of the Bible probably ought not to teach in our schools? You would say that you would have to define relationship between that and the religious?

Judge Pressler. I'm saying that if you'll let me know how much a person can disbelieve about the Bible and you think he should teach in our schools, I'll give you my opinion on it.

Educator. What I am trying to find out really is what your view is about a person who loves Jesus and loves the Bible as the Word of God, but not only does he not want to call the Bible "inerrant," but says on some things of the historical and scientific nature, "I'm not sure that the Bible is accurate."

Judge Pressler. Well, is he saying that he is sure that the Bible is wrong?

Educator. No, he is just not willing to affirm that he knows that it is accurate.

Judge Pressler. Once you say that the Bible could contain error, you make yourself the judge of what portions of the Bible are true and which portions are error. It is a presumptuous thing for an individual to edit God. Somebody has called it the spot theory of inspiration. The Bible was inspired in spots, and we are inspired to spot the spots. I think that is extremely presumptuous of man. And I have not yet heard any liberal who can define what he means by science or anything like that, where he would say the Scripture is wrong. Once you have crossed the theological Rubicon of saying that the Bible is sufficiently man's work so that it can be in error and make mistakes, then you have opened the floodgates for the individual to determine the categories which are error and the categories which are truth, and that is extremely presumptuous thing for a man to do. This is the crux of the whole discussion right here, and that's why when you ask questions you should give me a definition that is sufficiently concrete for me to be able to accurately answer your questions.

Educator. Let me follow up on this with a question then. This is very helpful because I think what the issue is, is often not understood.

Judge Pressler. I think that there has been a concerted effort on the part of liberals to keep people from knowing what the issue is.

Educator. Do you believe that the King James Version of the Bible is inerrant?

Judge Pressler. I believe that the original texts that God gave are inerrant. I believe that the King James Version is a very accurate translation. I believe that there are some even more accurate translations that have come later because we have been able to ascertain with even greater specificity what the original texts of Scripture are. I feel that it is completely reliable except in a few things that have been found, and nothing effects any doctrinal position.

Educator. Now, how does making a judgment about a few things that have been found in the King James Version to be mistaken, differ. . . .

Judge Pressler. Now wait a minute, not "mistaken"—"not in accordance with the original text." For instance, the first verse of the eighth chapter of Romans begins with the phrase, "who walk not after the flesh, but after the Spirit." That same phrase in the King James Version is repeated in the fourth verse. More ancient manuscripts have it only in the fourth verse. Therefore the King James does not accurately have that phrase in the first verse of the eighth chapter. No doctrinal error, no harm is caused, there is no erroneous fact presented by the fact that it is given twice in the Scripture rather than once. That is the type of thing where the King James might in small matter deviate from the original text but in nothing of substance.

Educator. How does making that kind of judgment differ from making the other kind of judgment that you described?

Judge Pressler. There is all the difference in the world because if you come to the text and say where it says that Melchizedek is the priest of the most high God but I believe that he is the priest of Baal, then you have called the Scripture wrong, and that is what Ralph Elliot did, and we paid him to teach at Midwestern Seminary until people realized what he was teaching at Midwestern Seminary. To say that a copyist made an error and put a phrase twice instead of once in the eighth chapter of Romans, is not to cast any doubt whatsoever of the validity of God's revelation but rather upon the accuracy of the scribe on something that makes no doctrinal difference whatsoever.

Educator. But it is still a human effort to judge what the Word of God really is?

Judge Pressler. No, it is an human effort to ascertain what the original texts are.

Educator. And the original texts were the Word of God?

Judge Pressler. God gave it as he gave it.

Educator. Therefore it is an human effort to judge what the original text, which is the Word of God, is?

Judge Pressler. It is an human effort to ascertain the accuracy of the text which we now have. Now, I have no trouble with anybody who would say that I believe that the King James Version is a hundred percent accurate, because he will not have any doctrinal error whatsoever. I think that he has an intellectual inconsistency, in that we have seen that there are a few minor scribal errors which do not effect any doctrine. And there is all the difference in the world in recognizing a couple of minor scribal errors, and in saying that, whatever the original text says, I don't believe that Melchizedek was the priest of the most high God, as Scripture says he is, because I am so smart that I can rewrite Scripture, and I can edit God, and I can tell where Scripture was wrong. There's all the difference in the world.

Educator. I certainly agree that there is a distinction, but is it not the case that in both instances we must make the most sincere effort we can to ascertain what the original texts were and therefore what the Word of God is?

Judge Pressler. We should make every effort to ascertain what the original texts are, but we can recognize at the time that we are doing it, that the texts we have are sufficiently accurate so that we have no doctrinal problem in those texts. And there is all the difference in the world between denying a portion of Scripture, denying the accuracy of Scripture, and saying that perhaps a scribe made a mistake in a word or two in getting it to us in the current form.

Educator. So it is acceptable to deny the accuracy of the current form; the critical thing is to affirm to accuracy of the original text?

Judge Pressler. The critical thing is to affirm the accuracy of everything that God has said in Scripture.

Educator. I still had some other questions that we didn't get to, but I think I'll proceed along with the other ones now. You have alerted us to the necessity of being attentive to the really central issue, Judge Pressler, which you see as Scripture. What about other issues that have been raised in recent years in the Convention? I'm thinking particularly about issues relating to the millennium, issues relating to the ordination of women, and so on? Are these not issues of concern to you?

Judge Pressler. They are not of concern to me at all. Russell Dilday is the one who raised the millennial issue when he declared that, in a talk on July 5, 1984, using the campus facilities at Southwestern Seminary, that dispensational premillennialism was a Southern Baptist heresy. Now, this to me is absolutely shocking, because conservatives have been talking about what Scripture is and that, under the priesthood of the believer, we are free to interpret Scripture. Now we have a man who is the head of one of our seminaries, who is branding a large number of Southern Baptists heretics because they do not believe in the eschatological interpretation to which he holds. Now this is shocking, it's disturbing, it cuts to the very basis of what Southern Baptists should believe. I believe that we can have pluralism about the eschatological position. Evidently, Dr. Dilday does not, because he says that those who hold to a dispensational premillennialism, that is a heresy, therefore those who hold to it are heretics. Now that brands a large number of ones in the Southern Baptist Convention as heretics. I think that is inexcusable. And he is going to something which the conservatives have never gone. I am interested personally in understanding what the Word of God says about the second coming of Jesus Christ. But my interpretation should never be forced upon anybody else, and I resent Dr. Dilday trying to force his interpretation of Scripture on somebody else.

Educator. So in your mind, these are, in some sense, not as central as the issue of Scripture?

Judge Pressler. These are derivative issues. If you do not believe the Scripture is accurate, then how can you come up with an accurate appraisal of what Scripture is saying about the second coming of Christ because you might come across something that you do not like and you can leave out anything you want to, to build the theory that you want? These are peripheral issues. The conservatives are talking about the basic issue of what Scripture is. It is Russell Dilday who is trying to impose his own eschatological position on other people.

Educator. A good many of the people in the Convention are concerned about issues like the millennium and the ordination of women.

Judge Pressler. Certainly. Those are interpretations of Scripture. But I don't know any conservative who is trying to push his interpretation of eschatology on anybody else. Russell Dilday is the only one that I've heard call somebody a heretic because he didn't hold to his particular eschatological position.

Educator. In your judgment, is the Baptist Faith and Message a satisfactory statement for Southern Baptists?

Judge Pressler. Splendid, splendid. As I said before, the problem we have is not with needing more creeds, but more integrity. The Baptist Faith and Message statement says that the Bible is truth without any mixture of error. How can anybody believe that there is error in Scripture and ascribe to a phrase that says that the Bible is truth without any mixture of error? If you have a way you can do that, then I would be interested in hearing it, but to me that is an absolute statement for inerrancy. I'd be very interested, if you could give me any way that somebody could believe the Baptist Faith and Message, that the Bible is truth without any mixture of error, and believe that there are errors in Scripture.

Educator. You were recently elected to the executive committee of the Southern Baptist Convention. Do you have hopes for particular goals that you want to achieve in that position?

Judge Pressler. The reason I agreed to run—and I didn't want to at first and I then prayed about it a good while, and the only reason I wanted to and decided to do it over really not wanting to—is that I thought it would give me an opportunity to know people and to get known. I felt that I had been so slandered and so mispresented in the Baptist press, that it would give me an opportunity to be known for what I believed and what I thought, rather than for what people were saying that I believed and thought. And my sole objective in serving on the executive committee is opening up the processes so we can communicate, so that we understand each other, and so that we are available to one another.

Educator. Thank you very much. These are the questions that I had. Would you like to add anything, a final comment?

Judge Pressler. The final comment I would make is: There is an adage at law, if the law is on your side, argue the law; if the facts are on our side, argue the facts; if you have neither the law or the facts, then you light into the opposing counsel and try to make the other side look as bad as possible. The issue in the Southern Baptist Convention has been, is, and always will be, as far as I am concerned, what Scripture is, not an interpretation of Scripture, not the personalities of individuals on the various sides. Now I think the liberals in the Convention have constantly tried to divert attention away from what the real issue is, away from the fact that the issue is what Scripture is and not any interpretation. I think that the issue is what Scripture is and not any interpretation. I think that their vehement attacks upon personalities in the conservative movement have been part of that diversionary tactic. I think that their throwing up straw men of eschatological interpretation has been part of that tactic. And I think it has been very disharmonious to the Convention, very hurtful to the unity of the Convention, and very hurtful to the cause of Christ. Ninety-five percent of Southern Baptists believe that the Bible doesn't have error in it. That is exactly what I believe, that is exactly what the conservatives believe, and that is what we are concerned about having taught in our institutions. If we did not have all the smokescreens, and if the people were allowed to understand the issue, this would have been over a long time ago, because Southern Baptists are so very united on the things that we who are conservatives are trying to emphasize in the Convention.

Document 33
SBC Motion to Establish a Peace Committee
SBC Annual 1985, 64-65

"Motion to Establish SBC 'Peace Committee' "

(1) That a Special Committee be authorized by this Convention, in session, in Dallas, June, 1985.

(2) This committee shall seek to determine the sources of the controversies in our Convention, and make findings and recommendations regarding these controversies, so that Southern Baptists might effect reconciliation and effectively discharge their responsibilities to God by cooperating together to accomplish evangelism, missions, Christian education and other causes authorized by our Constitution, all to the glory of God. "By this shall all men know that ye are my disciples, if ye have love one to another" (John 13:35; John 17:21).

(3) This committee shall follow the 1963 Baptist Faith and Message statement in regard to theological issues, and shall operate within the Constitution and Bylaws of the Southern Baptist Convention.

(4) To accomplish its work, this committee shall recognize the role of trustees and shall work with and through appropriate boards, commissions, and agencies of the Southern Baptist Convention. The committee shall report on the progress of its work to each meeting of the Executive Committee. The trustees, boards, and agencies of the Southern Baptist Convention, and their officers and employees, shall fully cooperate with the committee to accomplish the purposes outlined in this motion.

(5) Staffing and professional advice for this committee shall be in accord with the Business and Financial Plan of the Southern Baptist Convention. Funding shall come from Cooperative Program funds received by the Executive Committee as a priority item before the percentage division and allocation of Southern Baptist Convention Cooperative Program Allocation Budget.

(6) The committee may conduct its business in open sessions and may hold public hearings; but, the Committee may also hold executive sessions to accomplish its work.

(7) Any vacancy, or vacancies, on the Special Committee shall be filled by the Executive Committee at its next meeting after such vacancy occurs. In the filling of any such vacancy, balance of representation shall be maintained.

(8) The committee may make its final report and recommendations to the 1986 Southern Baptist Convention and request that it be discharged, or the committee may make a preliminary report to the 1986 Convention and may recommend that the Special Committee be continued in existence for an additional year, in which instance, the committee shall make its final report and recommendations to the 1987 Southern Baptist Convention.

(9) All Southern Baptists are urged to exercise restraint, to refrain from divisive action and comments, and to reflect Christian love while this committee is doing its work.

(10) The following shall be designated to serve on the Special Committee: Charles Fuller, chairman; Harmon Born, Doyle Carlton, Bill Crews, Robert E. Cuttino, Jim Henry, Bill Hull, H. H. Hobbs, Albert McClellan, Charles Pickering, William Poe, Ray Roberts, Adrian Rogers, Cecil Sherman, John Sullivan, Dan Vestal, Jerry Vines, and Ed Young. The SBC president shall serve as ex officio members with full rights (see items 111 and 197).

Document 34
The Slatton Motion to Amend the Committee on Committees
SBC Annual 1985, 78-79, 81

"The Slatton Motion"

George T. Schroeder (AR), chairman of the Committee on Committees, was recognized for the report of the committee. He moved the adoption of the report as printed in the Convention *Bulletin.* James Slatton (VA) moved to amend the committee's report by substituting present state convention presidents and Woman's Missionary Union presidents with the exception of New Mexico which would be the state convention president and first vice president. The Chair ruled that nominations would need to be dealt with on a state-by-state basis. Slatton moved to nominate Mrs. Carolyn (Jerry) Miller (AL) in place of Jane Riley Wiggins (AL). Al Jackson (AL) spoke against the nomination. John Dunaway (KY) asked if all proposed substitute nominees could be named at once and action then taken. Parliamentarian Wayne Allen (TN) shared the rationale for this being ruled improper. Slatton appealed to the messengers on a point of order. A vote was taken on whether to sustain the Chair, first by a standing vote and then by ballot. (See utem 204.)

204. Secretary Lee Porter (TN) reported results of the ballot on whether to sustain the ruling of the Chair (see item 200) on an earlier question. To sustain: 11,801 (48.41%); not to sustain 12,576 (51.59%). Continuation of the matter under discussion was scheduled for the Wednesday evening business period. (See items 210 and 227.)

210. President Charles Stanley (GA) announced the time for consideration of business matters. He recognized Bill Hickem (FL) who spoke against the pending Slatton motion (see item 200). Parliamentarian Wayne Allen (TN) gave interpretation of the Convention Bylaws pertaining to the motion. The Chair ruled the Slatton motion out of order. The original motion (item 200) of the Committee on Committees was submitted to the messengers for vote, first by raised hands and then by standing. A ballot was called for and cast. (See item 227.)

227. Secretary Lee Porter (TN) reported results of the ballot (see items 200 and 210) on the Committee on Committees motion: Yes - 13,123 (57.8%); No - 9,581 (42.2%).

1986

Chronology

April?. Gary North interviews Paul Pressler in "Firestorm Chats" and Pressler details strategy for taking control of SBC.

May 5. U.S. district judge decides in favor of SBC in the Crowder lawsuit, saying the first amendment of the U.S. Constitution prevents intrusion of secular courts into internal church disputes.

May 5. William G. Tanner, president of the Home Mission Board, elected executive director-treasurer of the Oklahoma Baptist Convention. His resignation creates first opportunity for fundamentalists to elect an executive of an SBC agency.

May. Moderate Foy Valentine, executive director of the SBC Christian Life Commission, requests that search process be initiated to select his successor with the obvious intent of selecting a moderate while moderates retain a majority on the SBC Commission. Search Committee appointed.

May. Theologian Clark Pinnock, former professor at New Orleans Baptist Theological Seminary, issues apology for fueling controversy in the late 1960s over inerrancy, a position he now claims is not "well supported exegetically."

June 10–12. SBC, Atlanta, 40,987 messengers (second largest in SBC history), Charles Stanley presiding.

—Fundamentalist Adrian Rogers elected president with 54.22% of the vote over moderate Winfred Moore 45.78%. (Both were members of the SBC Peace Committee.)

—Fundamentalist motion to deny funding to Baptist Joint Committee on Public Affairs resulted in "Fact Finding Committee" to study relationship of BJCPA to SBC.

—Upon recommendation of SBC Executive Committee the Convention approves amendment to bylaw 16 regarding nominations to the committee that recommends trustees of all SBC agencies. This action responds to the Slatton motion of the previous year and guarantees the enormous power in presidential committee appointments. A clear victory for fundamentalists. See document 35.

—Peace Committee presented progress report. See document 36.

June. Paige Patterson, in a statement following the fundamentalist victory in Atlanta, indicates that fundamentalists are expected to tie their positions on abortion, euthanasia, school prayer, and federal budget reduction to the hiring of denominational employees. Speaking of the fundamentalist social and moral agenda within the SBC, Patterson was quoted as saying, "I think it'll go over nearly as well as the inerrancy thing."

August. Moderate meeting in Macon GA where differing strategies for the future surface. Marks the beginning idea of the Southern Baptist Alliance and a clear signal that some moderates are growing weary with political warfare.

August 6. As a result of trustee elections at the Atlanta SBC, fundamentalists capture the balance of power on the Home Mission Board and force the resignation of a presidential search committee.

October 22. SBC seminary presidents present the "Glorieta Statement," which was affirmed by the Peace Committee and widely interpreted as a capitulation to the growing fundamentalist power within the SBC. Leading moderate spokesperson Cecil Sherman resigns in protest from the Peace Committee. See documents 37 and 38.

October 24. An eight-point peace proposal made by moderates rejected by fundamentalist leaders, indicating that fundamentalists wanted total control of the SBC.

December 1–2. Providence Baptist Church, Charlotte NC. Motion made to organize and incorporate the Southern Baptist Alliance.

Document 35
Amendment to Bylaw 16 regarding Nominations
to the Committee to Recommend SBC Agency Trustees
SBC Annual 1986, 37

"Recommendation 6: Southern Baptist Convention Bylaw 16,
Election of Board Members, Trustees, Commissioners,
or Members of Standing Committees."

The Executive Committee of the Southern Baptist Convention recommends that the Southern Baptist Convention adopt the amendment of bylaw 16, paragraph (1) of the Bylaws of the Southern Baptist Convention to read as follows (amendment in boldface italics; some word order changes):

(1) The Committee on Boards, Commissions, and Standing Committees shall be composed of two (2) members from each qualified state, who shall be elected by the Convention. Nominations *for each position* shall be made by the Committee on Committees. *Further nominations may be made from the floor. No messenger shall be allowed to nominate more than one person at one time for election to the Committee on Boards, Commissions, and Standing Committees.* One (1) person named to the committee from each state shall be a person not employed full-time by a church or denominational agency. Persons named to the Committee on Boards, Commissions, and Standing Committees shall have been resident members for at least one (1) year of Southern Baptist churches either geographically within the states or affiliated with the conventions of the states from which they are elected.

The present reading of the first paragraph in Bylaw 16 is as follows: (1) The Committee on Boards, Commissions, and Standing Committees shall be composed of two (2) members from each qualified state, who shall be nominated to the Convention by the Committee on Committees. One (1) person named to the committee from each state shall be a person not employed full time by a church or denominational agency. Persons named to the Committee on Boards, Commissions, and Standing Committees shall have been resident members for at least one (1) year of Southern Baptist churches either geographically within the states or affiliated with the conventions of the states from which they are elected.

Document 36
Progress Report of the Peace Committee
SBC Annual 1986, 250-57

"Southern Baptist Convention Peace Committee"

Action taken by the Convention in Dallas, Texas, 1985, involved a call for the committee to make progress reports in regular meetings of the SBC Executive Committee. The texts of reports made by the chairman to the Executive Committee in September 1985 and February 1986 are shared as background for the formal report made during the 1986 Convention sessions in Atlanta, June 10.

September 18, 1985

The Southern Baptist Convention Peace Committee will have its second meeting during October 8-9, 1985, at the Executive Committee building in Nashville, Tennessee, having had the first meeting on August 5-6 in Nashville. The next three committee meetings are scheduled as follows: December 10-11, 1985, in Atlanta; January 21-22, 1986 in Dallas; and February 25-26, 1986, in Nashville. Additional meetings of the committee will be announced later, and according to progress.

Seventeen of the twenty-two committee members were present for the first meeting, and eighteen are scheduled to attend the second. Attendance for the subsequent three meetings promises to be almost 100 percent. Special effort was made to arrange the dates for the second meeting to allow members absent from the first meeting to attend. Committee members are to be commended for the arrangements they have made in their personal commitments to be available for committee assignments. Needless to say, coordinating the schedules of twenty-two persons who compose the Peace Committee is a challenge in itself.

Although the Peace Committee is not oblivious to the difficult and delicate matters with which we must deal, we believe there is reason for optimism about our task. There are specific reasons for that optimism which, admittedly, prevails in varying degrees.

The *spirit* of the committee members was a source of encouragement during the first meeting and has been since. Despite sharp differences between us, there is a conviction that God will bless the honest attempts to face the facts of the controversy. By the October meeting date, each committee member is to have submitted a 350-word statement identifying the *theological* issues which beset our denomination.

Although a great deal of time, of necessity, was devoted to committee organization in the first meeting, an equal amount of time was devoted to prayer and the essential establishment of a relationship among the members. Prayer is not an item before the agenda, it is the priority item *on* the agenda.

These twenty-two committee members obviously represent constituencies as the committee is, in fact, the Convention-in-miniature. In the opinion of the Chairman, however, although committee members *represent* constituencies, they will not *serve* constituencies. We must function as individuals as the Lord gives us conviction and conscience to do so. The committee must become an entity itself, offering to the Convention findings and recommendations, leaving the final conclusions to the Convention family we serve.

The committee's readiness to deal with matters of substance is reflected in its decision to first address the theological issues which trouble us. This agreement on an early agenda is a cause for optimism. I might add, this is not to ignore the structural, political, and parliamentary matters which have been brought to our attention.

One *has* to be encouraged by the many reports of intercessory prayer, all across the Convention, for the Peace Committee. There are numerous letters sent to the committee each week pledging prayer support of churches, prayer groups, pastors' conferences, and individuals. A group of laypersons in Roanoke, Virginia, meets every Tuesday at six in the morning to pray for each of the Peace Committee members *by name*. The committee is an object of prayer in our own daily family prayer periods, as I am sure it is in yours. It is unthinkable that a member of the Southern Baptist Convention Executive Committee or anyone related to Convention leadership would *not pray daily* for the work of the Peace Committee and the *healing* of our denomination. Admittedly, the Peace Committee is just *beginning* to deal with some of the matters of controversy among us; nonetheless, we can see some beneficial outgrowths of our Convention's present situation.

(1) This is one of the most prayed-for periods in Southern Baptist Convention life.

(2) The desire to be informed about Southern Baptist life is at the highest level in years.

(3) Fewer Southern Baptists are inclined to take the Convention, its past and future, and the price of both, for granted.

(4) We are recognizing anew the *worth* of our fellowship and the importance of our *spirit*.

(5) It is more obvious than perhaps in years, if we are to *serve* Southern Baptists, we must *listen* to all Southern Baptists.

My requests of the Executive Committee are:

1. Pray daily for the Peace Committee and grow not weary in doing it.
2. Encourage others to pray, believing God can accomplish that otherwise [sic] could not be.
3. Communicate your concerns and suggestions directly to the committee.
4. Respect the request of the Convention to lower the profile and restrain unnecessary rhetoric regarding the controversies among us.
5. Turn a deaf ear to the cynics, skeptics, pessimists, and defeatists.

Cynicism and skepticism are not theological postures belonging to any *one* doctrinal persuasion. Cynical moderates and skeptical conservatives make strange bedfellows. Cynics and skeptics are *seldom* responsible for progress except as they fire the determination in those committed to accomplish what others deem futile.

Perhaps we would do well to remember the experience of Job whose companions were geared for such skepticism and cynicism they almost broke the back of a man of astounding faith. It was Elihu, with youthful tenacity, who called Job back to the realism of God's power to sustain and restore. Then, out of the whirlwind of his unbelievable circumstances, Job rediscovered the adequacy of a mighty God, and the last state of a once-shattered man became better than the first.

Out of the whirlwind of our recent experiences we too can find the adequacy of a mighty God and the last state of Southern Baptists will be better even than the first.

February 19, 1986

Since the report in September, the Peace Committee has met three times: in October and December 1985 and in January 1986. The next meeting will be February 24-25, 1986, in Atlanta. Since the first meeting, attendance for the sessions has been, in each instance, 100 percent or nearly 100 percent.

Following the meeting next month, two more meetings are scheduled: April 3-4 in Dallas and May 13-14 in Atlanta. It is likely the committee will also meet prior to the Southern Baptist Convention in June.

It is difficult to translate into words all that has transpired within the committee since its inception. The development of trust, freedom, and a sense of entity requires time and the emergence of a dynamic. The time has been invested and the needed dynamic has begun the yield of some productivity. Of late, that dynamic has produced even more than the planned agenda.

I am encouraged about the potential for a breakthrough in our pursuit for reconciliation. We have, by no means, *reached* a breakthrough, but we may very well be approaching some significant areas upon which we can come together and *honor our diversity while not dishonoring our convictions*.

The issue will, doubtless, eventually focus upon how courageous the committee will be, and Southern Baptists will be, in a willingness to make several hard decisions to *alter* our denominational garment in order not to *rend* it.

During the past two and one-half months, the Committee divided into five subcommittees assigned to visit the six seminaries and some of the denominational agencies. The leadership of those agencies and seminaries have been most cooperative and helpful in those visits. Regardless of how those committee visits have been perceived, they have *not* been designed to be *miniature inquisitions*. They were honest attempts to dialogue with Southern Baptist leaders about issues which the committee has been assigned to analyze. Frankly, it was in an attempt to *avoid* the atmosphere of an interrogation that we suggested our visits *to* the agencies and seminaries rather than asking their leaders to come to us. And regardless of *anyone's* speculation to the contrary, we will respect the trustee structure and process in any observations or recommendations resulting from our visits.

Preliminary reports on the subcommittee visits have been quite positive in the main. I am grateful there have been so few problems in these dialogue visits, and what few problems have been reported, I am convinced were inadvertent. In drafting our guidelines for these dialogue visits, we could not anticipate all situations, and didn't. We have discovered that learning how to be a Peace Committee is a great deal like learning to be a parent-the *doing* of it is the *learning* of it.

The Peace Committee has taken seriously what role it is to have in dealing with the Convention parliamentarian matter. We feel it is our responsibility to concentrate upon the future in this issue—not upon the past. Actually, Southern Baptists have no constitutional provisions for a parliamentarian, nor guidelines for the selection of one. Historically, it has been the option of the president if and when he used a parliamentarian. Our committee feels there is a need for some guidelines in the *future* selection of Convention parliamentarians, and we have asked three of our members to research the matter.

I continue to be encouraged by reports of efforts being made among some Southern Baptists to step beyond the levels of withdrawal, or even tolerant coexistence, and to attempt to communicate with each other instead of relying on what has been said *about* one another. To be sure, to those who are hardnosed, hardheaded, and hardhearted, such may be viewed as compromise or weakness. If I understand anything about Scripture, however, the *pursuit* of peace is both the biblical and promising approach for Christian to take in matters of reconciliation. The same Holy Spirit who inspired 2 Timothy 3:16 inspired 1 Peter 3:8-11. Being an inerrantist of what I hope is the consistent and wholeheartedly variety, I believe God not only *inspired* His Word, He meant for us to *obey* it.

Personally, I can see *no need for any additional theological or political position meetings among Southern Baptists at this time.* Our differences have been clearly stated and the flames have been fanned quite enough. It is our *spirit* which is in need of attention. The answer to our situation is not the *elimination* of politics, which is germane to the believer's own priesthood; rather, it is to reject *bad* politics in our midst and seek the wholesome, unembarrassing variety! It is no mere accident that when the Holy Spirit moved in Paul's heart, he wrote to Timothy, "give heed first to *yourself,* then take heed to the doctrine" (1 Tim. 4:10).

Because the Peace Committee recognizes the need for God's leadership and for His intervention in the task we have been given, I am asking Southern Baptists to enter into a period of prayer and fasting on Sunday afternoons, February 23, 1986, until noon February 24, 1986, seeking God's wisdom and power upon our meeting, February 24-25, in Atlanta. I ask you to claim with me, and *for* Southern Baptists, the prophet Zephaniah's promise:

> The Lord thy God in the midst of thee is mighty; He will save; He will rejoice over thee with joy; He will rest in His love; He will joy over you with singing . . . at that time will I bring you again, even in that time that I gather you: for I will make you a name and a praise among all people of the earth, when I turn back your captivity before your eyes, says the Lord.
>
> (Zephaniah 3:17, 20)

June 10, 1986

Since the Peace Committee received its assignment from the Southern Baptist Convention session in Dallas, June 1985, it has met eight times in a pattern of two-day meetings. Between the sessions various subcommittees have made eleven visits to selected agencies, and have held other meetings seeking information for reports to the committee.

Members of the Peace Committee have earnestly tried to talk *with* one another, not *at* one another. As a necessary part of the reconciliation process, members, in as Christlike a way as possible, have spent time in hearing and understanding the personal convictions of other members.

A major effort is necessary if Southern Baptists are to honor legitimate diversities without compromising established convictions. The legitimate diversities within the Convention are reflected in the membership of the Peace Committee. Some have said that it is a miniature of the Southern Baptist Convention. It is important that the members maintain an atmosphere of mutual respect and love even when they do not agree.

Good attendance has enhanced Peace Committee progress, as has active participation in discussions by the members. Reports of continuing intercessory prayer in the churches across the Convention have encouraged us. We commend all persons who have refrained from using harsh rhetoric and inflammatory statements during these challenging times. Prospects for real peace are increased when respect and Christian love are practiced by all. As we make this report, we are cautiously optimistic about the future. The report consists of five topics, as follows:

P urpose of the Peace Committee
E xamination of the Issues
A nxieties during the Controversy
C onclusions
E xhortations and Recommendations

I. Purpose of the Peace Committee

The purpose of the Peace Committee was made clear by the Southern Baptist Convention in its annual meeting in Dallas, June 11-13, 1985, and abbreviated as follows:

seek to determine the source of the controversies in our Convention and make findings and recommendations regarding these controversies, so that Southern Baptists might effect reconciliation and effectively discharge their responsibilities to God by cooperating together to accomplish evangelism, missions, Christian education, and other causes authorized by our Constitution, all to the Glory of God. . . .

. . . follow the 1963 Baptist Faith and Message statement in regard to theological issues, and operate within the Constitution and Bylaws of the Southern Baptist Convention. . . .

. . . to accomplish its work, this Committee shall recognize the role of trustees and shall work with and through appropriate boards, commissions, and agencies of the Southern Baptist Convention. . . .

. . . the Committee may make a preliminary report to the 1986 Convention and may recommend that the Special Committee be continued in existence for an additional year. . . .

. . . all Southern Baptists be urged to exercise restraint, to refrain from divisive action and comments, and to reflect Christian love while this Committee is doing its work. . . .

II. Examination of the Issues

The Peace Committee has examined many different issues of the controversy including all of the following: positive statements of doctrine on which Southern Baptists agree, theological diversities, the 1963 statement of Baptist Faith and Message and in particular the interpretation of article I, politics in the Southern Baptist Convention, Cooperative Program and selective support, press involvement in the controversy, parliamentarian(s), powers of the presidency, SBC committee appointments, messenger registration, voting process, and SBC agency publications.

III. Anxieties during the Controversy

The Peace Committee has noted and discussed widespread anxieties among Southern Baptists concerning the effect of the controversy on the work of the churches and the ministries of the denomination. These center in Christian witness to the world; evangelistic outreach in times of conflict; Southern Baptist example of Christian love for each other; missions outreach during the troublesome times; Cooperative Program and missions giving; the need for getting together in the spirit of Christ; and the effect of theological diversities and excessive political activities on the future of our denomination.

IV. Conclusions

The Peace Committee decided early in its work to arrange its study under two general headings: (1) theological concerns and (2) political activities.

Regarding the theological concerns, the committee appointed five sub-committees to conduct conversations with the executive officers of eleven SBC agencies, recognizing the role of trustees of the agencies as instructed by the Convention. Among Southern Baptists there are many points of doctrine on which all agree, and there are some on which all do not agree. After many months of study, the Peace Committee released to Baptist Press the following statement about the situation as they then saw it.

The Peace Committee has completed a preliminary investigation of the theological situation in our SBC seminaries. We have found significant theological diversity within our seminaries reflective of the theological diversity within our wider constituency. These divergences are found among those who claim to hold a high view of Scripture and to teach in accordance with and not contrary to the Baptist Faith and Message Statement of 1963. Examples of this diversity include the following, which are intended to be illustrative but not exhaustive: (1) Some accept and affirm the direct creation and historicity of Adam and Eve while others view them instead as representative of the human race in its creation and fall. (2) Some understand the historicity of every event in Scripture as reported by the original source while others hold that the historicity can be clarified and revised by the findings of modern historical scholarship. (3) Some hold to the stated authorship of every book in the Bible while others hold that in some cases such attribution may not refer to the final author or may be pseudonymous. (4) Some hold that every miracle in the Bible is intended to be taken as a historical event while others hold that some miracles are intended to be taken as parabolic.

The Peace Committee is working earnestly to find ways to build bridges between those holding divergent views so that we may all legitimately co-exist and work together in harmony to accomplish our common mission. Please pray that we may find ways to use our diversity to win the greatest number to faith in Christ as Saviour and Lord. We found many reasons to greatly affirm the work of our seminaries.

Some persons believe that theological differences are *the* source of controversy within the Convention. The limits of legitimate diversity are at the very heart of our ongoing process to bring about reconciliation. We seek solutions which honor our legitimate diversities without compromising our established convictions. Our diversities in common endeavors, however, must be limited to those beliefs which are consistent with the Convention-adopted 1963 statement of Baptist Faith and Message.

Concerning political activity, the Peace Committee finds that the extent of political activity with the Southern Baptist Convention at the present time creates distrust, diminishes our ability to do missions and evangelism, is detrimental to our influence, and impedes our ability to serve our Lord.

Political activity within the Convention since the late 1970s has reached a new level. Some inerrantists put together an effective political effort. Some moderates have attempted to match the effort of the inerrantists. A measure of political activity is inevitable in an organization that abides by democratic principles and processes.

Since the Southern Baptist Convention has never before been confronted with this degree of political activity, the Convention has never made a determination of what political activity is inappropriate and what measure of political activity must be retained consistent with our Baptist heritage, organization, and structure.

Regardless of what short-term measures are implemented, Southern Baptists must face this entire issue. The Peace Committee is continuing to receive input in this regard and to deliberate on the final recommendations in this area.

Charges of political excesses have been made against both groups by the opposite side. The Peace Committee has not completed all of its investigations into political activities, and although indications are that in many instances the charges are exaggerated, the committee finds that many people on both sides deplore the extent of political activity within the Southern Baptist Convention.

The Peace Committee has made preliminary findings as follows:

(1) Some spokesmen on both sides of the political spectrum have used intemperate, inflammatory and unguarded language, i.e., "going for the jugular," "Holy War," "Independent-fundamentalists," "flaming liberal" and other pejorative terms.

(2) Some spokesmen on both sides of the political spectrum and the autonomous independent journals on both sides of the issue have labeled and attributed improper motives to people with whom they disagree.

(3) Distribution of news is necessary in a democratic society. There have been instances when news releases have been altered, distorting the intent of the article and oftentimes creating confusion. In some denominational papers and in some autonomous independent journals, there has been prejudice against the conservative political activists and in some autonomous independent journals there has been prejudice against the moderate side.

(4) Although we have found indications of isolated voting irregularities at previous conventions, our preliminary finding concerning fraudulent voting has revealed no documented evidence of organized misuse of the ballot by any political groups.

(5) The continuation of political activity within the Convention at the present level will not serve the process of peace and reconciliation.

All groups like to be called conservative and evangelical. In addition to those identified as having views which are referred to as being to the left or right, there is a sizeable body of people who are mediating and nonaligned with any group. They resist the notion that they must choose a "side" in order to be of greater service to our common mission for the cause of Christ.

Some believe that political activity is the source of controversy within our Convention.

Besides theological concerns and political activities, the Peace Committee considered a number of other matters brought to its attention. These include:

Cooperative Program and Selective Support. We must find a way to function with our diversity without tampering with the magnificent gift of the Cooperative Program which God has allowed us to discover and refine. A new idea was advanced, which would allow persons dissatisfied with the programs of some agencies to designate Cooperative Program around those agencies. This was called selective support. Our unanimous conclusion is that we should not at this time make any changes in the Cooperative Program as it presently functions. Bold Mission Thrust must go forward for the cause of Christ as we join hearts and hands in spite of our known diversities. The Peace Committee encourages increased giving through the Cooperative Program that we may work together in our common ministry of missions, evangelism, and Christian education. We also recognize the historic Baptist right of individuals to designate any or all of their gifts.

Appointment of Persons to Convention Committees and Agencies. There seems always to be a popular perception that an "in group" is always unfair to an "out group" in appointments. Both feel excluded, ignored, and discriminated against when the other side controls the appointment powers of the presidency. We all "belong" and must be partners who continually seek ways to exhibit to each other our mutual respect, acceptance, and Christian love so that there might at all times result fairness for each other. A full place in SBC life must be given to all persons in our Convention whose beliefs are consistent with the Convention-adopted 1963 statement of Baptist Faith and Message.

The president of the Southern Baptist Convention appointed three parliamentarians for the 1986 Convention in Atlanta. One is a former SBC president, one is a former SBC vice president, and the third is a certified professional parliamentarian. Two assistant parliamentarians, both laymen, have also been appointed.

Subcommittee Visits. Five subcommittees were appointed to visit eleven agencies. The purpose was neither to accuse nor to gloss over. Members of the subcommittees sincerely tried to establish honest, open dialogue and straightforward communication. Visits were made in love and candor as members sought to identify issues and to enlist ideas from agency executives for resolution of the controversy. Each agency representative was given opportunity to express concerns and offer suggestions for peace.

The Peace Committee feels that administrators and appropriate trustee groups of some of the agencies have satisfactorily dealt with the matters submitted to them or they are dealing with them. There are concerns remaining that need further dialogue with some of the agencies, but none concerning the Home Mission Board, Sunday School Board, Historical Commission, and three of the seminaries.

Based on information gained in visits of the subcommittees to New Orleans, Southwestern, and Golden Gate seminaries, the Peace Committee has concluded that these schools are being operated in a manner consistent with the principles of the statement of the Baptist Faith and Message and in a manner consistent with the purpose for which they were founded. We commend the administrations and faculties for their commitment to the sound and effective education of our young people for Christian ministry. Dialogue is still in progress with Southern, Southeastern, and Midwestern seminaries. The Christian Life Commission has announced the appointment of a search committee for a new executive director. Questions still open for further discussion will be brought up again when the new executive director is elected. Our further item of information, which was not requested earlier, is needed and will be furnished by the Foreign Mission Board at an early meeting.

V. Exhortations

We can, we must, and will find peace that at times has seemed so elusive. God has high expectations for Southern Baptists. He has given us the opportunity, equipped us for the responsibility, and is now urging us to get on with the job at hand of winning the world for Christ. One day we will be held accountable, individually, for our response to His call to fulfill the Great Commission. God grant that we will be good stewards of the power of influence and the power of inspired leadership with which He has so richly endowed us, whether we be in full-time Christian service or whether we are committed lay servants at our various vocations in the marketplaces of life.

The Peace Committee has come far in its eight meetings, not to complete agreement or understanding, but to the beginning of understanding. We have done many things, but there are things yet to be done.

We plead for spiritual renewal throughout our Convention to provide the atmosphere in which we can expect reconciliation.

Let our love and respect for each other be second only to our love for God.

In our pursuit of peace, let each of us approach God with a sincere commitment to follow "His plan." We must abandon our pleas for God to bless "my plan" and put it into effect. Instead, we must be willing to commit to follow His guidance through the leadership of the Holy Spirit, to offer up an "empty cup" as it were. Let us individually ask Him to "*Fill My Cup, Lord*," as you would see fit to do it. . . . I trust you, dear God, to get us *together* with no prerequisites on my part. Throughout history, God has acted miraculously in the lives of His people *when conditions were right!* Today is no exception.

When all hope was gone for a desperate father whose little daughter had died, as recorded in Mark 5:36, Jesus said in effect, simply, Don't be afraid, just trust me! Meet the conditions . . . and believe! That is the message we have preached to the world all these centuries . . . it still works! God will never solve our problems, disagreements, lack of unity until and unless we are *ready* for Him to do so by committing our all to Him without reservation and with no preconditions.

Let's get ready . . . each and all of us! We must see that there is much bad in the good of us, and so much good in the worst of us, that it behooves none of us to talk about the rest of us. Romans 12:3 helps us in our personal evaluation of ourselves.

Let us work together with the common goal of winning the world to Jesus while actively emphasizing the major statements of faith on which we all agree wholeheartedly.

We must, by priority, concern ourselves with *being* what God wants us to *be* individually so that we will then *do* what he wants us to *do*. We will forget ourselves, our personal desires and ambitions, and work for the good of the whole as God leads and directs our paths.

We need to acknowledge that not only are there two groups with different theological interpretations, but there is also a group who in spite of theological differences is striving diligently to "bridge the gap" so that our ability to evangelize and do missions is not hindered.

Our seminaries should sincerely work toward progress in providing personnel and curriculum to teach our students theological and biblical interpretation points of view as represented by a significant part of our SBC constituency known as the conservatives. Agencies' publications should likewise include these views. Students are already exposed to many different theologies to help them understand and establish strong convictions of their own toward their ultimate and unshakable convictions for a lifetime of ministry in the kingdom of God.

We endorse the February 1986 action by the SBC Executive Committee to appoint a special committee to study the "messenger participatory process" at our annual conventions, including messenger registration, voting process, and how to better cope with the challenge of accommodating extremely large numbers of messengers.

The Peace Committee asks you to help restore *trust* among all Southern Baptists so that we may continue our journey toward reconciliation and peace. This is a worthy goal which we believe is attainable as we yield ourselves completely to the leadership of the Holy Spirit.

Recommendations

The Peace Committee is convinced that we must continue the current peace process. We therefore recommend:

(1) That the Southern Baptist Convention respectfully beseech all Southern Baptists to make 1986–1987 a year of intercession with periods of prayer, prayer rallies, and similar emphases for reconciliation and restoration in SBC life and work, etc.

(2) That the Convention respectfully request there be a one-year moratorium on theological/political position meetings and a deceleration, if not a dismantling, of the political power structures, allowing the Peace Committee and SBC agency leadership to work without distraction on the theological and political problems before us during the year 1986–1987.

(3) That the Convention deplore the use of the type of intemperate, inflammatory, and unguarded language used by some spokesmen on both sides of the political spectrum.

(4) That the Convention urge Baptist Press, the state Baptist papers, and the autonomous independent journals to be especially careful to be fair and accurate in reporting events in the Convention and refrain from labeling and attributing improper motives.

(5) That the Convention request its newly elected president, the Committee on Committees, and the Committee on Boards, Commissions, and Standing Committees, to be especially mindful of fairness in all appointments and nominations so that they are representative of the Convention.

(6) That this Convention strongly support the Peace Committee in a planned retreat with all its members joined by SBC agency executives and seminary presidents. We will come together for a time of dialogue, getting more closely acquainted in order to know and understand each other, and soliciting assistance in the peace-making process. This should be a fruitful event.

(7) And finally, that the Peace Committee be continued one year as originally authorized by the Dallas Convention action in June 1985 and that it report to the Southern Baptist Convention, meeting in St. Louis, June 16-18, 1987.

Oh, God, You are great . . . and we are grateful! May your matchless Name be honored and glorified by all that we are and all that we do or say from this day forward.

Other Committee Members:

Harmony M. Born	Charles Picketing
Dole E. Carton, Jr.	William Poe
Mrs. Morris H. Chapman	Ray Roberts
William Crews	Adrian P. Rogers
Robert E. Cuttino	Cecil Sherman
Mrs. A. Harrison Gregory	Charles F. Stanley
Jim Henry	John Sullivan
Herschel H. Hobbs	Daniel G. Vestal
William E. Hull	Jerry Vines
Albert McClellan	Edwin H. Young
W. Winfred Moore	

Document 37
The Glorieta Statement of the Seminary Presidents

"The Glorieta Statement" 22 October 1986

We, the presidents of the six SBC seminaries, through prayerful and careful reflection and dialogue, have unanimously agreed to declare these commitments regarding our lives and our work with Southern Baptists.

We believe that Christianity is supernatural in its origin and history. We repudiate every theory of religion which denies the supernatural elements in our faith. The miracles of the Old and New Testaments are historical evidences of God's judgment, love and redemption.

We believe that the Bible is fully inspired; it is "God-breathed" (2 Timothy 3:16), utterly unique. No other book or collection of books can justify that claim. The sixty-six books of the Bible are not errant in any area of reality. We hold to their infallible power and binding authority.

We believe that our six seminaries are fulfilling the purposes assigned to them by the Southern Baptist Convention. Nevertheless, we acknowledge that they are not perfect institutions. We recognize that there are legitimate concerns regarding them which we are addressing.

We commit ourselves therefore to the resolution of the problems which beset our beloved denomination. We are ready and eager to be partners in the peace process. Specifically,

(1) We reaffirm our seminary confessional statements, and we will enforce compliance by the persons signing them.

(2) We will foster in our classrooms a balanced, scholarly frame of reference for presenting fairly the entire spectrum of scriptural interpretations represented by our constituencies. We perceive this to be both good education and good cooperation.

(3) We respect the convictions of all Southern Baptists and we repudiate the caricature and intimidation of persons for their theological beliefs.

(4) We commit ourselves to fairness in selecting faculty, lecturers, and chapel speakers across the theological spectrum of our Baptist constituency.

(5) We will lead our seminary communities in spiritual revival, personal discipleship, Christian lifestyle, and active churchmanship.

(6) We will deepen and strengthen the spirit of evangelism and missions on our campuses while emphasizing afresh the distinctive doctrines of our Baptist heritage.

(7) We have scheduled for Southern Baptists three national conferences.

A Conference on Biblical Inerrancy, 1987

A Conference on Biblical Interpretation, 1988

A Conference on Biblical Imperatives, 1989

We share these commitments with the hope that all Southern Baptists will join us in seeking "the wisdom from above" in our efforts toward reconciliation: "The wisdom from above is first pure, then peaceable, gentle, open to reason, full of mercy and good fruits, without uncertainty or insincerity" (James 3:17).

Document 38
News Story: Cecil Sherman Resigns Peace Committee
Baptist Press, 24 October 1986, 5-6

"Sherman Resigns Peace Committee"
by Dan Martin

GLORIETA NM (BP)—Saying he cannot be part of the current process, Cecil Sherman has resigned from the Southern Baptist Convention Peace Committee.

Sherman, pastor of Broadway Baptist Church in Fort Worth, Texas, made his surprise resignation at the end of a three-day prayer retreat during which presidents of the six Southern Baptist seminaries issued a seven-point "commitment" aimed at resolving theological problems in the 14.5-million-member SBC. (See related stories.)

Although he said the resignation was not up for discussion, the Peace Committee accepted it, thanking him in their motion for faithful service during the 18 months the group has been meeting.

Sherman told Baptist Press he "absented" himself when the Peace Committee voted 19 to 0 to "affirm the seminary presidents" and to "express our appreciation to them for their effort at reconciliation."

Sherman resigned during the committee's executive session but gave a written statement to Baptist Press afterwards.

"The Peace Committee has begun to 'make progress'," he said. "Most of my friends in the Peace Committee are elated at the 'progress' we have made in the Glorieta meeting. I do not share their euphoria.

"The statement made by the six seminary presidents sets a course for theological education in the Southern Baptist convention for years to come. What fundamentalists have wanted, the Peace Committee has helped them get," he said.

Sherman added: "Fundamentalists began with the premise theological education was 'drifting into/towards liberalism.' The Peace Committee bought this premise and became one agent to bring pressure to bear on our seminaries.

"I started from a different place. Our six SBC seminaries are conservative by any normal use of the word, and they have been responsive to the constituency. Some of us on the Peace Committee have consistently made this case.

"Now the majority on the Peace Committee is of the opinion the way to make peace is to help fundamentalists toward their ends.

"I cannot be a part of this process."

The Fort Worth pastor noted the seminaries and some of the professors have been under heavy fire from critics within the denomination, and he said the visits of the Peace Committee subcommittees "pressured" the institutions into the statement.

"The seminaries have taken a long step toward their critics. They are trying to service us. What they have done will satisfy for a season, but fundamentalists will ask for more concessions from our educators. In the end, serious theological education will wither."

In his resignation statement, Sherman noted "some of us have offered the Peace Committee several ways to reduce tension and move down the long road to peace."

He said some of the suggestions are:

—"A restructuring of the Pastors' Conference, making it representative of all Southern Baptist pastors. In exchange, the Forum would be abandoned.

—"A division of both theological education and (Southern Baptist) Sunday School Board literature, with one track for moderates and another for fundamentalists.

—"Some serious, measurable way to make appointments in Southern Baptist life. Both sides would be represented to the strength of their vote in the last presidential election.

—"Design a better way to register and vote at the Southern Baptist Convention so the hint of irregularities could be reduced."

Sherman added: "To date, none of these proposals has much life in the Peace Committee. It seems to me a military model is at work. Peace will come not from reconciliation and mutual acceptance, but peace will come when one group defeats the other and drives it from the field."

He told Baptist Press he realizes the resignation "will appear to be 'sour grapes' and a sore loser. That may be."

"But," he added, "a few months from now I see a Peace Committee report coming that I cannot sign and hold a good conscience. At that point, I could be a part of a minority report should others hold my views.

"It seems to me it would be ironic to divide the St. Louis convention over the report of the Peace Committee.

"Resignation seems the better course to take."

He ended his written statement by asking Southern Baptists "to give a prayer for the few moderates on the Peace Committee. To this point, they are powerless."

Sherman has been a leading spokesman for the moderate/conservative political faction in the SBC, although he resigned from all responsibilities when he was named to the 22-member Peace Committee at the 1985 annual meeting of the SBC in Dallas.

Sherman was one of the organizers of a meeting in Gatlinburg, Tenn., in 1980, which was the first meeting of political moderates in the seven-year battle over the future of the denomination. One of the main efforts of the moderate/conservatives has been preservation of the seminaries as they are.

Peace Committee Chairman Charles Fuller told Baptist Press: "We regret Cecil's departure from the committee. He has been a vital part of our work from the beginning. He is a man of consistency and principle. He has kept before the committee an outspoken and earnest viewpoint to which he is deeply committed. I respect his integrity and commitment as a valuable part of our Southern Baptist family."

Fuller noted the action of the 1985 convention that created the Peace Committee "provides for the replacement of any vacancy by the action of the SBC Executive Committee."

"I will request them to take action quickly. If they choose to replace Cecil, the choice must be one who represents the moderate position," he said.

Sherman's departure comes at a point when the committee is nearing completion of its work. Fuller said the group plans to present a preliminary report to the Executive Committee at its February 1987 meeting and is aiming toward making public a final report in early April.

By convention action, the committee must make its final report at the St. Louis convention.

1987

Chronology

January. Baptist Press reports the beginning of new missions organization by fundamentalists.

January. Moderate Larry Baker elected to head the SBC Christian Life Commission by a 16–13 vote of the trustees. Vote is reflective of the growing power of fundamentalists and the weakening power of moderates.

Early 1987. "A Pastoral Plea for Peace among Southern Baptists: No Lord but Christ, No Creed but the Bible" statement released by moderate pastors. See document 39.

February. Patterson-Pressler issue statement to the SBC peace committee lauding developments in the SBC and noting their support for the Glorieta Statement and the Cooperative Program.

February 2–4. Trustees of the Sunday School Board authorize multi-volume inerrancy commentary on the Bible.

February 12. Announcement of formation of the Southern Baptist Alliance, one of the first organizational responses of moderates to the fundamentalist takeover of the SBC. The Alliance issues a "Covenant" composed of seven articles. See document 40.

February. SBC president Adrian Rogers's statement that, "If Southern Baptists believe that pickles have souls, the professors must teach that."

April 10. Fundamentalist Larry L. Lewis elected president of the Home Mission Board; first fundamentalist executive elected as a result of the Pressler-Patterson theological/political movement.

May 4-7. The Conference on Biblical Inerrancy sponsored by the six seminaries of the SBC.

May 14–15. First convocation of the Southern Baptist Alliance, Meredith College, Raleigh.

June 16–18. SBC, St. Louis, 25,607 messengers, Adrian Rogers presiding.

—Fundamentalist Adrian Rogers reelected president with 59.97% of the vote over moderate Richard Jackson with 40.03%.

—Adopted fundamentalist-dominated Peace Committee Report which takes on creedal nature in Southern Baptist life. See document 41.

June 26. Professional staffers of the Southern Baptist Home Mission Board asked by new fundamentalist president Larry Lewis to reaffirm their commitment to the Baptist Faith and Message Statement as interpreted by the Southern Baptist Convention Peace Committee.

August 25. SBC Public Affairs Committee endorses Robert H. Bork as Supreme Court Justice.

September 15. Moderate Larry Baker, executive-director of the Christian Life Commission of the SBC, avoids dismissal by a 15–15 tie vote. (Fundamentalist trustees sought Baker's dismissal because of displeasure with his views on abortion, capital punishment, and women in ministry.)

October 19. Shelby Baptist Association in Memphis TN withdraws fellowship from Prescott Memorial Baptist Church for calling a woman, Nancy Hastings Sehested, as pastor.

November 17. Southeastern Seminary President Randall Lolley and Dean Morris Ashcraft resign their positions in protest of the restrictive hiring policies mandated by fundamentalist trustees. See document 42.

December. Bill Moyers's PBS documentary entitled "God and Politics" highlights the SBC controversy, bringing Daniel Vestal to the forefront of moderate leadership and causing Paul Pressler to lodge later a protest against the series.

Document 39
**Moderates Issue a Pastoral Plea for Peace
Signed by 133 Pastors on the Subject of Bible and Creeds**

"A Pastoral Plea for Peace among Southern Baptists
No Lord by Christ, No Creed but the Bible"
January 1987

I. We hold to the Bible as the supreme and reliable source of authority in all matters of faith and practice, and we hold to the Bible first and foremost.

1. We hold to the Bible itself, high above all theories, doctrines, creeds, notions, and other such purely human inventions which attempt to explain how the Bible works. However helpful doctrines of biblical inspiration may be, they are only human rationalizations and explanations about the Bible. They are not the Bible, and our loyalty must be to the Scriptures and not to human notions about the Scriptures—our own or those of others.

2. This is the Baptist way. Baptists have always been suspicious of doctrinal statements as creeds, as *final expressions* about the Bible or Christian faith. *No creed but the Bible* has been the Baptist motto.

II. We hold to the duty and responsibility of every person to learn the Bible, to interpret the Bible, and to obey the Bible.

1. God speaks through the Bible, and each human soul has an inescapable duty to stand alone for himself before the Scriptures—learning, interpreting, and expressing faith in word and deed for himself alone. No one can rightly shirk this duty or leave it to another to fulfill.

2. No one can understand, interpret, or obey the Word of God for another. Therefore, it is wrong and harmful to pressure, impose, or otherwise require of others that they have our understandings, our experiences, or use our words to describe the nature or meaning of Scripture.

3. The duty of all Christians to interpret the Bible for themselves alone is, as Dr. George W. Truett said, "The crown jewel of the Baptists," and is the very meaning of the priesthood of believers and the freedom of conscience.

4. The right and burden of private interpretation is as binding upon teachers, preachers, and employees of the denomination as it is upon anyone else. One does not forego or escape this right and duty by accepting

denominational employment, any more than the preacher is bound to speak from the pulpit only the thoughts of the people who pay him.

III. The Holy Spirit is the true guide in interpreting the Bible to our hearts. The Spirit, and not human theories, is the sole defender of the authority of Scripture.

1. The role of the Holy Spirit as interpreter leads Baptists to depend upon the Spirit instead of creedal statements about the Bible to foster and preserve the authority of the Bible.

2. The persuasion of the Holy Spirit is the true way to religious conviction, and not the desire to please or agree with others. Because this is so, Baptists have valued the freedom of understanding and interpreting the Bible for themselves, and the free expression of differing views in our schools and churches.

3. Enforced uniformity in the interpretation of Scripture or in the way we express our beliefs about the Scriptures is distrust of the power of the Holy Spirit, the power and trustworthiness of the Word of God, and the competency of the individual to receive the Spirit's interpretation. It is an abandonment of the Baptist way.

IV. Southern Baptists always have gathered around the Bible itself and not around theories about the Bible. This is the true secret and foundational basis of our unity and cooperation.

1. Southern Baptists have cooperated for more than 140 years and have built an eminently successful missions enterprise without ever basing that unity and cooperation upon a creed or theory about the Bible. Our cooperative missions program is the envy of American Christianity.

2. Southern Baptists have never examined fellow Baptists for denominational employment of the basis of subscription to any one creedal or doctrinal statement about the Bible.

3. Since Southern Baptists have gathered around the Bible, the Bible itself, and the Bible alone, and the right and duty of personal interpretation, to make a theory of biblical inspiration the basis of unity would be to shift the grounds of cooperation away from that upon which we have worked together successfully.

4. The attempt to impose a human creed is a recent and different approach to Baptist unity.

By taking our stand upon the Bible itself, the Bible alone, and not upon a human notion about biblical inspiration, Southern Baptists can return to the basis of unity which gave us peace. By esteeming the Bible above theories about the Bible, and by esteeming the necessity of personal interpretation along with the centrality of the Bible, we choose for the Bible and for peace.

We call for a return to our roots, to the tried and true way of cooperation.

Sponsors

Ralph Langley, pastor	W. L. Lumpkin (retired)
First Baptist Church	Freemason Street Baptist
Huntsville AL	Norfolk VA
Paul W. Powell, pastor	Daniel John Yeary, pastor
Green Acres Baptist Church	University Baptist Church
Tyler TX	Coral Gables FL

(Second page contains a long list of "other supporting pastors.")

Document 40
The Covenant of the Alliance of Baptists

"The Covenant of the Alliance of Baptists"

In a time when historic Baptist principles, freedoms, and traditions need a clear voice, and in our personal and corporate response to the call of God in Jesus Christ to be disciples and servants in the world, we commit ourselves to:

—First, the freedom of the individual, led by God's Spirit within the family of faith, to read and interpret the Scriptures, relying on the historical understanding by the church and on the best methods of modern biblical study;

—Second, the freedom of the local church under the authority of Jesus Christ to shape its own life and mission, call its own leadership, and ordain whom it perceives as gifted for ministry, male or female;

—Third, the larger body of Jesus Christ, expressed in various Christian traditions, and to the cooperation with believers everywhere in giving full expression to the Gospel;

—Fourth, the servant role of leadership within the church, following the model of our Servant Lord, and to full partnership of all of God's people in mission and ministry;

—Fifth, theological education in congregations, colleges and seminaries characterized by reverence for biblical authority and respect for open inquiry and responsible scholarship;

—Sixth, the proclamation of the Good News of Jesus Christ and the calling of God to all peoples to repentance and faith, reconciliation and hope, social and economic justice;

—Seventh, the principle of a free church in a free state and to the opposition to any effect either by church or state to use the other for its own purposes.

Document 41
The SBC Peace Committee Report
SBC Annual 1987, 232-42

"Special Reports: Southern Baptist Convention Peace Committee"

Introduction

During the 1985 annual meeting of the Southern Baptist Convention in Dallas, 11-13 June 1985, a special committee was created to attempt to determine the sources of the current controversy in the Southern Baptist Convention and to make findings and recommendations to resolve it. The motion, overwhelmingly ádopted, says:

> With gratitude for God's bountiful blessings on us as Southern Baptists and with recognition of our unparalleled opportunity to confront every person on earth with the gospel of Christ by the year 2000 and with acknowledgement of divisions among us, which, if allowed to continue, inevitably will impede our progress, impair our fellowship and imperil our future; and after much prayer, we offer the following motion:
>
> That a special committee be authorized by this Convention, in session, in Dallas, June 1985; and
>
> That this committee seek to determine the sources of the controversies in our Convention, and make findings and recommendations regarding these controversies, so that Southern Baptists might effect reconciliation and effectively discharge their responsibilities to God by cooperating together to accomplish evangelism, missions, Christian education, and other causes authorized by our Constitution, all to the glory of God. "By this shall all men know that ye are my disciples, if ye have love one to another" (John 13:35) (John 17:21); and
>
> That this committee follow the 1963 Baptist Faith and Message Statement in regard to theological issues, and operate within the Constitution and Bylaws of the Southern Baptist Convention; and
>
> That to accomplish its work, this committee shall recognize the role of trustees and shall work with and through appropriate boards, commissions, and agencies of the Southern Baptist Convention. This committee shall report on the progress of its work to each meeting of the Executive Committee. The trustees, boards, and agencies of the Southern Baptist Convention, and their officers and employees, shall fully cooperate with the committee to accomplish the purposes outlined in this motion; and
>
> The staffing and professional advice for this committee shall be in accord with the Business and Financial Plan of the Southern Baptist

Convention. Funding shall come from Cooperative Program funds received by the Executive Committee as a priority item before the percentage division and allocation of the Southern Baptist Convention Cooperative Program Allocation Budget; and

That the committee may conduct its business in open sessions, and may hold public hearings, but, the committee may also hold executive sessions to accomplish its work; and

That any vacancy, or vacancies, on the special committee be filled by the Executive Committee at its next meeting after such vacancy occurs. In the filling of any such vacancy, balance of representation shall be maintained; and

That the committee may make its final report and recommendation to the 1986 Southern Baptist Convention and request that it be discharged, or the committee may make a preliminary report to the 1986 Convention and may recommend that the special committee be continued in existence for an additional year, in which instance the committee shall make its final report and recommendation to the 1987 Southern Baptist Convention; and

That all Southern Baptists be urged to exercise restraint, to refrain from divisive action and comments, and to reflect Christian love while this committee is doing its work; and

That the following persons be designated to serve on the special committee: Charles G. Fuller, chairman; Harmon M. Born, Doyle, E. Carlton, Jr., Mrs. Morris H. Chapman, *William O. Crews, Robert E. Cuttino, Mrs. A. Harrison Gregory, Jim Henry, William E. Hull, Herschel H. Hobbs, Albert McClellan, Charles W. Pickering, William E. Poe, Ray E. Roberts, Adrian P. Rogers, *Cecil E. Sherman, John Sullivan, Daniel G. Vestal, Jerry Vines, Edwin H. Young, *Charles F. Stanley, *Winfred Moore.

*Note: William O. Crews was elected president of Golden Gate Baptist Theological Seminary 13 October 1986 but was asked to remain as a member; Cecil E. Sherman resigned from the special committee 22 October 1986 and was replaced by Peter James Flamming; Charles F. Stanley and W. Winfred Moore served by virtue of office as president and first vice president of the Convention, and were asked to remain after their terms of office expired.

Since its creation, the Peace Committee has met fourteen times. Following each meeting, a report was given to Southern Baptists by Chairman Charles G. Fuller through the denominational news service Baptist Press.

In keeping with its assignment, the Peace Committee has determined what it believes to be the primary sources of the controversy, has made findings in reference to those sources, and, in this report, is making recommendations as to possible ways to effect reconciliation.

Sources of the Controversy

During its first meeting, the Peace Committee determined the primary source of the controversy is theological differences, but found there are political causes as well.

Theological Sources. In meeting after meeting of the Peace Committee, talk turned to the nature of inspiration of the Scriptures, often to the point of preempting the committee's established agenda. Gradually it became clear that while there might be other theological differences, the authority of the Word of God is the focus of differences. The primary source of the controversy in the Southern Baptist Convention is the Bible; more specifically, the ways in which the Bible is viewed.

All Baptists see the Bible as authoritative; the question is the extent and nature of its authority. The differences in recent years have developed around the phrase in Article I of the Baptist Faith and Message statement of 1963, that the Bible "has . . . truth without any mixture of error for its matter."

The action which created the Peace Committee instructed it to follow the Baptist Faith and Message statement of 1963 in regard to theological issues. Although the statement includes a preamble and seventeen articles, the committee has focused primarily on article 1, "The Scriptures":

> The Holy Bible was written by men divinely inspired and is the record of God's revelation of Himself to man. It is a perfect treasure of divine instruction. It has God for its author, salvation for its end, and truth, without any mixture of error, for its matter. It reveals the principles by which God judges us; and therefore is, and will remain to the end of the world, the true center of Christian union, and the supreme standard by which all human conduct, creeds, and religious opinions should be tried. The criterion by which the Bible is to be interpreted in Jesus Christ.

Herschel H. Hobbs, a member of the Peace Committee and chairman of the committee which wrote the 1963 Baptist Faith and Message statement, explained the phrase "truth without any mixture of error for its matter" by reference to 2 Timothy 3:16 which says, "all Scripture is given by inspiration of God." He explained: "The Greek New Testament reads 'all'—without the definite article—and that means every single part of the whole is God-breathed. And a God of truth does not breathe error." Dr. Hobbs made the comments during the 1981 annual meeting of the Southern Baptist Convention in Los Angeles, California.

Using article 1 of the Baptist Faith and Message statement of 1963 as a yardstick, Peace Committee subcommittees visited each of the Southern Baptist seminaries and five other agencies: the Foreign Mission Board, the Home Mission Board, Baptist Sunday School Board, Historical Commission, and Christian Life Commission. Following those visits, the committee adopted a "Statement of Theological Diversity."

> The Peace Committee has completed a preliminary investigation of the theological situation in our SBC seminaries. We have found significant theological diversity within our seminaries, reflective of the diversity within our wider constituency. These divergences are found among those who claim to hold a high view of Scripture and to teach in accordance with, and not contrary to, the Baptist Faith and Message statement of 1963.
>
> Examples of this diversity include the following, which are intended to be illustrative but not exhaustive.
>
> (1) Some accept and affirm the direct creation and historicity of Adam and Eve while others view them instead as representative of the human race in its creation and fall.
>
> (2) Some understand the historicity of every event in Scripture as reported by the original source while others hold that the historicity can be clarified and revised by the findings of modern historical scholarship.
>
> (3) Some hold to the stated authorship of every book in the Bible while others hold that in some cases such attribution may not refer to the final author or may be pseudonymous.
>
> (4) Some hold that every miracle in the Bible is intended to be taken as a historical event while others hold that some miracles are intended to be taken as parabolic.
>
> The Peace Committee is working earnestly to find ways to build bridges between those holding divergent views so that we may all legitimately coexist and work together in harmony to accomplish our common mission. Please pray that we may find ways to use our diversity to win the greatest number to faith in Christ as Savior and Lord.

Early in its second year, the Peace Committee continued to discuss theological concerns, including the fact that there are at least two separate and distinct interpretations of article 1 of the Baptist Faith and Message statement of 1963, reflective of the diversity present in the Convention. One view holds that when the article says the Bible has "truth without any mixture of error for its matter," it means *all* areas—historical, scientific, theological, and philosophical. The other holds the "truth" relates only to matters of faith and practice.

The Committee discussed whether the faculties of the SBC seminaries adequately reflect the views of many Southern Baptists who believe in the first interpretation. A Peace Committee subcommittee met with the six seminary presidents to communicate the need for the faculties to reflect the beliefs of these Southern Baptists.

In October 1986 the Peace Committee held a prayer retreat at Glorieta Baptist Conference Center near Santa Fe, New Mexico, attended by the Peace Committee and leaders of all national agencies. During that meeting, the seminary presidents presented a statement of their intentions which has become known as the "Glorieta Statement":

[The Glorieta Statement, 22 October 1986]
We, the presidents of the six SBC seminaries, through prayerful and careful reflection and dialogue, have unanimously agreed to declare these commitments regarding our lives and our work with Southern Baptists.

We believe that Christianity is supernatural in its origin and history. We repudiate every theory of religion which denies the supernatural elements in our faith. The miracles of the Old and New Testaments are historical evidences of God's judgment, love and redemption.

We believe that the Bible is fully inspired; it is "God-breathed" (2 Timothy 3:16), utterly unique. No other book or collection of books can justify that claim. The sixty-six books of the Bible are not errant in any area of reality. We hold to their infallible power and binding authority.

We believe that our six seminaries are fulfilling the purposes assigned to them by the Southern Baptist Convention. Nevertheless, we acknowledge that they are not perfect institutions. We recognize that there are legitimate concerns regarding them which we are addressing.

We commit ourselves therefore to the resolution of the problems which beset our beloved denomination. We are ready and eager to be partners in the peace process. Specifically

(1) We reaffirm our seminary confessional statements, and we will enforce compliance by the persons signing them.

(2) We will foster in our classrooms a balanced, scholarly frame of reference for presenting fairly the entire spectrum of scriptural interpretations represented by our constituencies. We perceive this to be both good education and good cooperation.

(3) We respect the convictions of all Southern Baptists and we repudiate the caricature and intimidation of persons for their theological beliefs.

(4) We commit ourselves to fairness in selecting faculty, lecturers, and chapel speakers across the theological spectrum of our Baptist constituency.

(5) We will lead our seminary communities in spiritual revival, personal discipleship, Christian lifestyle, and active churchmanship.

(6) We will deepen and strengthen the spirit of evangelism and missions on our campuses while emphasizing afresh the distinctive doctrines of our Baptist heritage.

(7) We have scheduled for Southern Baptists three national conferences.

A Conference on Biblical Inerrancy, 1987*

A Conference on Biblical Interpretation, 1988

A Conference on Biblical Imperatives, 1989

*Note: The first conference, focusing on biblical inerrancy, was held at Ridgecrest Baptist Conference Center 4-7 May 1987 with more than 1,000 in attendance.

We share these commitments with the hope that all Southern Baptists will join us in seeking "the wisdom from above" in our efforts toward reconciliation: "The wisdom from above is first pure, then peaceable, gentle, open to reason, full of mercy and good fruits, without uncertainty or insincerity" (James 3:17).

The Peace Committee affirmed the Glorieta Statement and ceased its official inquiry, referring unanswered questions and unresolved issues back to the administrators and trustees of Southern Baptist Theological Seminary, Southeastern Baptist Theological Seminary, and Midwestern Baptist Theological Seminary, hoping the results of their actions would be satisfactory to the Convention at large.

During the committee's December 1986 meeting, additional questions arose as to the meaning and the implementation of the Glorieta Statement.

The seminary presidents report that their efforts to implement the Statement have included an effort to recruit conservative scholars to fill faculty vacancies, expansion of reading lists, invitations to conservative scholars to address chapel and other events, a commitment to treat all persons fairly, and expanded evangelistic and missions activities on campus.

The question for the majority of the Peace Committee, however, remains not whether there is diversity in the Southern Baptist Convention, but how broad that diversity can be while still continuing to cooperate.

Political Sources. In the opinion of the Peace Committee, the controversy of the last decade began as a theological concern. When people of good intention became frustrated because they felt their convictions on Scripture were not seriously dealt with, they organized politically to make themselves heard. Soon, another group formed to counter the first and the political process intensified.

The Peace Committee, primarily through its Political Activities Subcommittee, has studied charges and countercharges regarding political activity. It has looked at many issues, including:

Restructuring the Constitution and Bylaws of the Southern Baptist Convention to limit the appointive powers of the president; restructuring the way in which the annual meeting is held, specifically shifting the pre-Convention meetings to post-Convention meetings; cooperation between the Pastors' Conference and the SBC Forum; discussing the coverage of personalities and issues in the controversy by the official and unofficial news media outlets; the use of descriptive terms and labels for the various groups; "de-politicizing" the Convention by asking the various groups to "stand down" from political activities; instituting stricter means of messenger registration and voting to prevent misuse of the registration and voting processes at annual meetings.

A primary area of discussion was changing the Constitution and Bylaws of the Convention to restrict the appointive powers of the president. However, the majority of the committee's members feel the basic Convention structure has served Southern Baptists well and should not now be changed.

The Committee investigated numerous charges of political malfeasance and voter irregularity. It heard a detailed report, complete with statistical analysis, on messenger participation at annual meetings, presented by the SBC registration secretary and Convention manager, as well as the chairman of a special study committee appointed by the SBC Executive Committee. Although the reports included isolated instances of registration and ballot abuse, there was no evidence of widespread or organized misuse of the ballot by any political group and no evidence of massive voter irregularities related to annual meetings.

The Political Activities Subcommittee, as well as a special ad hoc committee, dealt with the question of a parliamentarian for the annual meeting. The matter was deferred in 1986, because then SBC president Charles F. Stanley appointed a certified parliamentarian to assist him at the Atlanta annual meeting. The Committee is recommending a new bylaw be prepared concerning the appointment of a certified parliamentarian and two assistant parliamentarians for the annual meeting.

A special subcommittee also looked into the possibility of "negative designation" or "selective support" of agencies through the Cooperative Program, but concluded that a change in the basic structure of the unified giving plan would not provide significant help in resolving the crisis.

Some of the issues have been brought forward as recommendations from the Peace Committee. Others were not deemed sufficiently significant to warrant recommendations at this time.

Findings

The Peace Committee has made findings on Scripture and on politics.

On Theology. The Committee found there is significant diversity in the understanding of article 1 "On Scripture" of the Baptist Faith and Message statement of 1963. The Committee found there are at least two separate and distinct interpretations of the article. One holding "truth without any mixture of error for its matter" means *all* areas—historical, scientific, theological, and philosophical. The other holds "truth" relates only to matters of faith and practice.

The Committee, discussing whether the faculties of the SBC seminaries adequately reflect the views of many Southern Baptists who believe in the first interpretation, found there was not a theological balance represented in the faculties at Southern Baptist Theological Seminary or Southeastern Baptist Theological Seminary.

The Committee adopted two statements concerning its findings on theology, one a "foundational" statement, and the other a more elaborate statement.

1. *The Foundational Statement on Theology.* The Committee agreed the following Scripture references should be read as an introduction to the "Foundational Statement on Theology": Deuteronomy 4:2; Joshua 1:7; Psalm 119:160; Matthew 5:18; 2 Timothy 3:16; Revelation 22:10.

It is the conclusion of the majority of the Peace Committee that the cause of peace within the Southern Baptist Convention will be greatly enhanced by the affirmation of the whole Bible as being "not errant in any area of reality."

Therefore, we exhort the trustees and administrators of our seminaries and other agencies affiliated with or supported by the Southern Baptist Convention to faithfully discharge their responsibility to carefully preserve the doctrinal integrity of our institutions receiving our support, and only employ professional staff who believe in the divine inspiration of the whole Bible and that the Bible is "truth without any mixture of error."

The Committee also adopted the more elaborate statement on Scripture.

2. *The Statement on Scripture.* We, as a Peace Committee, affirm biblical authority for all of life and for all fields of knowledge. The Bible is a book of redemption, not a book of science, psychology, sociology, or economics. But, where the Bible speaks, the Bible speaks truth in all realms of reality and to all fields of knowledge. The Bible, when properly interpreted, is authoritative to all of life.

We, as a Peace Committee, reaffirm the Baptist commitment to the absolute authority of Scripture and to the historic Baptist position that the Bible has "truth without any mixture of error for its matter." We affirm that the narratives of Scripture are historically and factually accurate. We affirm that the historic accounts of the miraculous and the supernatural are truthful as given by God and recorded by the biblical writers.

We, as a Peace Committee, have found that most Southern Baptists see "truth without any mixture of error for its matter" as meaning, for example, that

(1) They believe in direct creation of mankind and therefore they believe Adam and Eve were real persons.

(2) They believe the named authors did indeed write the biblical books attributed to them by those books.

(3) They believe the miracles described in Scripture did indeed occur as supernatural events in history.

(4) They believe that the historical narratives given by biblical authors are indeed accurate and reliable as given by those authors.

We call upon Southern Baptist institutions to recognize the great number of Southern Baptists who believe this interpretation of our confessional statement and, in the future, to build their professional staffs and faculties from those who clearly reflect such dominant convictions and beliefs held by Southern Baptists at large.

However, some members of the Peace Committee differ from this viewpoint. They would hold that "truth without any mixture of error" relates only to faith and practice. They would also prefer a broader theological perspective. Yet, we have learned to live together on the Peace Committee in mutual charity and commitment to each other. We pledge our mutual efforts to fulfill the Great Commission, and we call on others within our Convention to make the same pledge.

On Politics. The Committee has found that the sources of the political aspect of the controversy are long-standing. Historically, informal political groups or coalitions have emerged in Southern Baptist life. Prior to the last decade, most of these groups operated informally by word of mouth among mutual acquaintances interested in selecting the leadership of the Southern Baptist Convention. More recently, these groups have developed organized coalitions centered around theological perceptions and committed to electing leadership committed to a particular viewpoint. The effort has been largely successful, but led to the formation of a countereffort which has increased hostility and turned up the heat on the controversy.

After its investigation, the Peace Committee found "that the extent of political activity . . . at the present time creates distrust, diminishes our ability to do missions and evangelism, is detrimental to our influence, and impedes our ability to serve our Lord."

The Committee adopted two statements, one a "foundational" statement and the other a more elaborate statement.

1. *The Foundational Statement on Politics.* It is the unanimous conclusion of the Peace Committee that fairness in the appointive process will contribute to peace.

Therefore, we exhort the present and future presidents of the Southern Baptist Convention, the Committee on Committees, and the Committee on Boards to select nominees who endorse the Baptist Faith and Message statement and are drawn in balanced fashion from the broad spectrum of loyal, cooperative Southern Baptists, representative of the diversity of our denomination.

The more elaborate statement on politics was also adopted.

2. *The Statement on Politics.* Politics are intrinsically a part of congregational polity, that is, voting, public and private discussions, influencing others to share one's view.

Historically, informal political groups or coalitions have emerged in Southern Baptist life. Prior to the last decade, most of these groups operated informally by word of mouth among mutual acquaintances interested in selecting the leadership of the Southern Baptist Convention. More recently, these groups have developed organized coalitions centered on theological perceptions and individual leaders committed to a defined viewpoint. These coalitions have adopted political strategies for electing officers of the Convention, appointing committees, and changing or preserving the character of accepted institutions. These strategies have included extensive travel, numerous informational and ideological meetings, mailouts, network of representatives who share in this common strategy, and sustained efforts to recruit messengers to attend the Convention.

We as a Peace Committee recognize that these political coalitions and strategies were born in part, at least, out of deep conviction and concern for theological issues.

But, we believe that the time has come for the Convention to move beyond this kind of politics. We find that the extent of political activity within the Southern Baptist Convention at the present time promotes a party spirit; creates discord, division, and distrust; diminishes our ability to do missions and evangelism; is detrimental to our influence; and impedes our ability to serve our Lord.

If allowed to continue unchecked, such political activity in the Convention can had disastrous consequences affecting our ability to serve our Lord and do His work.

Steps have been taken and additional steps are recommended in this report to resolve the theological issues involved in our present controversy. Because of our fear of the consequences of continued organized political activity within our Convention, and since steps have been and will continue to be taken to resolve theological issues, we feel that continued organized political activity within the Southern Baptist Convention is no longer necessary, desirable, or appropriate. We think the continuation of such political activity in the future would be unacceptable and could be disastrous.

We recommend that the Southern Baptist Convention request all organized political factions to discontinue the organized political activity in which they are now engaged. We think the following specific activities are out of place and request all groups to discontinue these specific political activities:

(1) Organized political activity;

(2) Political strategies developed by a group with central control;

(3) Holding information/ideological meetings;

(4) Extensive travel on behalf of political objectives within the Convention; and

(5) Extensive mailouts to promote political objectives in the Convention.

In 1986 the Southern Baptist Convention adopted the report of the Peace Committee which found:

(1) Some spokesmen on both sides of the political spectrum have used intemperate, inflammatory, and unguarded language, is that, "going

for the jugular," "Holy War," "independent fundamentalists," "flaming liberal," and other pejorative terms.

(2) Some spokesmen on both sides of the political spectrum and the autonomous independent journals on both sides of the issues have labeled and attributed improper motives to people with whom they disagree.

(3) Distributions of news is necessary in a democratic society. There have been instances when news releases have been altered, distorting the intent of the article and oftentimes creating confusion. In some denominational papers and in some autonomous independent journals, there has been prejudice against the conservative political activists and in some autonomous independent journals there has been prejudice against the moderate side.

The Convention in Atlanta [1986] adopted the recommendations of the Peace Committee as follows:

—That the Convention deplore the use of the type of intemperate, inflammatory, and unguarded language used by some spokesmen on both sides of the political spectrum.

—That the Convention urge Baptist Press, the state Baptist papers, and the autonomous independent journals to be especially careful to be fair and accurate in reporting events in the Convention and refrain from labeling and attributing improper motives.

Despite these recommendations approved by the Southern Baptist Convention, the Peace Committee finds that some of the state Baptist papers and the autonomous journal—the *Southern Baptist Advocate, SBC Today, Baptists United News,* and the *Baptist Laity Journal*—have continued to use intemperate, inflammatory language and have labeled individuals and impugned motives.

We renew again our request to these papers and journals to contribute to the process of reconciliation and the promotion of our cooperative work together as we seek to do the work of Christ. We again call upon all state Baptist papers and the independent autonomous journals to comply with the action taken at the Atlanta Convention and outlined above. We call upon individual Southern Baptists to use their influence to help stop these divisive actions.

We the Peace Committee ask Baptist Press, all Baptist state papers, Baptist publications, and independent autonomous journals to refrain from using terms and labels, specifically terms such as fundamentalist, liberal, fundamental-conservative, and moderate-conservative.

Conclusions

The enabling resolution of the Southern Baptist Convention at the 1985 Dallas Convention commissioned this special committee to determine the sources of the controversies within the Convention and to make findings and recommendations that would make it possible for Southern Baptists to effect reconciliation and to continue to cooperate in carrying out evangelism, missions, Christian education, and other causes.

Making peace among all Southern Baptists was not to be the work of the committee. *Reconciliation* was, and still is, the key word. Surely, there must be peace; that is, there must be an end to hostility among us, which is peace. Committed Christians must live in peace. No recommendation of the committee is needed to effect peace—it is found in the heart of the believer.

Reconciliation may be a first cousin to peace, but it rests on a different foundation. To reconcile is to harmonize, to cause to be friendly again, to reunite, to accept our differences, and to cooperate in all undertakings which enhance our mutual interests and goals. It was only through a subtle process of reconciliation, taking place over 142 years of history, that Southern Baptists have with God's blessing, and His help, achieved a preeminent position in missions, education, and evangelism. We have kept our differences from creating hostility, until recently, and not only have we lived in peace, but with remarkable harmony and cooperation.

We must never try to impose upon individual Southern Baptists nor local congregations a specific view of how Scripture must be interpreted. If such an attempt is made, then reconciliation is not the goal nor is it possible to achieve.

There is but one way for us to survive *intact* as a denomination. It involves recognition of some basic facts, among which are these:

(1) Changes are now taking place in the leadership of many Southern Baptist Convention boards.

(2) These changes will impact these boards and agencies for years to come.

(3) The role of many who have exercised leadership in the past will change as colleagues of different persuasions will fill leadership roles.

(4) This change will mean that some who have been in general agreement with Convention programs in the past will have less involvement, while those who previously have had difficulty in agreement with certain Convention programs will have more involvement.

(5) We have seen changes in Southern Baptist life in the past and we will see changes in the future. The important issue is that we must continue to be faithful stewards of the opportunities God has given Southern Baptists.

How then can we survive intact or substantially that way?

First, the hostility must cease within the heart of each of us. That brings peace.

Second, our leaders must have and must demonstrate a view of Baptist life that reaches beyond the limits of their own personal theology. No effort should be made or should be permitted to be made which would seek to eliminate from Baptist life theological beliefs or practices which are consistent with the Baptist Faith and Message statement and which have found traditional acceptance by substantial numbers of our people. Proponents of extreme positions at each end of the current Baptist theological spectrum should be encouraged to major on those things which lead to cooperative efforts and to minimize divisive issues and controversies.

Third, and most important, nothing must be allowed to stand in the way of genuine cooperation in missions, Christian education, evangelism, and our other traditional causes. While different leaders may arise, the nature and work of our Christian cooperative enterprise must continue unabated.

Finally, we should recognize and freely admit that the greatest source of our strength as a denomination lies in the thousands of local church congregations that support our cooperative undertakings. Through long years of experience, they have learned to trust our leaders, our agencies and institutions, and, because of that trust, they have provided magnificent support and responded to that leadership.

We have proclaimed this to be God's way of doing His work. Through continued cooperation in His enterprises, we can continue this mighty work. If we insist on having our way, drawing lines which exclude from places of leadership and responsibility those who do not hold our specific viewpoint, we can destroy what God has created in the Southern Baptist Convention. If, however, we can maintain a cooperative spirit and let our sense of Christian love bridge the gap of the diversity among us, we can continue to bear effective witness to His kingdom enterprise throughout all the world.

Recommendations

We make the following recommendations:

1. Although the Baptist Faith and Message statement of 1963 is a statement of basic belief, it is not a creed. Baptists are noncreedal in that they do not impose a man-made interpretation of Scripture on others. Baptists, however, declare their commitment to commonly held interpretations which then become parameters for cooperation. Therefore, we recommend that we,

(1) Reaffirm the 1963 Baptist Faith and Message statement as the guideline by which all the agencies of the Southern Baptist Convention are to conduct their work.

(2) Request, respectfully, all Southern Baptists to continue their high view of Scripture as "given by inspiration of God" (2 Tim 3:16), and to diligently teach and proclaim the truthfulness, the reliability, and the authority of the Bible.

2. Although all Southern Baptists do not understand the Baptist Faith and Message statement on Scripture the same way, this diversity should not create hostility toward each other, stand in the way of genuine cooperation, or interfere with the rights and privileges of all Southern Baptists within the denomination to participate in its affairs.

Because fairness in the process of making committee and board appointments is essential to the process of reconciliation and peace, the committee recommends that the present and all future presidents of the Southern Baptist Convention, the Committee on Committees, and the Committee on Boards select nominees who endorse the Baptist Faith and Message statement, and are drawn in balanced fashion from the broad spectrum of loyal, cooperative Southern Baptists, representative of the diversity of our denomination.

Recognizing the nature of our diversity and the rightful place of biblical interpretation, we believe we can learn from each other and, in the long run, we can protect each other from unwanted extremes.

We, therefore, further recommend that the Southern Baptist Convention continue in every attempt to remain a unified fellowship, rejecting the notion of any official division of our body.

3. We recommend that the Southern Baptist Convention Executive Committee study and report to the Southern Baptist Convention in 1988 a Convention bylaw establishing an office of parliamentarian, and that the study include the following considerations:

(1) The president and two vice presidents, acting together, shall annually appoint a chief parliamentarian and two assistant parliamentari-

ans to advise the presiding officer of the Convention on matters of parliamentary procedure.

(2) The chief parliamentarian shall be a fully certified member of the American Institute of Parliamentarians who has the experience to serve effectively at annual sessions of the Southern Baptist Convention.

4. In view of the fact that the Cooperative Program is the lifeline of all that we are doing as Southern Baptists, we commend our churches and state conventions for their increased giving through the Cooperative Program and we recommend to our people that they continue their strong support of the Cooperative Program.

We recognize the historic right of each Southern Baptist church to give to the work of the agencies, in keeping with its deeply held convictions, without intimidation or criticism.

We recommend that the Cooperative Program be continued unchanged.

5. We recommend, in view of the intense public discussions of the last few years, that trustees determine the theological positions of the seminary administrators and faculty members in order to guide them in renewing their determination to stand by the Baptist Faith and Message statement of 1963, to the Glorieta Statement of their intention to work toward reconciliation of the conflict in the Convention, and to their own institutional declarations of faith as the guidelines by which they will teach their students in preparation for gospel ministry in the churches, mission fields, and service to the denomination.

The Bible is a book of redemption, not a book of science, psychology, sociology, or economics. But, where the Bible speaks, the Bible speaks truth in all realms of reality and to all fields of knowledge. The Bible, when properly interpreted, is authoritative to all of life.

We call upon Southern Baptist institutions to recognize the great number of Southern Baptists who believe this interpretation of article 1 of the Baptist Faith and Message statement of 1963, and, in the future, to build their professional staffs and faculties from those who clearly reflect such dominant convictions and beliefs held by Southern Baptists at large.

We, as a Peace Committee, recognize and respect those in Southern Baptist life whose view of Scripture differs from this one and pledge to continue to cooperate. We pledge the highest regard, charity, and commitment to them in our combined efforts to fulfill the Great Commission and we call upon them to make the same pledge.

6. We recommend that the Southern Baptist Convention request all organized political factions to discontinue the organized political activity in which they are now engaged. At this time, we think the following specific political activity is out of place and we request all groups to discontinue the following specific political activities:

(1) Organized political activity.

(2) Political strategies developed by a group with central control.

(3) Holding information/ideological meetings.

(4) Extensive travel on behalf of political objectives within the Convention.

(5) Extensive mailouts to promote political objectives in the Convention.

7. We recommend that Baptist Press, all state Baptist papers, independent autonomous journals, and individual Southern Baptists refrain from the use of intemperate and inflammatory language, labeling individuals and impugning motives.

Specifically, we request that all Baptist writers and individual Baptists refrain from characterizing fellow Southern Baptists in terms such as "fundamentalist," "liberal," "fundamental-conservative," "moderate-conservative."

We request all Southern Baptists to take a positive view of Southern Baptist life, to use their influence to help stop the above divisive actions, and to contribute to the process of reconciliation and the promotion of our cooperative endeavors as we seek to do the work of Christ.

8. We recommend that the Southern Baptist Convention request the SBC Committee on Resolutions to continue its policy of not presenting resolutions that are divisive in Southern Baptist life for at least the next three years.

9. We recommend that the leadership of the Pastors' Conference and the SBC Forum take immediate steps to explore the possibility of "getting together" in ways that will enhance and promote our mutually strong beliefs as expressed in the Baptist Faith and Message statement.

10. We recommend that the Southern Baptist Convention continue the present twenty-two members of the SBC Peace Committee to serve for up to, but not to exceed, three years for the purpose of observing the response of all agencies, officers, and other participants to the recommendations of the Peace Committee in an effort to encourage compliance and foster harmonious working relationships among all segments of our Baptist family. The Peace Committee would meet once each year at a

time of its own choosing and would make an appropriate report to each annual session of the Convention.

Acknowledgments

1. The Peace Committee wishes to acknowledge the assistance provided us by the office and staff of Harold C. Bennett, president-treasurer of the Executive Committee of the Southern Baptist Convention. Special appreciation is due Martha T. Gaddis, administrative assistant to Dr. Bennett, and to Dan Martin, news editor of Baptist Press.

2. The Peace Committee expresses gratitude to the host of Southern Baptists and to Christians of other denominations who have faithfully prayed for the work of the committee throughout its existence.

Charles G. Fuller, chairman
Southern Baptist Convention Peace Committee

SBC Peace Committee

Charles G. Fuller, chairman	Albert McClellan
Harmon M. Born*	Charles W. Pickering*
Doyle E. Carlton, Jr.*	William E. Poe*
Mrs. Morris H. Chapman (Jodi)*	Ray E. Roberts
William O. Crews	Adrian P. Rogers
Robert E. Cuttino	Charles F. Stanley
P. James Flamming	John Sullivan
Mrs. A. Harrison Gregory (Christine)*	Daniel G. Vestal
Jim Henry	Jerry Vines
Herschel H. Hobbs	Edwin H. Young
William E. Hull	

*Indicates nonchurch-related vocation

Document 42
News Story: Lolley and Ashcraft Quit
Baptist Press, 23 October 1987, 9-11

"Southeastern Seminary President, Dean Set Plans to Terminate Roles"
by Larry E. High and R. G. Puckett

WAKE FOREST NC (BP)—In a surprise announcement which stunned the faculty, student body, and the community, W. Randall Lolley announced his plans to terminate his presidency at Southeastern Baptist Theological Seminary, a post he has held for 13 years.

The 56-year-old native of Alabama—who holds two degrees from Southeastern and is the only alumnus to serve as its president—told a tearful and stunned student body Oct. 22 that action taken by seminary trustees the preceding week left him no alternative. Trustees removed all power for selecting new faculty members from the faculty and gave it completely to Lolley and trustees.

"I cannot fan into flame a vision which I believe to be contradictory to the dream which formed Southeastern in 1951 and has nourished me as a student and alumnus of the school," Lolley said at the conclusion of his chapel sermon. "I have reached some conclusions that make it necessary to begin discussing with the appropriate persons the termination of my presidency."

Lolley gave no date when the resignation would be effective. He tentatively has scheduled a Nov. 3 meeting with four members of the trustee board. They are Robert E. Rowley, chairman; James R. DeLoach, vice chairman; Jesse P. Chapman, immediate past chairman; and W. Lee Beaver Jr., chairman immediately before Chapman.

Lolley also revealed he had received a letter from Morris Ashcraft requesting that he be relieved of the role of dean but be permitted to continue on the faculty as professor of theology.

Lolley has no faculty status nor tenure, but Ashcraft has both. In his letter to Lolley, Ashcraft wrote: "The recent actions and stated intentions of the majority of our board of trustees indicate to me that I will not be able to implement their guidelines for the instruction unit of the seminary. Therefore, I hereby request that you plan for me to relinquish my position as dean of the faculty."

Lolley prepared a statement but would not make printed copies of it available because he will make it his official resignation which must go to the trustees. He left the campus immediately after the chapel service to go to the bedside of his father who is seriously ill.

"In these resignations (Lolley and Ashcraft), we suffer two grievous losses," Professor Richard Hester told a crowd of students and friends at a press conference held on the steps of Broyhill Hall, the building where the trustees met the week before.

"We are deeply saddened but not terribly surprised," Hester read from a prepared statement. "President Lolley and Dean Ashcraft have both made it abundantly clear that they will not implement the policies of political fundamentalism now being enacted by a narrow majority of our board of trustees.

"The president and the dean have told us they will not serve as agents of the persons who want to overturn this school's distinguished 37-year tradition of competent, open, responsible theological education. They have told us they refuse to preside over a fundamentalist school," Hester, president of the local chapter of the American Association of University Professors, told several hundred students and media representatives.

With the faculty assembled behind him, Hester said, "We respond to their resignations with grief and a profound sense of loss, but we also respond with affirmation of their values, their integrity and their courage."

Robert D. Crowley, a pastor in Rockville, Md.—who was elected chairman of the board of trustees, unseating Chapman, who could have served another year—repeatedly has said trustees have no plans to fire any existing faculty members. However, he did indicate all new faculty members will be inerrantists.

Crowley said he was shocked that the president's resignation was "announced so emphatically to the student body."

"The message that sends is that the decision is nonnegotiable," Crowley said in a telephone interview with Todd Ackerman of the *Raleigh News and Observer*. "Our major task now will be to find someone who will be able to assume the leadership Dr. Lolley so effectively provided."

About the search for a new president, Crowley said, "I would be an imbecile if I tried to tell you I didn't have some names going through my mind. I can assure that whoever he is, he will be an inerrantist."

Other trustees also reacted. Chapman, a retired surgeon in Asheville NC, said resignation came as a surprise, but expressed his regrets and called the situation a tragedy.

"I felt it would be very difficult for President Lolley to keep his own sense of what was appropriate and right after the trustees' meeting Oct. 12-14," Chapman said. "Dean Ashcraft is also a man of high principles."

"I am real surprised at this," said William D. Delahoyde, an assistant U.S. attorney from Raleigh, N.C. "This subject did not come up during the board meeting. . . . Perhaps this is a function of the thought he had given to his administration between the end of the board meeting and now."

Delahoyde reported Lolley had "said to me in the past that he was willing to work with the board. He realized conservatives need to be included in the board." Delahoyde also said he was surprised Lolley reacted negatively to the recent trustee action concerning faculty selection, because the change "enhanced his authority in that area."

"I was not surprised" at the resignation, said Mark Caldwell, a pastor from Hyattsville, Md. "There is no way Randall Lolley can administer that school under these directives of the present board of trustees. He could not maintain his honor, his integrity—he just could not do it. His announcement that he plans to resign is an act of integrity and honor."

"I'm just bleeding a little bit. I'm a Southeastern graduate myself," said W. Jerry Holcomb, a pastor from Virginia Beach, Va.

He said he was not shocked by the announcement: "I had suspected it in light of the last board meeting. If the deacons I serve with had shown what the trustees showed . . . it would have been fairly obvious that the working conditions would have been very difficult to operate in."

"I was absolutely shocked and flabbergasted," said DeLoach, an associate pastor from Houston. "When we left the campus, there was a spirit of reconciliation and openness I've always found with Randall Lolley."

Reports that Lolley "could not work with fundamentalist trustees" do not sound like the Lolley he has come to know, DeLoach added. "Something must have happened to make him feel this way," he said.

DeLoach said he is sympathetic with the Southeastern community: "Randall Lolley is a very popular president, a very popular colleague. I would be greatly disappointed if the students and faculty were not disappointed. . . . My spirit grieves with the students. Right now, all they can see is blood and thunder."

He also reiterated the pledge that faculty will not be fired. "Every time anything has been said about firing, we have tried to squelch that rumor," he said, noting the issue of professors who are inerrantists is "a hiring matter," not a question of dismissing faculty.

The faculty at Southeastern has no plans to resign en masse, Hester reported: "We do not intend to give up our prophetic voice. We do not intend to give up our academic freedom. We do not intend to abandon this school's 37-year tradition of quality theological education. We intend to continue our classes today, tomorrow, and the months ahead, fulfilling our responsibility to our students."

He added only occasionally in history does this kind of "opportunity come to the faculty, the staff, and the students of a theological school."

"Only occasionally does an opportunity come to join together in proclaiming the truth in the face of a stifling, oppressive, and powerful political movement," he said. "The events of the past 11 days have shaped this campus into the clearest and most determined opposition New Right fundamentalism in the Southern Baptist Convention has ever faced. The loses of a great president and a great dean make us all the more determined to continue this fight."

Following Lolley's announcement, students gathered outside to pray, to share testimonies and feelings, read Scripture and sing.

Student Council president Beverly Hardgrove told her fellow students, "Dr. Lolley wrote me a letter last week of one sentence and it was very special, 'We don't know what the future holds, but we know Who holds our future.'

"I knew last Tuesday (Oct. 13) afternoon in the trustees meeting that something here had died and some idea that we were experiencing had been lost. We are called to a new hope and our hope is in God," she said.

Part III

1988–1991

Introduction to Part III

Despite the thriving momentum of the right wing of the denomination, moderates would not quit—not yet, at least. Conditions had gotten so bad for them, however, fundamentalist patriarch W. A. Criswell could savagely and publicly malign them as "skunks" in his 1988 Pastors' Conference address. Nonetheless, moderates made their best showing in the presidential election at San Antonio in 1988. Jerry Vines, the fundamentalist candidate, beat Richard Jackson, the moderate candidate, by a razor-thin vote of 15,804 to 15,112, a margin of 692 and a percentage of 50.53% to 48.32%.

Fundamentalists would often claim that ninety-five percent of Southern Baptists agreed with them on the issues. The presidential elections, the best barometer of the divided Southern Baptist house, belied this claim. When nonincumbents competed for the presidency during the decade-long controversy, fundamentalists won by the following margins: 1979, 51.36%; 1980, 51.67%; 1982, 56.97%; 1984, 52.18%; 1986, 54.22%; 1988, 50.53%; 1990, 57.68%. Impressive to be sure, but the nearest thing to a rout came in the final year of the conflict and this with fundamentalists' weakest candidate for the decade, demonstrating only that fundamentalist momentum mushroomed by 1990. For fundamentalists to claim 95% of the SBC family at least proves that their mathematics were not inerrant!

With newly discovered might fundamentalists took bold steps to solidify their power, even to the point of revising the Baptist heritage. At the 1988 meeting of the SBC in San Antonio messengers adopted a resolution that virtually debaptistified the SBC. Known as "On the Priesthood of the Believer," it was presented by and voted for by people who simply did not know the Baptist heritage. The resolution actually diminished and perverted the historic Baptist principle of the priesthood of all believers, misrepresented Baptist theologians who had written on the subject, falsified the position of the "Baptist Faith and Message" on the topic, and nonbaptistically exalted the authority of the pastor.[1] And it passed by a 54.75% majority! No wonder Randall Lolley led a group of moderates from the convention center to the Alamo and ceremonially tore up that resolution! "Resolution 5" did not represent anything in the Baptist heritage.

As a result of Bill Moyers's December 1987 PBS documentary entitled "God and Politics," Daniel Vestal, pastor of First Baptist Church, Midland, Texas, emerged to the forefront of the moderate movement. He challenged Vines for the SBC presidency at Las Vegas in 1989, garnering an impressive 43.39% of the votes against an incumbent president. It was not enough, however. At New Orleans the next year, 1990, Vestal went head to head with Morris Chapman, fundamentalist pastor of First Baptist Church, Wichita Falls, Texas, and was soundly defeated by Chapman 57.68% to 42.32%.

After New Orleans moderates were exhausted by their decade of losing. They quit the politics of the SBC. They continued, however, a process which they had begun as early as 1983, creating their own structures. In historical order moderates created *Baptists Today* (April 1983), Southern Baptist Women in Ministry (June, 1983) the Forum (June 1984), the Southern Baptist Alliance (December 1986), Baptists Committed (December 1988), the Associated Baptist Press (July 1990), Baptist Cooperative Missions Program, Inc. (August 1990), the Cooperative Baptist Fellowship (August 1990), Smyth & Helwys Publishing (November 1990), the Baptist Center for Ethics (May 1991), the Baptist Theological Seminary in Richmond (September 1991), and the William H. Whitsitt Baptist Heritage Society (October 1992). The Cooperative Baptist Fellowship (CBF), called into being by Daniel Vestal in 1990, is the glue that holds the moderate movement together. In 1991 the Coordinating Council of CBF issued "An Address to the Public," a brief document outlining the origin of CBF and some of the major differences between it and the SBC.

On the other side of the SBC aisle, fundamentalists had captured by August 1986 the balance of power on the first SBC agency board of

---

[1]For an extended analysis and historical treatment, see my article "The Priesthood of All Believers and Pastoral Authority in Baptist Thought," *Faith and Mission* 7/1 (Fall 1989): 24-45, or in my book *Proclaiming the Baptist Vision: The Priesthood of All Believers* (Macon GA: Smyth & Helwys Publishing, Inc., 1993) 131-54.

trustees. After that the "domino theory" came into operation. One agency after another came under the domination of aggressive proteges of Rogers, Patterson, and Pressler. With a majority on the boards of trustees, fundamentalists began electing their denominational agency heads: Larry Lewis at the Home Mission Board (April 1987), Lewis Drummond at Southeastern Seminary (March 1988), Richard Land at the Christian Life Commission (September 1988), James Draper at the Baptist Sunday School Board (July 1991), Morris Chapman at the Executive Committee (February 1992), Paige Patterson at Southeastern to replace Drummond (May 1992), Al Mohler at Southern Seminary (1993), and by the end of 1995 the fundamentalist lock on the denomination was virtually complete.

1988

Chronology

<u>February 24.</u> Former SBC presidents Adrian Rogers, Bailey Smith, James Draper, and Charles Stanley issue "An Inerrantist Manifesto," claiming inerrancy the position of the Baptist Faith and Message, the Hobbs interpretation of the Baptist Faith and Message, the Glorieta Statement, and the Peace Committee Report.

<u>March.</u> Paige Patterson proposes agency status for WMU.

<u>March 14.</u> Lewis Drummond elected president of Southeastern Seminary by fundamentalist trustees.

<u>May 15.</u> Moderate Larry Baker, director of Christian Life Commission, accepts pastorate of First Baptist Church, Pineville LA, sixteen months after accepting the CLC post.

<u>June 1.</u> Moderate Jack U. Harwell becomes editor of *SBC Today*, succeeding Walker L. Knight.

<u>June 14–16.</u> SBC, San Antonio, 32,727 messengers, Adrian Rogers presiding.

—At SBC Pastors' Conference, W. A. Criswell groups "moderates" with "liberals," saying, "A skunk by any other name still stinks." See document 43.

—Fundamentalist Jerry Vines elected president with 50.53% of the vote over moderate candidate Richard Jackson (48.32%) and two other independent candidates.

—Resolution "On the Priesthood of the Believer" adopted by 54.75% to 45.25% of the vote. This resolution diminished the historic Baptist principle of the priesthood of all believers and advocated pastoral authority in an unprecedented way in Baptist life. See document 44.

<u>July 21.</u> SBC Foreign Mission Board terminates Michael E. Willett, missionary to Venezuela, because of Willett's "doctrinal ambiguity."

<u>September 12.</u> Fundamentalist Richard Land elected head of the SBC Christian Life Commission following moderate Larry Baker's resignation in the spring.

<u>December 15–16.</u> Continuation of the moderate political network through the formation of "Baptists Committed to the Southern Baptist Convention." See document 45.

Document 43
News Story: W. A. Criswell's "Skunk" Sermon
The Christian Index, 23 June 1988, 2

"SBC Pastors' Conference"
"Criswell Lambasts 'Liberals'; Georgians Share Platform"
by Ken Camp and Jim Lowry For Baptist Press

A fiery indictment of "the curse of liberalism" by W. A. Criswell, former president of the Southern Baptist Convention, highlighted the closing session of the annual Southern Baptist Pastors' Conference. "Building the Greatest Churches since Pentecost" was the theme of the meeting.

"The curse of liberalism" has led to the downward spiral of mainline denominations and to the declining number of baptisms within the SBC, Criswell, pastor of the 20,000-member First Church in Dallas TX, told an estimated 16,000 preachers at the conference.

Criswell grouped "liberals" with "moderates" in the SBC, saying, "A skunk by any other name still stinks."

Pointing to the "inroads" made by liberalism and secularism, Criswell said, "We have taken the doctrine of the priesthood of the believer and made it to cover every damnable heresy you can imagine."

Criswell, whose church is the largest in the 14.7-million-member SBC, denied that ongoing controversy in the convention has been the cause of a declining number of Southern Baptist baptisms.

Evangelist Bailey Smith, of Atlanta, another former SBC president, challenged preachers to stand against formalism, secularism and liberalism. Smith said churches in America face a crisis of apathy and of cold formalism.

"You cannot marry high church music and a burden for souls," he said, observing that liturgy leads to lethargy.

Smith warned against the crisis of liberalism, comparing the choice between theological conservatism and liberalism to a choice between health and cancer. He admonished Southern Baptist preachers never to compromise with the forces of liberalism and secularism.

"Every problem in this country could be laid at the feet of a compromising pulpit," Smith said.

Numerous speakers explored possible reasons for the declining number of baptisms in Southern Baptist churches.

Freddie Gage, evangelist from Euless TX, rejected the notion that the declining number of baptisms are due to controversy.

"That is absurd. That is a scapegoat," he said. Gage said the solution to the problem of a drop in baptisms is for "Southern Baptist seminaries to crank out soul winners."

Gage lambasted those whom he termed "pussyfooting preachers" who refuse to use the word "inerrant" to describe Scripture.

Richard Lee, pastor of Rehoboth Church in Tucker, cited a survey conducted by Western Reserve University in which 57 percent of the Baptist clergymen interviewed said they did not believe the Bible is the inspired word of God.

"No wonder our baptisms are down. Let's put the blame where it belongs," Lee said. "It's not politics or programs. It's puny preaching from powerless pulpits by men who don't believe the word of God."

Charles Stanley, pastor of Atlanta First Church and former SBC president, said that pastors wanting to build great churches need a strong awareness of their accountability to God; a preaching ministry based on the unquestioned authority of the Bible; personal self-discipline; ability to endure hardship; and willingness to fulfill their calling to do the work of an evangelist.

Morris Chapman, pastor of First Church of Wichita Falls, Texas, called for a Christ-like spirit in maintaining convictions about the Word of God.

"I will never change my conviction about the Word of God, but as I stand for what I believe, may I stand in such a manner people will see Jesus in me," he said. "My heart breaks when I hear rhetoric bouncing off the walls; when I see sensational headlines; and when I hear character assassination."

Paige Patterson, president of Criswell Center for Biblical Studies in Dallas, addressed the importance of preaching the atonement of Christ.

"If we want peace in the denomination, we will have it not through compromise, but in the peace that is found at the foot of the cross," Patterson said.

Document 44
SBC Resolution on Priesthood of All Believers
SBC Annual 1988, 68-69

"Resolution No. 5—On The Priesthood of the Believer"

WHEREAS, None of the five major writing systematic theologians in Southern Baptist history have given more than passing reference to the doctrine of the priesthood of the believer in their systematic theologies; and

WHEREAS, The Baptist Faith and Message preamble refers to the priesthood of the believer, but provides no definition or content to the terms; and

WHEREAS, The high profile emphasis on the doctrine of the Priesthood of the Believer is a term which is subject to both misunderstanding and abuse; and

WHEREAS, The doctrine of the priesthood of the believer has been used to justify wrongly the attitude that a Christian may believe whatever he so chooses and still be considered a loyal Southern Baptist; and

WHEREAS, The doctrine of the priesthood of the believer can be used to justify the undermining of pastoral authority in the local church.

Be it therefore, *Resolved*, That the Southern Baptist Convention meeting in San Antonio, Texas, June 14-16, 1988, affirm its belief in the biblical doctrine of the priesthood of the believer (1 Peter 2:9 and Revelation 1:6); and

Be it further *Resolved*, That we affirm that this doctrine in no way gives license to misinterpret, explain away, demythologize, or extrapolate out elements of the supernatural from the Bible; and

Be it further *Resolved*, That the doctrine of the priesthood of the believer in no way contradicts the biblical understanding of the role, responsibility, and authority of the pastor which is seen in the command of the local church in Hebrews 13:17, "Obey your leaders, and submit to them; for they keep watch over your souls, as those who will give you an account;" and

Be it further *Resolved*, That we affirm the truth that elders or pastors are called of God to lead the local church (Acts 20:28).

Document 45
News Story: The Formation of "Baptists Committed"
Baptist Press, 29 December 1988

"SBC 'Centrist' Coalition Forms; Coordinator Named"
by Dan Martin

DALLAS (BP)—About two dozen Southern Baptists from around the nation—saying they represent the mainstream in the Southern Baptist Convention—met in Dallas in mid-December to form what they call a "centrist" coalition.

The organization, to be called Baptists Committed to the Southern Baptist Convention, also hired a full-time "coordinator," David Currie of Paint Rock, Texas, to "get the movement underway in the states."

A news release issued by Currie after the Dec. 15-16 meeting said the group will "direct its message toward the 'broad center' of Southern Baptists who are disenchanted with the fundamentalist takeover of the convention and yet do not wish to abandon the convention or start a new denomination."

Winfred Moore, pastor of First Baptist Church of Amarillo, Texas, called the December meeting and will be chairman of the group. An executive committee will be named later, he said.

Moore, former first vice president of the SBC and twice candidate for president, said: "We are traditional, mainstream, conservative Southern Baptists who are deeply committed to this convention and its historic principles. These principles, which are our heritage and legacy, and which must be preserved if our convention is to survive, include the priesthood of the believer, the autonomy of the local church, the separation of church and state and cooperative missions.

"Surely Southern Baptists can stop fighting and unite under these principles which have historically defined us as a group.

"With contributions down, baptisms down and unity shattered, enough is enough. Southern Baptists want and deserve a group to lead us out of this despair, a group which is truly committed to all that Southern Baptists have been in the past and which has a vision of cooperative mission for the future which includes all Southern Baptists.

"We support the restoration of our convention, not its destruction."

Although the news release said the group formally organized at the December meeting, a group also calling itself Baptists Committed to the

Southern Baptist Convention sent out a mass mailing to more than 34,000 Southern Baptists churches in advance of the 1988 annual meeting of the SBC.

The mailing included a 10-minute recorded cassette tape from Moore and a brochure produced by Baptists Committed to the Southern Baptist Convention. The mailing stirred controversy in the SBC because of various charges the brochure made against conservative leaders.

Paul Pressler, a Houston appeals court judge who was specifically mentioned in the brochure, responded to Baptists Committed by noting: "It appears to be a reorganization of the same people who for 10 years have been resisting a return to Biblical theology."

"Baptists need to be working together to promote the Cooperative Program, evangelism and missions, not starting new political organizations that will be decisive and counterproductive to the welfare of the convention."

John Baugh, a Houston businessman who has been active in Laity For the Baptist Faith and Message, one of the founders of the coalition, said the name comes from "two things: first, Baptists Committed to the Southern Baptist Convention means we are Baptists committed to being a part of the SBC and assisting in causing it to be what it should become. Second, without any doubt, the people whom I know in that group are traditional, mainstream Southern Baptists."

Moore told Baptist Press that although he called the December meeting and invited the 25 or so participants, he was unable to attend because of a schedule conflict.

James Slatton, pastor of River Road Baptist Church in Richmond, Va., who chaired the two-day session, said: "This is an attempt to form a centrist coalition which stands as an alternative between the political right wing on one hand and just checking out of denominational participation on the other."

"We feel there are people who wish to rally to that alternative. We feel there is a need for an emphasis on the essentials of Baptists. We think the Baptist understanding of the priesthood of the believer is in jeopardy; that the democracy of the local congregation is being threatened by pastoral autocracy."

"Southern Baptists are now a large national body with many constituencies and subgroups. The attempt to exclude from denominational service any who will not kiss the frog of creedal conformity and cooperation with one political group is dividing and destroying the denomination."

Slatton, who declined to identify the other participants in the meeting, said Baptists Committed is "a coalition which includes fundamentalists, moderates and anybody who is willing to work together around a commitment to the faith that honors Baptist freedom."

He added: "Ten years ago zealous people—give them credit for their sincerity—thought they could save the Bible by attacking the denominational structure. What they did was not save the Bible but destroy our unity and our trust.

"I think a great deal of damage has been done. Our denomination is like the Titanic after it hit the iceberg. It will take a long time to determine how much; but we know there has been damage and there is a decided list to the old ship."

He said the new organization will be "issues oriented. We are going to preach the Baptists essentials. We are not candidate oriented. Our major agenda will be to campaign on the issues."

Potential candidates for the presidency of the SBC at the 1989 annual meeting in Las Vegas were not discussed, he said. "This (the organization) is not about candidates; it is about the issues which are at stake."

Moore said the new organization, however, will have a political dimension and the group will continue to try to elect a candidate "who will personify the centrist position of where I think the great majority of Southern Baptists are."

Richard Jackson, pastor of North Phoenix (Ariz.) Baptist Church, said he attended a small meeting of six people in advance of the larger meeting to discuss the issues but did not attend the organizational meeting.

"We talked about what they were going to talk about," Jackson said. "I went to the meeting because I want a place for loyal, committed Southern Baptists to belong.

"We are in an identity crisis. The ordinary Southern Baptist has nowhere to go. Either he is identified with the group in charge or he is called a liberal or a moderate. This group (Baptists Committed) is trying to provide a place for mainline Southern Baptists who believe the Bible is the Word of God and in our missions endeavor."

Randy Fields, a San Antonio, Texas, attorney and chairman of Laity For the Baptist Faith and Message, said the meeting was "similar to other meetings we have had a couple of times a year. It was an organizational meeting to reassess what has happened since San Antonio (site of the 1988 annual meeting of the SBC) and to gear up for Las Vegas."

"I see Baptists Committed as a loose cooperative effort between many groups. We are not a monolithic body, but various groups who do not agree on everything. We see ourselves as centrists, representing the mainstream."

Norman Cavendar, a Claxton, Ga., businessman, said the meeting and organization "is an expression of all that has gone on before," and added he is encouraged because of "the new people who are beginning to get involved because they now believe we have a problem."

"I wish I could say I see profound change happening to bring us back to our roots, but I don't. There is incremental change. There is some new energy and new effort," he added.

1989

Chronology

<u>January 1.</u> Moderate Stan Hastey becomes the first permanent executive-director of the Southern Baptist Alliance.

<u>February 21-22.</u> The SBC Executive Committee approves a Paul Pressler motion by a vote of 40-14 expressing concern about "the biased content of Bill Moyers special TV series 'God and Politics'," urging individuals to protest to the Public Broadcasting System.

—The SBC EC approves by a vote of 42-27 to establish a new SBC agency in Washington to be called the Religious Liberty Commission. An effort to separate the SBC from the BJC.

<u>March.</u> Third annual convocation of the Southern Baptist Alliance in Greenville, SC.

—SBA approves opening of Baptist Theological Seminary at Richmond.

<u>April 10-11.</u> Moderate Jimmy Allen resigns as president of the SBC Radio and Television Commission.

<u>April 16.</u> Moderate Daniel Vestal announces he will be a candidate for the SBC presidency in Las Vegas. See document 46.

<u>May.</u> SBC president Jerry Vines asks EC to withdraw motion regarding the establishment of the Religious Liberty Commission and EC complies in June meeting.

<u>May 25.</u> Seventy "Young Conservatives" promote the fundamentalist cause with militant rhetoric at a meeting at James Draper's church in Euless TX.

<u>June 11.</u> Bill Moyers withdraws request to appear before the SBC Executive Committee in June to discuss his special TV series with Paul Pressler. The EC chairman had refused Moyers's request, indicating that the chair would ask the committee if they wished to hear Moyers in September. Moyers's letter of withdrawal to the chairman described Pressler as a "secular politician who has infected this Christian fellowship with the partisan tactics of malice, manipulation,

and untruth." Pressler was elected vice chair of the EC at later meeting in Las Vegas.

June 13-15. SBC, Las Vegas, 20,411 messengers, Jerry Vines presiding.

—Fundamentalist Jerry Vines reelected president with 56.58% of the vote over moderate Daniel Vestal with 43.39%.

—Effort to defund Baptist Joint Committee failed by narrow margin but precipitated fierce debate.

—The Baptist General Association of Virginia dispatched memorial to the SBC requesting the following: (1) continuation of the historic relationship between SBC and Baptist Joint Committee, (2) creation of a financial plan permitting negative designations to the Cooperative Program, (3) commitment to responsible theological education, and (4) the election of persons from Virginia to SBC committees proposed by the state convention of Virginia.

June 27. FMB trustees rejected staff recommendation to appoint Greg and Katrina Pennington as missionaries, because she was ordained.

July 22. Dellanna W. O'Brien elected WMU national executive director.

August 7. Baptist Sunday School Board trustees rebuke president Lloyd Elder for alleged denominational politics but turn back attempt to fire him. The BSSB also approved projected forty-volume inerrancy commentary to be edited by Paige Patterson and others.

September. In an address to the EC, president Jerry Vines indicated it was time to settle the issue of the BJCPA, calling for a vote on the agency at the 1990 convention in New Orleans.

Document 46
News Story: Vestal's Presidential Bid
Baptist Press, 20 April 1989, 1-3

"Vestal To Permit SBC Nomination"
by Mark Baggett & Toby Druin

NASHVILLE (BP)—Offering himself as a "responsible reconciler, a bridge to call our people back together," Daniel Vestal announced April 16 that he will permit his nomination as president of the Southern Baptist Convention in Las Vegas, Nev., June 13.

Vestal made the announcement to Dunwoody (GA) Baptist Church in suburban Atlanta, where he has been pastor since October 1988, following a 12-year pastorate at First Baptist Church of Midland, Texas.

"After going through a great deal of soul searching and prayer, I've come to a conviction that this is God's will for me," Vestal said.

He described his decision as a personal conviction and said he is "not anybody's candidate." However, he said he is a "centrist" in the SBC theological/political controversy.

"I am theologically and biblically conservative and have proven that I am committed to the cooperative approach to missions," Vestal said.

He hopes to return to the "time-honored principles of Southern Baptists: the authority of Scripture, the priesthood of believers, the autonomy of the local church, the separation of church and state, and the cooperative approach to missions rather than the independent approach," he said. "Because of our allegiance to those principles, we have thrived. But we are no longer thriving, because we are drifting away from those principles."

Interviewed April 18 in Corsicana, Texas, where he was conducting a revival meeting, Vestal said his decision to allow his nomination is born out of conviction that the SBC is "in danger of losing its viability as a denomination."

"We are languishing," he said. "Cooperative Program (unified budget) giving is down; mission budgets are being cut; seminary budgets have been cut. It's not because of the economy. It's because we have forsaken (the convention's) basic principles."

Southern Baptists also have thrived because of their commitment to freedom, which has eroded during the years of the SBC controversy, he said: "For 10 years, there has been a deliberate intentional campaign to discredit people's convictions which has intimidated them. It has created fear and threatened free expression. The intimidation has been like this: If you don't vote a certain way, you are portrayed as not believing the Bible. If you don't vote a certain way, you are portrayed as supporting liberals.

"Well, no Southern Baptist wants to be accused of not believing the Bible. No Southern Baptist wants to be accused of harboring liberalism. That kind of constant rhetoric threatens the environment of freedom.

"The convention has been under a kind of tight control of those who say if you don't vote a certain way then you don't believe the Bible and you can't be a part of the decision-making process. Well, I am Baptist enough to say that when our freedom is being threatened, I am going to stand up and speak against that. It has to stop; it must cease."

Vestal, who in February was among several people who spoke at a meeting sponsored by Baptists Committed to the Southern Baptist Convention in Nashville, said he welcomed the group's support of his nomination, but insisted he does not belong to Baptists Committed or any group: "I am not owned by anybody. I am owned by Jesus Christ. I welcome the support of others, but I am my own person."

He does not know who will nominate him in Las Vegas, he said, but he has had several offers.

Reaction from his church has been "positive, overwhelming, supportive, affirmative," he said. He has told members that being their pastor will be his first priority, but he has asked them "to let me do some traveling during the next two months."

Vestal plans to "be vocal" before the SBC meeting, June 13-15: "I will speak up and out to groups, churches and individuals. I think a lot of people in this convention want to hear from someone like me, from someone who is both biblically conservative and denominationally involved."

His decision is "not so much to run against Jerry Vines personally," Vestal said. Vines, pastor of First Baptist Church of Jacksonville, Fla., is completing his first year as SBC president and said in February he is willing to be nominated for a second term.

"I served with Jerry Vines on the Peace Committee for two years and love him as a Christian brother and value his friendship and his ministry," said Vestal.

"What I am doing is not a calculated political move, but a matter of conscience and conviction for me because I think this denomination is in serious trouble. I feel we are dangerously close to losing our viability as a denomination for world evangelization."

He will offer "convictions that ring true and harmonize with the convictions of most Southern Baptist people," he said. "That is, being in the middle doctrinally, biblically conservative and cooperative in my approach to world missions . . . where I believe most Southern Baptists are."

Vestal, 44, noted his Southern Baptist roots. He is the son of the late Southern Baptist evangelist Dan Vestal and was an evangelist as a boy and young man himself, preaching more than 300 revivals.

He earned two degrees each from Baylor University in Waco, Texas, and Southwestern Baptist Theological Seminary in Fort Worth, Texas. He was pastor of two churches before moving to First Baptist Church of Midland in 1976. The Midland church has led the SBC in Cooperative Program giving over the past decade and gave more than $1 million in 1988.

The 3,500-member Dunwoody church gave $295,036 to the Cooperative Program in 1988 and will give 12 percent of undesignated receipts this year, Vestal said. He has baptized more than 100 people since moving there last October.

Vestal served on the SBC Cooperative Program Study Committee in the early 1980s, the SBC Peace Committee, and he was chairman of the SBC Committee on Boards, now the Committee on Nominations, in 1982.

Those are "very conservative" roots, he said, calling himself a biblical inerrantist.

He has tried to be a "responsible reconciler" in all of his roles, he said. "If God has given me a gift, it is to be able to listen to people of different persuasions and not sacrifice my own convictions, to be a bridge, one to call people together."

If he should be elected SBC president, he said, he would try to be a "reconciler." He added he would favor looking at the powers of the president or at least sharing the president's appointive powers. The SBC controversy has swirled around the election of a president, who appoints the Committee on Committees, which nominates the Committee on Nominations, which recommends people for election to SBC boards, commissions and committees.

"This crisis we have had does not need to happen again," Vestal said. "I would favor an investigation into that by the Executive Committee or by an appointed committee."

His appointments would be "men and women who are Bible-believing Southern Baptists who have proven in their churches and by their personal lives a commitment to and an involvement in the denomination and in cooperative missions."

The constant "harangue" about "liberals" in the SBC has concerned him, he said: "I know many of these men (professors) personally and owe them a great debt myself. I know what kind of men they are, their commitment to Scripture, their commitment to this denomination, their commitment to God.

"They have influenced my life. When I hear this innuendo, these slurs that 'these liberals are in our seminaries,' it grieves me and angers me, because that is not true."

With some 600 professors at the six Southern Baptist seminaries, Vestal noted, "there may have been some need for theological renewal in some instances, maybe even correction, but the way this movement (now in control of the SBC) has tried to make that correction is wrong. It has created a party spirit and more divisiveness in the SBC than perhaps we have ever known, at least more than we have known in our recent past."

"It has taken away our focus on evangelism; it has removed our trust; and now I think it is causing us to lose our viability as a denomination."

"It is no more a theological issue. It is a power or control issue, and Southern Baptists have got to resist it. We have got to stand up and say enough is enough or we are going to destroy this denomination. The hour is late."

1990

Chronology

<u>April.</u> Southern Seminary trustee Jerry Johnson unleashes attack on President Roy Honeycutt and faculty members at Southern in paper entitled "The Cover-Up at Southern Seminary." Among other charges, Johnson said, "One would have to be blind as a mole not to see that Dr. Honeycutt just does not believe the Bible." Johnson later apologized for the document but said he had not changed his mind.

<u>June 11.</u> Randall Lolley's Bramble Bush Sermon at the Forum. See document 47.

<u>June 12-14.</u> SBC, New Orleans, 38,403 messengers, Jerry Vines presiding.

—Fundamentalist Morris Chapman elected president with 57.68% of the vote over Daniel Vestal with 42.32%.

—SBC cuts budget support for BJCPA from $391,000 to $50,000.

—Fundamentalists celebrate their control of SBC on Wednesday night at Cafe du Monde where convention parliamentarian Barry McCarty presides and Patterson and Pressler are presented with certificates of appreciation.

<u>July 17.</u> In closed session behind armed security guards, fundamentalist-dominated SBC executive committee fires Al Shackleford, director of Baptist Press, and Dan Martin, Baptist Press news editor; immediately, Nashville attorney Jeff Mobley announces the beginning of Associated Baptist Press.

<u>August.</u> Meetings by concerned Baptist professors, pastors, and laypersons to consider forming an alternative Baptist publishing house (Smyth & Helwys).

<u>August 13-15.</u> Fundamentalist-dominated Sunday School Board trustees vote to destroy all copies but one of a manuscript of that board's centennial history written by Southwestern Seminary esteemed church historian Leon McBeth.

August 23–25. Consultation of Concerned Southern Baptists, the Inforum, Atlanta, called by Daniel Vestal, presided over by Jimmy Allen, head of Baptists Committed.

—Formation of the Baptist Cooperative Missions Program, Inc. (BCMP), a funding mechansim for moderate SBC causes.

—Daniel Vestal, elected first moderator of later named Cooperative Baptist Fellowship, leads 60-member interim steering committee. See documents 48 and 49.

September 21. BCMP offices open in *SBC Today* facilities in Decatur GA.

September 21. Baylor University amends charter to replace trustees with regents who will have sole governance of the institution. The change established three-fourths of the board of regents as self-perpetuating, with only one-fourth of the regents elected by the Texas Baptist Convention.

September 24–25. Fundamentalist-dominated board of trustees imposes Peace Committee report as new creedal statement for hiring at Southern Seminary.

October 15. Furman University amends charter to give the board of trustees rather than the South Carolina Baptist Convention the power to elect trustees.

November 9. News release announces beginning of Smyth & Helwys Publishing, Inc., a free press for Baptists.

Document 47
Randall Lolley's Bramble Bush Sermon at the 1990 Forum

"Lest a Bramble Rule over Us"
Judges 9:7-15
by W. Randall Lolley, 11 June 1990

Remember Gideon? Not the one who puts Bibles in all the motels, but the one highlighted in the Old Testament, during the period of the Judges (Judges 6–8). Gideon was a hero in Israel, ridding the land of dominance by the Midianites. Gideon was quite a family man. Listen: "Now Gideon had seventy sons, his own offspring, for he had many wives. And his concubine who was in Shechem also bore him a son, and he called his name Abimelech" (Judges 8:30). Gideon died "in a good old age" and was buried in the tomb of Joash his father.

Gideon's corpse was scarcely cold, when his son Abimelech, off-spring of his concubine at Shechem, and half-brother of Gideon's other seventy sons, became embarrassed by his inferior status. He conspired with his mother's kinsmen to help him seize power. They contributed the funds with which Abimelech "hired worthless and reckless fellows who followed him" (Judges 9:4). In time they massacred every one of the seventy sons of Gideon, Abimelech's half brothers, and potential rivals for power in Shechem after the death of Gideon. Only Jotham, Gideon's youngest son, escaped the bloodbath. He hid himself from the assassins. Abimelech took no prisoners, ruled with a big stick, and could not tell the truth. So the Shechemites anointed him king.

In time, Jotham, the only kinsman escapee, assembled the people of Shechem in that natural amphitheater by Mount Gerizim, and without benefit of microphone or megaphone shouted out the famed Jotham's parable (Judges 9:7-15). Morris Ashcraft only recently reminded me of it. The olive tree refused to enter politics by saying, "Shall I leave my fatness, by which gods and men are honored, and go to sway over the trees?" The fig tree declined to run for office, justifying the refusal by saying, "Shall I leave my sweetness and my good fruit, and go to sway over the trees?" The vine turned thumbs down on a call to leadership, saying, "Shall I leave my wine which cheers gods and men and go to sway over the trees?" But the bramble bush drove a hard bargain and agreed to become the ruler of the forest.

The bramble is really a briar, prickly and thorny, with spines and runners forming tangled masses of vegetation. It is an ugly, useless, undesirable plant which bears no fruit and appears to serve no redeeming purpose. Jesus spoke of it in Luke 6:44: "For figs are not gathered from thorns, nor are grapes picked from a bramble bush."

Jotham outlined a political reality for every age. When the olive trees, fig trees, and grape vines refuse to provide leadership, albeit they may be busy producing fatness, sweetness, and cheer, then the bramble bushes, who have nothing to give up anyway, are always ready to rule over us. Good people, by default, allow ambitious and fruitless folks to fill leadership voids. Since 1979 Jotham's parable has played a rerun in our beloved Southern Baptist Convention.

Thus the timeliness of this 1990 Forum theme: "Recapturing the Future." It is high time that a new breed of leaders, blending our heritage and our hope, lead us "back to the future."

Meet Baptist A. He is conservative and proud of it. In fact, he is quite comfortable with being called a fundamentalist. He is sick and tired of being caricatured as uncaring, unthinking, unintelligent blockhead. And he is weary of feeling cut out of the Caribbean cruises and the high command of past presidents in whose grip political decision making is held vice-like just now. He is looking for leaders.

Meet Baptist B. He prefers to call himself moderate—progressive is even better. He has passion and is sick and tired of being labeled "liberal" just because he happens to be open on several theological issues. He supports the Baptist cooperative technique because it is a far better way of doing missions and education than any other way yet devised. He is looking for leaders.

Meet Baptist C. She is young, bright, articulate. She bears no special label except the one she inevitably wears with her gender. She is a Christian Baptist female. She is sick and tired of all the chatter which surrounds her efforts to pursue her calling—the intimidations and threats to monitor her witness. She knows that there is a hand on her shoulder, a fire in her bones, and a mandate to her mission from which she cannot escape. She is looking for leaders.

Meet Baptist D. She is one of Southern Baptists' 6,000 home and overseas missionaries. She is frightened, frustrated, and hurt with her people. She feels like a chip in a terrible game of political intrigue. Let her tell you how she feels: "Our hardest times as missionaries have not been when we have worked isolated at our station, without friends or family, and sometimes in physical danger. We have suffered most when we have felt helpless as Christian friends we depended on for prayer and other support were more concerned over biblical inerrancy and political maneuverings than with missions and their covenant with us." She is looking for leaders.

These four, and millions more, all over this world, now raising its freedom cries, are looking for leaders to claim their futures. Where will they come from—the fruit bearers or the briars? Those of you in this room—the olive trees, the fig trees, the grape vines of this Convention—hold the answer to that question squarely in your hands.

One of the lingering questions, fascinating both young and old, is, "Where did all the dinosaurs go? What ever happened to those huge creatures which roamed the earth eons ago? Well, students of dinosaurs disagree; but there is some consensus that something cataclysmic affected the climate, which affected their food supply, which affected their lifestyle, which eventually wiped out all of them. In short, the dinosaurs disappeared when their food supply failed, when that which fueled them disappeared.

So with our Southern Baptist family recapturing the future. Our leaders recently have been elected, and they have led us with a dinosaur rhetoric. And their rhetoric is soon to die out in three crucial areas (biblical authority, pastoral authority, and Christian femaleness) as the fresh winds of a recovered biblical free-church rhetoric displaces the very forces which have fueled the past.

1. *Listen to the dinosaur rhetoric of the past regarding biblical authority:*

> The theological doctrine of biblical inerrancy is the only force sufficient to correct a dangerous theological drift in our denomination. (Essence of several quotations from a variety of fundamental-conservative leaders.)

Listen to the biblical rhetoric of the future regarding biblical authority:

> The law of the Lord is *perfect*
>   reviving the soul,
> the testimony of the Lord is *sure,*
>   making wise the simple;
> the precepts of the Lord are *right,*
>   rejoicing the heart;
> the commandment of the Lord is *pure,*
>   enlightening the eyes;
> the fear of the Lord is *clean,*
>   enduring forever;

the ordinances of the Lord are *true,*
    and *righteous* altogether.
More to be *desired* are they than gold,
    even much fine gold;
sweeter also than honey
    and drippings of the honeycomb (Psa. 19:7-10).

Here in one Old Testament text are nine words describing the Word of the Lord—perfect, sure, right, pure, clean, true, righteous, desirable, and sweet. And the word "inerrant" is not among them. Inerrant is a man-word, not a God-word.

Listen again: "All Scripture is inspired by God" (2 Tim. 3:16). "There are some things in (Paul's letters) hard to understand, which the ignorant and unstable twist to their own destruction, as they do the other Scriptures. You therefore, beloved, knowing this beforehand, beware lest you be carried away with the error of lawless men and lose your own stability" (2 Peter 3:16-17). Here Peter serves commentary on some of Paul's inspired statements. Here, precisely, is the error of inerrantists. They "twist to their own destruction" perfect words from a perfect Bible because everyone of them is an imperfect interpreter. And they have used our Bible to bludgeon persons into submission to their imperfect interpretations. That is the dinosaur way, and its days are numbered. That which fuels it is fast becoming fossil.

Here is the biblical way of appealing to biblical authority. Listen. Paul speaks to Timothy in 2 Timothy 2:15; "Do your best to present yourself to God as one approved, a workman who has no need to be ashamed, rightly handling the word of truth."

Paul's word here is *orthotomeo*, which literally means "to cut straight, to cut rightly." The idea expressed is that the servant of God is to teach the Word of God straight without bending or distorting it to fit his/her own prejudgments. Paul's word conjures many pictures. We use the same prefix in words like *orthodontist* (one who straightens teeth) and *orthopedist* (one who straightens bones). The early church fathers likened Paul's word *orthotomeo* to *orthodoxy*—that is, straight thinking, straight teaching, and straight responding to the Word of God. John Calvin connected Paul's word with a father dividing out (cutting rightly) food at a meal, cutting it up so that each member of the family received the fitting and necessary portion. The Greeks in Paul's day used this word in three different connections: for driving a straight road across country; for plowing a straight furrow in a field; for cutting and squaring a stone so that it fitted properly into its place in the structure of a building.

So, you see, Paul's word *orthotomeo* ("rightly handling the word of truth") is a many-faceted concept. Christians who "rightly divide the word of truth" (KJV) drive a straight road through the whole of biblical revelation and refuse to be lured down fascinating but irresponsible proof texting by paths. They plow a straight furrow, following a lineup on biblical truth, through all the fields of human endeavor—and that includes modern science. They take each portion of biblical truth and fit it into its correct position as a skilled stonemason does a stone, allowing no part to usurp an undue place or an undue emphasis, and so to knock the whole structure of truth out of balance.

Here is the wave of the future.

Have you noticed within recent weeks that the rallying call of the present SBC leadership has shifted from "inerrancy" to the rhetoric of a "perfect Bible?" That is a predictable move—even a shrewd political move. "Perfect" is a fine biblical word describing Scripture. But I do wonder whether our leaders know the New Testament meaning of "perfect." It refers not to nature, but to function. It means performance, not perfection in any ethical sense. In short, "perfect" describes an entity doing exactly what it was intended to do. A "perfect" Bible functions perfectly only when handled as Paul mandates in 2 Timothy 2:15. The future belongs to this understanding of biblical authority. Let us seize together this moment for truth.

2. *Listen to the dinosaur rhetoric of the past regarding pastoral authority:*

> The pastor is the ruler of the church. There is no other thing than that in the Bible. . . . A laity-led church will be a weak church every time.
>
> (W. A. Criswell)

> If they (laypersons) will get where they ought to be, they'll be where I am.
>
> (Jerry Vines)

Listen to the biblical rhetoric of the future regarding participatory servant leadership.

> And (Jesus) said to them, The kings of the Gentiles exercise lordship over them. . . . But not so with you; rather let the greatest among you become as the youngest, and the leader as one who serves. . . . I am among you as one who serves (Luke 22:25-27).

> When (Jesus) had washed their feet, and taken his garments, and resumed his place, he said to them "Do you know what I have done to you? You call me Teacher and Lord; and you are right, for so I am. If I then, your Lord

and Teacher, have washed your feet, you also ought to wash one another's feet. For I have given you an example, that you also should do as I have done to you" (John 13:12-15).

Have you noticed that many pastors who use the dinosaur rhetoric wear cowboy boots? Now there is nothing wrong with cowboy boots, unless you lose your towel while looking for your lariat. Bolstered by their holsters, the cowboys run roughshod throughout the flock of God. They rule from their saddles. Never expect a cowboy to do a shepherd's job. There were as many cattle as there were sheep in Jesus' day; and perhaps just as many cowboys as shepherds. Listen: "I am the good cowboy." Does that sound like our Lord? No! It struts too much. Too much macho. Cowboys *drive* cattle. Jesus said, "I am the good shepherd" (John 10:11). Shepherds *lead* sheep; and die for them if they have to. It sounds so like our Lord who took up his towel twelve hours before he took up his cross. Toweling is the servant way of Golgotha.

Christian ministry is not something you *do*. It is someone you *are*. All ministry in the name of Christ is cruciform. It is nailed to a cross.

Priesting means "bridge building" (coming as it does from the Latin *pontifex*, bridge). At the clergy/laity interface, the differentiation is in role, not rank. It tapers off into gifting. The night before he died, Jesus Christ washed the feet of a dozen prima donnas arguing over which ones of them would be greatest when their movement prevailed. Priesting: the key is "authority," *exousia* (out of being), based on influence, energy from within, not "power," *danumis*, from without. Priesting is never by way of the special few. It is always by way of all the servant people of God (the *laos*). Pastors are leaders, not rulers, in a partnership of servants (no matter how many present-day leaders twist and distort Hebrews 13:7 to their own destruction). The tides of history run against authoritarians/totalitarians. The future belongs to servant leaders who democratize their churches and their agencies. Let us seize together this moment of truth.

3. *Listen to the dinosaur rhetoric of the past regarding Christian femaleness:*

Whereas, the Scriptures, attest to God's delegated order of authority (God the head of Christ, Christ the head of man, man the head of woman) . . . ; and Whereas, the Scriptures teach that women are not in public worship to assume a role of authority over men . . . ; and Whereas, while Paul commends women and men alike in other roles of ministry and service (Titus 2:1-10) he excludes women from pastoral leadership (1 Tim. 2:12) to preserve a submission God requires because the man was first in creation and the woman was first in the Edenic fall. . . . "

(SBC Resolution #3, Kansas City MO, 1984)

Listen to the biblical rhetoric of the future regarding Christian femaleness:

For in Christ Jesus you are all sons (and daughters) of God through faith. For as many of you as were baptized into Christ have put on Christ. There is neither Jew nor Greek, there is neither slave nor free, there is neither male nor female; for you are all one in Christ Jesus (Galatians 3:26-28).

Now there are varieties of gifts, but the same Spirit. . . . For just as the body is one and has many members, and all the members of the body, though many, are one body, so it is with Christ. . . . Now you are the body of Christ and individually members of it. And God has appointed in the church first apostles, second prophets, third teachers, then workers of miracles, then healers, helpers, administrators, speakers in various kinds of tongues. . . . But earnestly desire the higher gift (1 Corinthians 12).

The 1984 SBC Resolution consists of 86 lines, and 542 words. Eight times it mentions "ministry." Fifteen times it mentions "women." Thus the real agenda in that resolution was not ministry, but women—females themselves—all the women in all the churches of the Southern Baptist Convention. And in that hotly controverted resolution, the most contested concept is in the tenth "whereas": "the woman was last in creation and first in the Edenic fall." That phrase makes plain the real issue before Southern Baptist churches today. It is not vocation, mission, ministry, or ordination. It is womanhood itself. The churches of this Convention must hammer out for themselves—one and all—a doctrine of Christian femaleness.

And sincere students of Scripture will not resort to proof texting from a few isolated and imprecise verses for such a profound doctrine. They will rely on the total sweep of biblical revelation—including the doctrines of creation, salvation, gifting, calling, equipping, and ministering.

Anybody who takes the time to do it can write just as strong a resolution against men as the Kansas City resolution was against women—while using Scripture in precisely the same way. For example, the Bible says: "Sin came into the world through *one man* (Adam), and death through sin, and so death spread to all men" (Romans 5:12). The first blamer was a man—"she gave me and I did eat . . . " (Genesis 3:12). The first liar was a man (Genesis 3:10). So was the first murderer (Genesis 4:8). Jesus was denied by a man, betrayed by a man, and doubted by a man. He was condemned to death by men; and men drove the nails into his hands, and shoved the spear into his side. If we want to add up the Bible's testimonies and divide them up according to gender then man does not come out any better than woman. But we are not likely either to bring in the Kingdom or better it on the earth by such an endeavor.

Close examination of the biblical passages cited in the Kansas City resolution reveals several crucial things. There are twelve biblical texts cited. The most striking thing about them is the high degree of selectivity used in deciding that these verses are to apply literally as "an order of creation" to women today, while other equally specific passages are overlooked. Every sect has established itself in this same way, whether "the Moonies," "the Mormons," Jim Jones in Guyana, or Father Divine in New York. They select a few texts, disregard their context, bend their interpretation, and make them normative for faith and practice. That is the "heresy" in the Kansas City resolution. That resolution writer was not a literalist. He was a selectionist.

The simple plain fact is that in both the Old Testament and the New Testament women play a surprisingly prominent role in male-dominated religion. For example, two books in our Bible bear the names of women: Ruth and Esther. Miriam, Aaron's sister, was a prophetess who celebrated Israel's Exodus from Egypt in the dawn of Hebrew history (Exodus 15:20). Deborah, a judge in Israel, so represented the Spirit of the Lord, that the mighty general Barack refused to go into battle without her blessing (Judges 4:4-10). Huldah, the prophetess, played a profound part through her preaching, in the great reforms under King Josiah (2 Kings 22). Priscilla took the powerful preacher Apollos to her home in Ephesus and "taught him the way of God more accurately" (Acts 18:26). Lydia, seller of purple goods, was converted on the river bank at Philippi, and helped Paul plant the first church in Europe (Acts 16:14). Phoebe, "a deaconess of the church at Cenchrea," was sent by Paul on a preaching mission to Rome (Romans 16:1-2). Four unmarried daughters of Philip the Evangelist at Caesarea, were effective preachers throughout that entire region (Acts 21:8-10). Elizabeth was the first human being to know that the time of Messiah's coming was at hand, and that her son John would be the forerunner (Luke 1:57ff.). Mary, Elizabeth's cousin, actually bore the miracle-conceived Son of God (Luke 2:1ff.). Anna, the prophetess, at age eighty-four, proclaimed Jesus the Messiah in the temple when he was only forty days old (Luke 2:36-40). The women were last at the cross (Matthew 27:55-56) and first at the tomb (Luke 24:1-12).

"Last in creation, first in the Edenic fall"—is that the best the dinosaur rhetoric can muster to put Christian femaleness down, and keep women "in their place" out of the mainstream of God's futures for God's people? The biblical rhetoric of the future has another word—a word of grace. Women have been loosed from the bondage of the law (and of culture) and liberated into the power of the Gospel, just like men. God has no grandchildren; but all who believe are freed to be the sons and the daughters of God. The future belongs to Christians who embrace that call to freedom. Let us claim together this moment of truth. We started this message with Abimelech. Let me conclude with him:

> Then Abimelech went to Thebez, and took it. But there was a strong tower with in the city, and all the people of the city fled to it, all the men and women, and shut themselves in; and they went to the roof of the tower. And Abimelech came to the tower, and fought against it, and drew near to the door of the tower to burn it with fire. And a certain woman threw an upper millstone upon Abimelech's head, and crushed his skull. Then he called hastily to the young man his armor-bearer, and said to him, "Draw your sword and kill me, lest men say of me, a women killed him." And his young man thrust him through, and he died (Judges 9:50-54).

Thus ended the career of the consummate male chauvinist. You know what, the future does not belong to Abimelech Baptists! Amen.

Document 48
Daniel Vestal's Description of the Beginning of the CBF
The Struggle for the Soul of the SBC, 253-56

"The History of the Cooperative Baptist Fellowship"
by Daniel Vestal

I was elected to the Peace Committee in 1985 because I was theologically conservative but politically nonaligned. I had resisted the fundamentalist takeover both publicly and privately but had not engaged in any organized effort to stop it. If anyone came to the Peace Committee assignment with a sincere desire for reconciliation, it was I. And I honestly thought we could achieve that goal. I argued for theological renewal, and I argued for a cessation of the organized political efforts by the fundamentalists to control the convention.

After a year of sincere effort at being a "man in the middle" reaching out to both sides, I realized that only one side really wanted reconciliation. I realized that the fundamentalists only desired control, total control, absolute control and that they wanted no participation except with those who had that same desire.

In the 1987 SBC meeting in St. Louis I sat on the platform next to a trusted friend as the Peace Committee report was being given. I looked over at him and saw that he was crying. He said to me, "This is not the SBC I have always known." And indeed it wasn't. Shared decision making, open communication, acceptance of diversity were gone. In its place was a political machine that governed committee appointments, trustee selection, platform speeches and even floor debate.

I left the 1987 Convention in a state of depression and grief. In August of that year Bill Moyers contacted me about participating in the PBS documentary, *God and Politics*. My appearance on that program in December 1987 thrust me into a public role I had not known. I received hundreds of responses by phone, mail, and personal visit. Everywhere I turned, people were saying to me. "Something must be done." I was aware of the previous moderate efforts, but now I was being urged and encouraged to get involved. In February 1989, I attended a press conference in Nashville sponsored by Baptists Committed, knowing full well what that meant. I knew it would now involve me politically in a way I had not been involved. When asked to be nominated for the presidency of the SBC in Las Vegas by several close friends and respected colleagues I prayerfully consented.

From the beginning, my willingness to be nominated was motivated by the same desire that caused me to serve on the Peace Committee or appear in the Moyers' special. I genuinely wanted reconciliation. I had come to the conviction that there could be no reconciliation without political reconciliation, that is, there had to be inclusion of all Southern Baptists in the decision-making process. I made the open pledge that if elected I would purposely choose individuals from both sides of the controversy for the Committee on Committees. I promised inclusion instead of exclusion with the desire for genuine renewal. That was not enough, and I was defeated in Las Vegas.

I weighed what I would do during the summer, and I decided to try again in New Orleans. I had decided to be nominated in Las Vegas only six weeks before the Convention. I felt that if I could have nine months to get out the message of hope, inclusivity, and cooperation, I could surely be elected in New Orleans in 1990. It was not to be so. I was defeated more decisively in New Orleans then in Las Vegas.

The Call for a Convocation

The night after the election, I attended a reception with friends from Dunwoody Baptist Church, Atlanta, and First Baptist Church, Midland, Texas. Afterwards, Jim Denison, Pastor of FBC Midland, and I went to the hotel room of Jimmy Allen. We talked about the events of the day and the significance of those events in Baptist life. I felt the mantle of responsibility for the many who had voted for me and expressed their conscience in that vote. I sensed this defeat was an end to the moderate political effort. It was the end for many reasons, the primary one being that this was the twelfth straight defeat and the people were tired of the conflict. I realized that what I would say and do the next day would voice the feelings and concerns of a lot of disenfranchised and discouraged Southern Baptists. I felt accountability to them, but most of all I felt accountability to the convictions of my own conscience. Late in the evening I penned the following words to be delivered the next day.

> The election this year in New Orleans was not about who believes the Bible as the Word of God. I believe the Bible is the Word of God. Our presidents, administrators, professors, and denominational employees believe the Bible is the Word of God. Rather, the election this year was about our mission for the future—whether or not we will forge a united and inclusive

denomination for world missions. On June 12, 1990 that vision failed. And to say that I am not disappointed would be dishonest. I am deeply disappointed.

Why did it fail? Why did we lose the election? I confess to you that I don't have all the answers. I've searched and questioned, but I am not emotionally or intellectually prepared at this time to offer an analysis. But this I do know: What we did was right. I will not say that everything we did was perfect, but it was right. We spoke to the issues that are crucial to our day: openness, fairness, missions, trust and freedom. We resisted a political movement that excludes people from decision making, assassinates people's character, questions people's integrity and commitment to the Word of God. We resisted it, and we responded: "It's wrong, it's wrong, it's wrong." We called for a return to Baptist distinctives: the priesthood of the individual believer, religious liberty, separation of church and state. We called for a return to our Southern Baptist heritage: cooperative missions, unity in diversity.

The one overriding emotion I had on that Tuesday night was hope. Of course, I was sad and disappointed. But beyond that sadness and disappointment was a genuine conviction that God was at work. I honestly didn't know what ought to be done, but I felt that in the collective experience of Baptist people we could discern the will and work of God. I decided that the next morning at the Baptists Committed Breakfast I would call for a convocation of concerned Baptists. I determined to ask Baptists Committed to convene and plan the meeting. Its purpose would be renewal, and in it we would find ways to cooperate for the cause of Christ.

The next morning was a sober, but at the same time, a positive event. I remember the almost immediate response to the call for a convocation. It was a resounding affirmation that the time had come to move beyond political contest and theological debate. We somehow realized that the time had come to forge the future, to act instead of react, to find ways to cooperate without sacrificing our Baptist distinctives.

We all felt the need for a collective and corporate experience that would seek renewal. I was tired of the conflict. All of us were tired. We needed ways to be healed and to give healing. We needed a place to be accepted for who we are, true followers of Christ with a worldwide mission vision, Baptists who believe in the Bible but also believe in the freedom to interpret it. We needed a time to celebrate those distinctives and a time to deliberate together on how to implement those distinctives into action.

Document 49
News Story: Election of CBF Steering Committee
Baptist Press, 27 August 1990, 6

"Moderate Fellowship Elects 60 to Steering Committee"

ATLANTA (BP)—Moderate Southern Baptists attending a national consultation elected 60 members to an interim steering committee assigned to plan a national convocation next spring when a permanent steering committee would be elected.

Daniel Vestal, pastor of Dunwoody Baptist Church in suburban Atlanta, was elected chairman of the interim steering committee. Vestal had sought the presidency of the Southern Baptist Convention for the two previous years, but had been defeated.

The steering committee of the organization, which has no official name other than "the fellowship," will be comprised of up to 70 members when elected next spring. The interim committee will have authority to fill vacancies and enlist 10 additional members, using criteria developed by a nominating committee.

Seven "at-large" members were selected to serve on the interim committee because of their involvement in planning the consultation in Atlanta Aug. 23-25. They are:

Winfred Moore of Amarillo, Texas, now a visiting professor at Baylor University, Waco, Texas; Jimmy Allen of Fort Worth, Texas, chairman of Baptists Committed and former president of the Southern Baptist Radio and Television Commission, Fort Worth; Stan Hastey, executive director of the Southern Baptist Alliance, Washington; Carolyn Cole Bucy, of Waco, Texas, president of Women in Ministry; Cecil Sherman, pastor of Broadway Baptist Church, Fort Worth, Texas; Richard Groves, pastor of Wake Forest Baptist Church, Wake Forest, N.C.; and Vestal.

Fifty-three members were elected to represent 23 states. They are:

ARKANSAS: John McClanahan and Billie Sharp; ALABAMA: Dotson Nelson and Steve Tondera; CALIFORNIA: Cherry Chang and E.W. McCall; DISTRICT OF COLUMBIA: Joe Hairston, Jeanette Holt, and Diane Williams; FLORIDA: James Graves and Dan Yeary;

GEORGIA: Nancy Ammerman, Wink Hinks, and Walter Shurden; HAWAII: Rudy Zachery; ILLINOIS: Bill Trautman; KENTUCKY: Ken Chafin, Reba Cobb, and Gabe Payne; LOUISIANA: Relma Hargus and

Jon Stubblefield; MARYLAND/DELAWARE: Frank Heintz and John Roberts;

MICHIGAN: Dot Sample; MISSISSIPPI: Mary Jane Nethery, Tom Sims and Joe Tuten; MISSOURI: John Hughes and Joy Steincross; NEW MEXICO: Charles Price; NEW YORK: Jamie Munro and Virginia Neely;

NORTH CAROLINA: Peggy Haymes, John Hewett, and Anne Neil; OKLAHOMA: Stephen Earle and Bill Owen; PENNSYLVANIA/SOUTH JERSEY: Dwight Moody; SOUTH CAROLINA: John Cothran, David Hull and Barbara McClain; TENNESSEE: Calvin Metcalf, Anne Nolan and Bill Sherman;

TEXAS: Patsy Ayres, Jim Lacy, George May, Margarita Trevino, and Charles Wade; and VIRGINIA: Ray Allen, Paula Clayton Dempsey, Ray Spence and Jean Woodward.

1991

Chronology

January 7. Thomas H. Graves elected president of the Baptist Theological Seminary at Richmond.

January 17. Lloyd Elder, president of the Baptist Sunday School Board, forced to retire by fundamentalist-dominated board of trustees.

February. Smyth & Helwys announces commitment to publish alternative church-curriculum resources.

March 14–16. The Southern Baptist Alliance eliminates reference to the Southern Baptist Convention in its statement of purpose.

April 8. Trustees of Southern Seminary adopt a "Covenant Renewal between Trustees, Faculty, and Administration" which replaces the SBC Peace Committee report as guidelines for hiring faculty but commits faculty and trustees to a document other than the historic "Abstract of Principles."

May 9–11. Cooperative Baptist Fellowship convocation, Omni Coliseum, Atlanta, Daniel Vestal, presiding.

—"An Address to the Public" presented by the Fellowship's interim steering committee. See document 50.

—The Fellowship adopts the name "The Cooperative Baptist Fellowship" rather than the recommended "United Baptist Fellowship."

—John H. Hewett, pastor, First Baptist Church, Asheville, elected second CBF moderator.

May 20. News release announces Cecil P. Staton, Jr. has become first full-time publisher of Smyth & Helwys.

May. *SBC Today* changes to *Baptists Today*.

May. Meeting held at Woodmont Baptist Church in Nashville, at which was born the Baptist Center for Ethics. (The name "Southern Baptist Center for Ethics" rejected as too provincial.)

June 4–6. SBC, Atlanta, 23,465 messengers, Morris Chapman presiding.

—Fundamentalist Morris Chapman unopposed for president and reelected by acclamation. Moderates drop out of political process.

—SBC dropped all financial support for the BJCPA.

July 18. Fundamentalist James T. Draper elected president of the Baptist Sunday School Board.

September. Smyth & Helwys moves to the campus of Mercer University and begins period of cooperation with Mercer University Press; Cecil P. Staton, Jr. becomes publisher of MUP as well as of S&H.

September 10. Baptist Theological Seminary at Richmond begins classes.

October 9. Fundamentalist-dominated Foreign Mission Board trustees vote to delete from budget $365,000 previously promised to the Baptist Theological Seminary in Rüschlikon, Switzerland.

Document 50
CBFs "An Address to the Public"
The Baptist Identity, by Walter B. Shurden, 97-102

"An Address to the Public" from the Interim Steering Committee
of the Cooperative Baptist Fellowship
adopted 9 May 1991

Introduction

Forming something as fragile as the Cooperative Baptist Fellowship is
not a move we make lightly. We are obligated to give some explanation
for why we are doing what we are doing. Our children will know what
we have done; they may not know why we have done what we have
done. We have reasons for our actions. They are:

I. Our Reasons Are Larger than Losing

For twelve years the Southern Baptist Convention in annual session
has voted to sustain the people who lead the fundamentalist wing of the
SBC. For twelve years the SBC in annual session has endorsed the arguments and the rationale of the fundamentalists. What has happened is not
a quirk or a flash or an accident. It has been done again and again.

If inclined, one could conclude that the losers have tired of losing.
But the formation of the Cooperative Baptist Fellowship does not spring
from petty rivalry. If the old moderate wing of the SBC were represented
in making policy and were treated as welcomed representatives of
competing ideas in the Baptist mission task, then we would coexist, as
we did for years, alongside fundamentalism and continue to argue our
ideas before Southern Baptists.

But this is not the way things are. When fundamentalists won in
1979, they immediately began a policy of exclusion. Nonfundamentalists
are not appointed to any denominational positions. Rarely are gentle fundamentalists appointed. Usually only doctrinaire fundamentalists, hostile
to the purposes of the very institutions they control, are rewarded for service by appointment. Thus, the boards of SBC agencies are filled by only
one kind of Baptist. And this is true whether the vote to elect was 60-40
or 52-48. It has been since 1979 a "winner take all." We have no voice.

In another day Pilgrims and Quakers and Baptists came to America
for the same reason. As a minority, they had no way to get a hearing.
They found a place where they would not be second-class citizens. All

who intended the annual meeting of the SBC in New Orleans in June of 1990 will have an enlarged understanding of why our ancestors left their homes and dear ones and all that was familiar. So forming the Cooperative Baptist Fellowship is not something we do lightly. Being Baptist should ensure that no one is ever excluded who confesses, "Jesus is Lord" (Philippians 2:11).

II. Our Understandings Are Different

Occasionally, someone accuses Baptists of being merely a contentious, controversial people. That may be. But the ideas that divide Baptists in the present "controversy" are the same ideas that have divided Presbyterians, Lutherans, and Episcopalians. These ideas are strong and they are central; these ideas will not be papered over. Here are some of these basic ideas:

I. Bible. Many of our differences come from a different understanding and interpretation of Holy Scripture. But the difference is not at the point of the inspiration or authority of the Bible. We interpret the Bible differently, as will be seen below in our treatment of the biblical understanding of women and pastors. We also, however, have a different understanding of the nature of the Bible. We want to be biblical—especially in our view of the Bible. That means that we dare not claim less for the Bible than the Bible claims for itself. The Bible neither claims nor reveals inerrancy as a Christian teaching. Bible claims must be based on the Bible, not on human interpretations of the Bible.

2. Education. What should happen in colleges and seminaries is a major bone of contention between fundamentalists and moderates. Fundamentalists educate by indoctrination. They have the truth and all the truth. As they see it, their job is to pass along the truth they have. They must not change it. They are certain that their understandings of the truth are correct, complete, and to be adopted by others.

Moderates, too, are concerned with truth, but we do not claim a monopoly. We seek to enlarge and build upon such truth as we have. The task of education is to take the past and review it, even criticize it. We work to give our children a larger understanding of spiritual and physical reality. We know we will always live in faith; our understandings will not be complete until we get to heaven and are loosed from the limitations of our mortality and sin.

3. Mission. What ought to be the task of the missionary is another difference between us. We think the mission task is to reach people for

faith in Jesus Christ by preaching, teaching, healing, and other ministries of mercy and justice. We believe this to be the model of Jesus in Galilee. That is the way he went about his mission task. Fundamentalists make the mission assignment narrower than Jesus did. They allow their emphasis on direct evangelism to undercut other biblical ministries of mercy and justice. This narrowed definition of what a missionary ought to be and do is a contention between us.

4. Pastor. What is the task of the pastor? They argue the pastor should be the ruler of a congregation. This smacks of the bishops's task in the Middle Ages. It also sounds much like the kind of church leadership Baptists revolted against in the seventeenth century.

Our understanding of the role of the pastor is to be a servant/shepherd. Respecting lay leadership is our assignment. Allowing the congregation to make real decisions is of the very nature of Baptist congregationalism. And using corporate business models to "get results" is building the Church by the rules of a secular world rather than witnessing to the secular world by way of a servant Church.

5. Women. The New Testament gives two signals about the role of women. A literal interpretation of Paul can build a case for making women submissive to men in the Church. But another body of scripture points toward another place for women. In Galatians 3:27-28 Paul wrote, "As many of you as are baptized into Christ have clothed yourselves with Christ. There is no longer Jew or Greek, there is no longer slave or free, there is no longer male and female; for all of you are one Christ Jesus" (NRSV).

We take Galatians as a clue to the way the Church should be ordered. We interpret the reference to women the same way we interpret the reference to slaves. If we have submissive roles for women, we must also have a place for the slaves in the Church.

In Galatians Paul follows the spirit of Jesus who courageously challenged the conventional wisdom of his day. It was a wisdom with rigid boundaries between men and women in religion and in public life. Jesus deliberately broke those barriers. He called women to follow him; he treated women as equally capable of dealing with sacred issues. Our model for the role of women in matters of faith is the Lord Jesus.

6. Church. An ecumenical and inclusive attitude is basic to our fellowship. The great ideas of theology are the common property of all the Church. Baptists are only a part of that great and inclusive Church. So, we are eager to have fellowship with our brothers and sisters in the faith and to recognize their work for our Savior. We do not try to make

them conform to us; we try to include them in our design for mission. Mending the torn fabric of both Baptist and Christian fellowship is important to us. God willing, we will bind together the broken parts into a new company in preview of the great fellowship we shall have with each other in heaven.

It should be apparent that the points of difference are critical. They are the stuff around which a fellowship such as the Southern Baptist Convention is made. We are different. It is regrettable, but we are different. And perhaps we are most different at the point of spirit. At no place have we been able to negotiate about these differences. Were our fundamentalist brethren to negotiate, they would compromise. And that would be a sin by their understandings. So, we can either come to their position, or we can form a new fellowship.

III. We Are Called to Do More than Politic

Some people would have us continue as we have over the last twelve years, and continue to work within the SBC with a point of view to change the SBC. On the face of it this argument sounds reasonable. Acting it out is more difficult.

To change the SBC requires a majority vote. To effect a majority in annual session requires massive, expensive, contentious activity. We have done this, and we have done it repeatedly.

But we have never enjoyed doing it. Something is wrong with a religious body that spends such energy in overt political activity. Our time is unwisely invested in beating people or trying to beat people. We have to define the other side as bad and we are good. There is division. The existence of the Cooperative Baptist Fellowship is a simple confession of that division; it is not the cause of that division.

We can no longer devote our major energies to SBC politics. We would rejoice, however, to see the SBC return to its historic Baptist convictions. Our primary call is to be true to our understanding of the gospel. We are to advance the gospel in our time. When we get to heaven, God is not going to ask us, "Did you win in Atlanta in June of 1991?" If we understand the orders we are under, we will be asked larger questions. And to spend our time trying to reclaim a human institution (people made the SBC; it is not a scriptural entity) is to make more of that institution than we ought to make. A denomination is a missions delivery system; it is not meant to be an idol. When we make more of the SBC than we ought, we risk falling into idolatry. Twelve years is too long to engage in political activity. We are called to higher purposes.

Conclusion

*That we may have a voice in our Baptist mission . . . for that is our Baptist birthright.

*That we may work by ideas consistent with our understanding of the gospel rather than fund ideas than are not our gospel.

*That we may give our energies to the advancement of the Kingdom of God rather than in divisive, destructive politics. . . . For these reasons we form the Cooperative Baptist Fellowship. This does not require that we sever ties with the old Southern Baptist Convention. It does give us another mission delivery system, one more like our understanding of what it means to be Baptist and what it means to do gospel. Therefore, we create a new instrument to further the Kingdom and enlarge the Body of Christ.

Conclusion

by Walter B. Shurden

After both living through the controversy and studying its remains, I have a hunch that fundamentalists got far more than they ever expected.[1] Surely it was not more than they wanted, for even though their words vigorously deny it, their actions clearly demonstrate what they wanted: absolute control of a denomination which biblically, theologically, ethically, and politically reflects their fundamentalist view of the world. But I seriously doubt that even Pressler or Patterson anticipated in 1979 getting absolute control of the denomination. Moreover, while it was a gargantuan struggle, my guess is that in the end it was far easier than fundamentalists would have ever imagined.

Why and how did they win? Fundamentalism had never been able to capture the conservative SBC before. Why during the 1980s? By now many answers—wise and unwise—have been given.

One simple answer, of course, is that *God willed it*. Paige Patterson, not surprisingly, has used this interpretation. The movement he and Pressler launched was not only "right," but "the commandment of God."[2] Patterson himself, however, stops short of saying that either "winning" or "losing" are necessarily signs of God's will. Some of his colleagues were not as careful. Charles Stanley said, according to James Hefley, "God has turned our denomination around. . . ."[3]

Another less transcendent explanation is available. *Fundamentalists persuaded more messengers to attend the annual conventions and vote for their presidential candidate than did the moderates.* Based on sheer

---

[1]My hunch is documented. At a meeting of 100 fundamentalist leaders at the First Baptist Church in Atlanta on 3 March 1989, James T. Draper said, "I don't think anybody back in 1978–1979 would have dreamed that we [would] come as far as we have." See James Carl Hefley, *The Truth in Crisis*, 5 vols. (Dallas: Clarion Publications, and Hannibal MO: Hannibal Books, 1986–1990) 4:206.

[2]Paige Patterson, "My Vision of the Twenty-First Century SBC," *Review and Expositor* 88/1 (Winter 1991): 50.

[3]Hefley, 4:206.

numbers of people voting it is now easy to say, "Moderates could never have won." As a matter of fact SBC history itself contradicts that. While no such thing as "moderates" existed before 1980, traditional Southern Baptists, the ancestors of moderates, had always successfully resisted extremism such as J. R. Graves's Landmarkism and Frank Norris's fundamentalism.

More to the question at hand is why traditional Southern Baptists were unsuccessful in the 1980s. While other factors may have been important, I suggest fundamentalists won because of the following factors: emotional passion, theological clarity, cultural congruity, organizational unity, and personal leadership. A word about each.

Emotional Passion. This factor ought to be the one most instructive for other denominations threatened by extremists of whatever kind. James Slatton, a passionate moderate, said, "We always worked with the disadvantage that moderates were, by definition, *moderate.*"[4] He meant passion won, moderation lost. Cecil Sherman echoed Slatton even more passionately:

> Moderates did not have enough moral energy to win. We could not bring ourselves to use moral language to describe our cause. Truth was butchered. We said nothing. Good people were defamed. We were silent. Baptist principles were mangled and Baptist history was replaced, rewritten. All the while, teachers who could have written about the problems in calling the Bible inerrant, did not. And preachers who could have called us to arms, said nothing. The want of moral energy was the undoing of the moderate movement.[5]

Samuel Hill, a leading interpreter of religion in the American South, has a helpful analysis of Southern Evangelical Protestantism which is applicable at this point. Hill says that there are four types of evangelicalism in the South: (1) the truth oriented, rightly called "fundamentalist"; (2) the conversion oriented who are "evangelistic"; (3) the spiritually oriented, "devotional" in nature; and (4) the service oriented, "ethical" in

---

[4]James H. Slatton, "The History of the Political Network of the Moderate Movement," in Walter B. Shurden, ed., *The Struggle for the Soul of the SBC: Moderate Responses to the Fundamentalist Movement* (Macon GA: Mercer University Press, 1993) 56.

[5]Cecil E. Sherman, "An Overview of the Moderate Movement," in Shurden, ed , *The Struggle for the Soul of the SBC*, 44.

nature and concerned with justice issues.[6] While one may find all four types in a single denomination and certainly in the old SBC, one should also note a very significant attitudinal difference among the four types. Types 2, 3, and 4 tend to be inclusive, relational, and nonabsolutist. Type 1, the truth oriented, tends to be exclusive, rationalistic, and dogmatic.

It is a descriptive not a derogatory statement to say that this is the very nature of the type of fundamentalism that captured the Southern Baptist Convention. When a Christian believes he or she has a monopoly on the gospel and others err because they do not agree with a certain interpretation, trust is out the window, reconciliation is impossible, and Christians with a different point of view are labeled dangerous and heretical. The uncompromising, nonnegotiating aspect of fundamentalism can only be understood in light of their passionate conviction that fundamentalists and fundamentalists alone are the truth-people. They think they *are* being "fair" when they do not appoint people to committees who disagree with them. They think they *are* being "fair" when they want people fired from faculties who do not agree with them. They think they *are* being "fair" when they want only their kind appointed to positions of leadership in the denomination.

Some among them, to be sure, are simply small and petulant people. We all have names of people who fall into this category. Fundamentalists are not alone in this moral shortfall, however. On the other hand, I would argue that some among them are people of conscience. More convicted by a particular understanding of truth than they are mean in spirit, their passionate and unbending and inflexible understanding of truth makes them appear mean in spirit. Their understanding of truth simply must exclude rather than include because for them truth is more important than love, a point that most moderates think they would have trouble reconciling with Jesus' understanding of authentic religious faith. It should come as no surprise that the multivolume, celebrated fundamentalist interpretation of the controversy is entitled *The Truth in Crisis*. As a matter of fact, Christian "truth" was never at risk, unless by the fundamentalists themselves.

Theological Clarity. Extremism of whatever kind rides to the front of the parade pontificating shibboleths, simplistic slogans, and watchwords.

---

[6]Samuel S. Hill, Jr., "The Shape and Shapes of Popular Southern Piety," in *Varieties of Southern Evangelicalism*, ed. David E. Harrell, Jr. (Macon GA: Mercer University Press, 1981) 99.

"Inerrancy" as it relates to the Bible is such a word, and most of fundamentalist scholarship knows this. Push them hard and they will qualify it nine different ways. But "bumper sticker theology" which is brief, unambiguous, and passionate communicates. It even intimidates.

Moderates got tongue-tied in their nonresponses to the theological oversimplifications of fundamentalism. Fundamentalists spoke in spades; moderates could not speak in spades. They honestly knew the subject was too knotty and ambiguous for that kind of sleight of the theological hand. To say that one reads the Bible, studies the Bible, tries to live by the Bible, and loves the Bible was not enough for inerrantist fundamentalists. Moderates did not say soon enough or loudly enough or simply enough what Cecil Sherman wrote in italics: *Inerrancy is not the truth.* In their address to the public in 1990 the interim steering committee of the Cooperative Baptist Fellowship asserted that "The Bible neither claims nor reveals inerrancy as a Christian teaching." That candor early in the controversy would have been a better offense for moderates than always being forced into theological defensiveness. Moreover, for moderates to take such a position on inerrancy did not mean that they took a position *against* inerrantists. The fact is that some inerrantists identified with, even were leaders, in the moderate movement.

Cultural Congruity. By the 1980s America, indeed the world, appeared to be moving away from toleration. Just as Islamic fundamentalism gained power throughout the world, Christian fundamentalism ascended in America. Jerry Falwell, Jim Bakker, Jimmy Swaggart, Charles Stanley, Oral Roberts, and a host of other television preachers bombarded the nation's airways, and for the most part went unchallenged by mainstream American religion. This trend only reinforced the swing to the right wing in Southern Baptist life.

It is a truism, of course, that what was happening religiously was happening also in national politics. Carter was out. Reagan was coming in. When Bailey Smith made his "God Almighty does not hear the prayer of a Jew" statement, he was on the platform with several other past or future Southern Baptist Convention presidents. Together they and other leaders of the religious right listened and applauded when Ronald Reagan addressed some 20,000 participants. Reagan's election reflected and strengthened the fundamentalist ascendancy within the SBC. The extremist movement within Southern Baptist life in the 1980s had a stronger ally in the culture than any previous controversy in the denomination. Moderates, on the other hand, were constantly swimming upstream.

Organizational Unity. Moderates never had the apparent lockstep unanimity that fundamentalists had. That is understandable. Moderates don't think as militarily. When a group of the fundamentalist leaders began to lead some cruises together, they facetiously were dubbed by moderates as the "Caribbean Cardinals." As Sherman pointed out, however, a cruise ship was not necessary to transport the fundamentalist decision makers. Sherman said they could have ridden in a minivan. Personally, I think they could have been comfortable in a pickup truck if it did not have bucket seats. By the middle of the decade they needed room for only three—Rogers, Patterson, and Pressler—and Rogers was driving.

While Cecil Sherman was the single most important, consistent, and clearest moderate voice throughout the decade, he was not followed by all moderates the way fundamentalists followed Rogers. At one point Sherman relinquished the leadership to Don Harbuck, then James Slatton, then John Jeffers. At another point Foy Valentine was responsible for "getting out the vote," and for a brief period the seminary presidents, Dilday, Lolley, and Honeycutt, led the moderate procession.

Personal Leadership. While the personal leadership factor is closely connected to the issue of organizationally unity, they are not necessarily the same. Thus far in most of the interpretations explaining why the controversy turned out as it did, too little attention has been given to the dimension of personal leadership.

Often overlooked is the fact that the SBC was in a "generational crease" immediately prior to and in the early years of the controversy. Southern Baptists had a changing of the guard in many of its agencies and institutions as well as in some of the larger pulpits in SBC life. In the evolution controversy of the 1920s the denomination solidified around E. Y. Mullins, while in the turbulent 1960s Herschel H. Hobbs commanded a hearing. During the fundamentalist-moderate conflict Porter Routh, Baker James Cauthen, James Sullivan, Duke McCall, Grady Cothen, Albert McClellan, all prominent denominational leaders, retired within a matter of a few years of each other, either immediately before or in the early years of the epic struggle. Naturally, those who replaced them did not have comparable influence in the denomination. When moderates called upon some of these revered leaders—McCall and Cothen, especially—who had given their lives to the SBC, they were disdainfully dismissed by the fundamentalists as being part of the problem.

If one generation was passing off the scene, much of the rising generation of traditional Baptists on the scene chose silence over confrontation. In a recent book on *The New SBC* Grady Cothen bemoaned the deafening

silence from the multitudes in the SBC regarding the new fundamentalism. And then he released two paragraphs that blistered denominational
leadership from directors of missions to presidents of national agencies,
including all the college presidents, state executive directors, and state
denominational employees in between. In addition, Cothen notes that
many pastors did not educate their members about the problems and/or
blindly held to the view that the controversy did not affect them.[7] A
major part of the story of this controversy is relatively simple. It had to
do with the absence of the courage to resist.

In Sherman, Slatton, Chafin, Vestal, and others, moderates had courageous and convicted leadership. But it appears that fundamentalists had
even more of that kind. In compliment rather than criticism, someone
said that Pressler and Patterson were theological pit bulldogs. Charles
Stanley had a national audience by virtue of television ministry. W. A.
Criswell probably does not deserve as much credit for the triumph of the
new fundamentalism as history will grant him, but he certainly was the
granddaddy of the movement. While I do not subscribe to a simple and
singular biographical view of history, I sincerely doubt, as I said earlier
in this chapter, that fundamentalism could have known its measure of
success apart from Adrian Rogers. Three times the president of the SBC
in a span of nine years, he was crucial in the profundamentalist outcome
of the Peace Committee. No other fundamentalist could rival him as
preacher, debater, or intransigent believer. When the leadership of the
fundamentalists met for their strategy sessions, the press releases often
read, "Adrian Rogers presided." He was by far fundamentalists' most
capable leader and moderates' most formidable opponent.

What have been the results of the fundamentalist-moderate controversy for the SBC? In his study, William Stone said that the conflict "rede-
fined Southern Baptists, revised their history, remythologized their future,
and reformed their values, beliefs, and social relationships."[8] Grady
Cothen, a man who knows the SBC inside out, said, "Whatever else can

---

[7]Grady C. Cothen, *The New SBC: Fundamentalism's Impact on the Southern
Baptist Convention* (Macon GA: Smyth & Helwys Publishing, Inc., 1995) 121-
22. On this same point see Cecil Sherman's forthright indictment of those "who
sat out the public part of the fight" in "An Overview of the Moderate Movement," in Shurden, ed., *The Struggle for the Soul of the SBC*, 39-40, 43-44.

[8]William S. Stone, Jr., "The Southern Baptist Convention Reformation,
1979–1990" (Ph.D. diss., Louisiana State University, Baton Rouge LA, May
1993) 3.

be said about the SBC, it is no longer the same body in doctrine, polity, procedures, or cooperative effort in education and missions."[9] Fisher Humphreys wrote his superb book based on the premise "that Southern Baptists will never again be exactly the kind of people they were before the controversy."[10] Stone, Cothen, Humphreys, and other interpreters confirm my earlier assertion that the controversy changed almost everything in SBC life. To dismiss the controversy in a cavalier fashion as "a preacher's fuss," is simply to miss the transformation of the SBC.

Space precludes a description of all the changes in the SBC brought about by the new fundamentalist leaders and their triumph. These changes are yet in process, so the final story cannot be told. To this point, however, the following summary is clear: theologically and ideologically the SBC has been *fundamentalized*; ecclesiologically the SBC has been *centralized*; culturally, in terms of gender issues, the SBC has been *chauvinized*; ecumenically the SBC has been *sectarianized*; and denominationally the SBC has been *debaptistified*.

Theologically and ideologically the new SBC has been *fundamentalized*. For years the SBC was a "conservative" denomination. While the present fundamentalist leadership want to maintain the "conservative" terminology and apply it to themselves, they have great difficulty doing this because the difference between them and the traditional conservative leadership is so radically stark. Pressler, Patterson, Rogers, and Stanley are much closer to independent fundamentalist Jerry Falwell and the descendants of Frank Norris at First Baptist Church in Ft. Worth than they are to traditional Southern Baptists such as George W. Truett, E. Y. Mullins, Baker James Cauthen, or even Herschel H. Hobbs. By no means does this mean that all Southern Baptists are now fundamentalists. They most certainly are not. But increasingly the nonfundamentalists within the SBC will have problems establishing an identity apart from the powerful new leadership.

Basic to the fundamentalizing of the SBC is the theological constrictionism, the narrowing theology which expresses itself in creedalism. Baptists of the South organized the SBC in 1845, so 1995 marked the one hundred and fiftieth anniversary of the convention. In 1845 at

---

[9]Cothen, *The New SBC*, 177.

[10]Fisher Humphreys, *The Way We Were: How Southern Baptist Theology Has Changed and What It Means to Us All* (New York: McCracken Press, 1994) ix.

Augusta messengers to the first meeting of the SBC claimed that they had no creed but the Bible. By the mid-1990s, however, that disclaimer, while yet a part of denominational rhetoric, has been effectively shelved.

The SBC has become a creedalistic structure. This is a charge the fundamentalists bristle at and deny, because they know they have stepped outside the Baptist heritage. While eschewing the word "creeds," they now speak of doctrinal "parameters." Their public statements and actions, however, support the assessment that the SBC is increasingly creedal. In the interest of integrity and clarity, the fundamentalist leadership would be better served to state this publicly. In addition to the 1963 "Statement of the Baptist Faith and Message," fundamentalists now call for compliance to the "Glorieta Statement," the "Peace Committee Report," and "The Chicago Statement on Biblical Inerrancy," and the resolutions and motions adopted at annual meetings of the SBC.

Ecclesiologically, the SBC has become *centralized*. Increasingly, the term "The Southern Baptist Church" appears in letters to the editor. While that term represents a gross misinterpretation of the Baptist doctrine of the church, it reflects many developments in Southern Baptist life since 1979. Historically, resolutions adopted at the annual sessions were never considered "denominational law" for SBC agencies and institutions. Since 1979 such resolutions have increasingly been interpreted as "directives," centralizing all agencies around SBC actions. In June 1994 administrators at Southern Seminary told Professor Molly Marshall that she should resign or suffer the possibility of dismissal from her position on the faculty. The vice president for academic affairs indicated that her alleged disregard for the content of motions and resolutions passed at the SBC constituted one of the possible charges against her.

SBC constitutional changes, SBC actions which in effect deny the liberty of the local churches to channel funds according to the church's desires, legislative actions of the Executive Committee toward individual SBC agencies, and intrusions by SBC agencies into state convention life are further examples of a growing centralization in the Southern Baptist Convention.[11] A new federalism accompanies the new fundamentalism in SBC life. Just as constrictionism is at work in matters of theology, centripetal forces are operative in the denominational machinery. Voices which began in 1979 bemoaning "denominational bureaucracy" end up intensifying it. The present centralization process within the SBC

---

[11]Ibid., 154-68.

substantiates the early moderate contention that "control" was a major feature of the controversy.

No fundamentalist has been more outspoken or articulate in roundly condemning denominational centralization than Paige Patterson. At this point I find myself in solid agreement with Patterson. When arguing persuasively in his 1985 article[12] against "the growing centralization of the Southern Baptist Convention," Patterson quoted extensively from William Wright Barnes's insightful 1934 monograph *The Southern Baptist Convention: A Study in the Development of Ecclesiology*, one of the most prophetic books ever written about the SBC. Patterson's quotations were highly selective, however. He quotes Barnes approvingly when Barnes writes disapprovingly of "denominational ownership of religious papers." Barnes and Patterson are correct. The denomination would be healthier without denominational control of the press, and that includes both state Baptist papers as well as the Baptist Press news agency. Now that Patterson's group is in control of the Baptist Press, however, Patterson's prophetic comments in the Barnes tradition have apparently grown silent. Why? Will Patterson and those who now control Baptist Press object to denominational ownership of the press as "another link in the chain of centralization," as Barnes described it, or was Patterson speaking earlier out of principle or expediency?

Above, I indicated that Patterson's selection from Barnes's legitimate tirade against denominational centralization was highly selective. Patterson significantly omitted Barnes's lament regarding the centralization of power within the SBC Executive Committee, the centralization of power by the elevation of the SBC presidency into an ecclesiastical position, and the centralization of power through theological creed making in the SBC, all significantly increased by the recent fundamentalist movement.[13]

In a 1991 article in the *Review and Expositor* Patterson reaffirmed his wise appraisal that "there is an unhealthy and subtle form of connectionalism in our ecclesiastical structure which must be resisted." Here Patterson bemoans the fact that a local church, because of the monetary connectionalism of the Cooperative Program centered in the state conventions, is not autonomous in "deciding about the percentage of mission

---

[12]See document 31, p. 141, above.

[13]See William Wright Barnes, *The Southern Baptist Convention: A Study in the Development in Ecclesiology* (Ft. Worth TX: published by the author, 1934) 8, 59-60.

money it wishes to invest in local, associational, state, and international mission causes." Patterson is on target again when he says, "*Unfortunately*, state conventions then decide what percent of the church's gifts to the Cooperative Program remain in the state and what portion is sent on to the national convention."[14] Each local church, as Patterson insists, should be responsible, apart from the state conventions, in deciding about the disbursement of its mission money. If the new fundamentalist leadership would now push for such a change, "Baptists of varying theological stripes," as Patterson said, would be enabled "to find continued cooperative giving much more palatable."

Culturally, in terms of gender equality, the SBC has become *chauvinized* by its male fundamentalist leadership. Since Adrian Rogers's glib "Satan's fib about women's lib" line in 1979 to the adoption of the 1984 Kansas City resolution and increasingly since, women have been relegated to second-class citizens in SBC life. All the jokes, one-liners, and feigned deference to women to one side, the SBC has become as chauvinistic in the 1990s as it was racist in the 1890s. Indeed, the same approach to biblical interpretation used to justify slavery in a previous century has been utilized in this century on women. Not only has male "headship" been affirmed by fundamentalists, but women, so the new SBC leadership contend, have no role as deacons or pastors in a local church. When new seminary president Ken Hemphill of Southwestern Seminary announced the addition of a woman to the faculty of the theology school, he noted that she would be teaching only church history and not theology, and he also assured the SBC constituency that she was "under" the authority of the seminary president at work and her husband at home. At Southern Seminary in Louisville, Kentucky, Al Mohler, fundamentalist president, announced in April 1995 a litmus test for hiring faculty which included opposition to women serving as pastors. I predict that, just as the SBC apologized for racism in 1995, it will one day apologize for its chauvinism.

Ecumenically, the fundamentalist leadership has *sectarianized* the Southern Baptist Convention. Long before 1979 and the rise of the new fundamentalism in SBC life, ecumenists generally viewed the SBC as one of the major problem children of American Protestantism. One of the results of the recent controversy, however, is that the SBC has been taken further out of the mainstream of American Christianity, increasingly

---

[14]See Patterson, "My Vision of the Twenty-First Century SBC," 46.

relating itself to the radical right wing of American Protestantism. This sectarianism is expressed not only in the groups with which they associate, but with the Baptist groups, such as the Cooperative Baptist Fellowship, which they have repudiated.

Denominationally, the new fundamentalism has *debaptistified* the SBC. Examples are abundant: the growing creedalism, the novel emphasis on pastoral authority and the corresponding diminishing of the priesthood of all believers and congregational church government, and the incredible notion of W. A. Criswell that the separation of church and state was the figment of some infidel's imagination. This debaptistification of the SBC is obviously something that the new SBC leadership denies.

While not calling it debaptistification, Humphreys speaks to this issue in the closing pages of his book. Posing a question in Reagan-like fashion, he asks, "Are you better off than you were before 1979?" Acknowledging that some Southern Baptists think they are, this careful and objective theologian answers for himself saying:

> I do not believe this. I believe that the loss of the Protestant belief in the priesthood of all believers is unfortunate and that the loss of the distinctively Baptist beliefs in congregational decision making by democratic means, in the careful separation of church and state, and in the rejection of all creeds but the Bible, are theological tragedies as great as any in the history of the Convention.[15]

One would not be surprised if William Brackney, a non-Southern Baptist historian, was thinking of the new SBC when he said of Baptists today:

> They have strayed from their beginnings. The loudest and most obvious and most often quoted Baptists in the United States seem to be nowhere near the historic principles of older Baptist bodies.[16]

---

[15]Humphreys, *The Way We Were*, 173.
[16]Ibid., 178.

Going for the Jugular.
A Documentary History of the SBC Holy War.
  compiled and edited by Walter B. Shurden and Randy Shepley

ISBN 0-86554-456-5. Catalog and warehouse pick number MUP/H377.
Mercer University Press, 6316 Peake Road, Macon, Georgia 31210-3960.
Text, interior, titles, cover, and jacket designs, and composition and layout
  by Edd Rowell.
Camera-ready pages composed on a Gateway 2000 386/33C (via WordPerfect
  dos 5.1 and wpwin 5.1/5.2) and printed on a LaserMaster 1000.
Text font: TimesNewRomanPS 11/13 and 10/12.
Display fonts: Helvetica and TimesNewRomanPS.
Titles (cover and dust jacket): Present.
Printed and bound by McNaughton & Gunn, Inc., Saline, Michigan 48176.
  Printed via offset lithography on 50# Natural Offset (500 ppi).
  Smyth sewn and cased in with 80# natural endsheets
    in Holliston Roxite grade C 57560 cloth (sand) over .080 binders boards,
      stamped one hit (PMS 216, dark red) on c. 1 and spine.
  Dust jacket printed PMS 216 (dark red) and black on 80# Litho Label c1s,
    and film laminated.
  Individually shrinkwrapped and bulk packed in standard cartons on skids.

[First printing June 1996 1m]